I0606367

DAVID

The Man After God's Own Heart

Unless otherwise noted, all Scripture quotations are taken from the New American Standard Bible. Nashville: Thomas Nelson Publishers, 1978; the Complete Jewish Bible, Baltimore: Messianic Jewish Publishers, 1998; or the New International Version Bible, New York: International Bible Society, 2002.

Printed in the United States of America

Cover design by Lisa Rubin,
Messianic Jewish Publishers
Graphic Design by Yvonne Vermillion,
MagicGraphix.com

About the cover art: The Psalms of King David, engraving of Nazarene School, published in The Holy Bible, St.Vojtech Publishing, Trnava, Slovakia, 19. The Nazarene School was a group of German Romantic-era painters who sought to revive Christian art.

1 2026
ISBN 9781951833091

Published by:
Lederer Books
An imprint of Messianic Jewish Publishers
6120 Day Long Lane
Clarksville, MD 21029

Distributed by:
Messianic Jewish Publishers & Resources
Order line: (800) 410-7367
lederer@messianicjewish.net
www.MessianicJewish.net

Dedication

For my great-grandsons:

Herman Issac Heinen
Malakai Tyler-James Murphy
Easton James Hendrikse
Judah Dale Stecker
Kahenn Knox Hendriske
Jayce Thomas Stecker
Hayes Believer Hendriske
Luke John Guillen
Landon Robert Guillen
Addison Bruce Heinen

Table of Contents

PART II: David as King

PART I

David's Rise to Power

1 Samuel 16 - 2 Samuel 1
&
Eight Fugitive Psalms by David

Lesson 1

Demonstrating That God is the Living God

1 Samuel 16:1- 17:54

A young shepherd named David, from the family of Jesse, makes his first full appearance in 1 Samuel 16, but his story and appointment by God will go on into all of 2 Samuel. This section of Scripture from 1 Samuel 16 to chapter 31may be labelled as "The History of David's Rise," and will form part I of our character study of David, "the man after God's own heart."

The narrative begins with Samuel the prophet receiving God's instruction in 1 Samuel 16:1-13 to stop grieving over the divine rejection of Israel's first king Saul, whom Samuel helped appoint as king, and instead Samuel was to go to Bethlehem to anoint Saul's successor. But once this successor to the kingship of Israel was found, he was not left with nothing to do for a good while; instead, vv. 14-23 in the second half of this chapter 16 relates how this successor, though he came from humble and somewhat uncultured circumstances of the shepherd's fields outside Bethlehem, he nevertheless found his way immediately into the court of King Saul by the providence working of God.

In the previously coronation, the initiation of the Israelite monarchy in I Samuel 8-15 began with the account of King Saul at the demand of the people, so now the establishment of the monarchy under David begins with the narrative of his slow rise to power. However, David's careful rise relates to the decline of Saul's tenure as king. As a result, the narratives of Saul and David intersect throughout the remaining chapters of 1 Samuel, contributing to the most complex and compelling sections of the text. We will now examine these passages in greater detail.

David Is Anointed as King of Israel – 16:1-13

I Samuel 16:1 continues where chapter fifteen ended, with the prophet Samuel still mourning for Saul. So, what was the prophet's problem? God had to tell Samuel to "Let bygones be bygones." However, perhaps Samuel was grieving over the fact that he had failed as a mentor to Saul;

after all, Samuel had devoted a good deal of his life to instructing Saul, and it was he who had anointed him as king when Israel screamed for a king to rule over them just like the other nations. But Samuel may have feared that with Saul's failure, the failure of the nations might not be far behind in time. Did this change in the leader of the government mean Israel's enemies would now take advantage of them or would civil war break out on the nation during this unknown change in leadership?

But the Lord clearly instructed Samuel to "Get over it." Samuel was to take "horn with oil" and go to a man named "Jesse of Bethlehem," (a phrase that appears again in 17:58, which forms an inclusion that ties together chapters 16 and 17), for God had chosen one of Jesse's sons as the new king (1b). Samuel obeyed, even though he was apprehensive as to what Saul would do if he learned why he had come to Bethlehem. The Lord understood his problem, for he instructed Samuel to take a "heifer" with him as a sacrifice (2). Then he was to invite Jesse to the sacrifice, and from there on God would tell him what to do (3).

The key word in chapter 16 is the word to "see," (Hebrew, *ra'ah*), the Hebrew root of which appears nine times in chapter 16. [1] In v. 1 the verb to "see" is best translated as "chosen," as in the election of a king (cf. 2 Kings 10:3).

Samuel followed God's instructions; however, he feared what Saul would do when he heard what he had come to do (2). Therefore, the Lord told him to take along a sacrifice of a heifer as a secondary reason for his making the trip and offer it as a fellowship offering along with the ritual of anointing. The elders of the town "trembled [or: "quaked with fear"] when they met [Samuel]" and asked him, "Do you come in peace?" (16:4; cf. same question in 1 Kings 2:13; 2 Kings 9:22). Uppermost in their minds was their hearing of Samuel's recent execution of King Agag (15:33). But Samuel's calm answer assuaged their immediate anxieties.

Samuel seemed eager to start the process of anointing a king (6), for as soon as he cast his eyes on the stately appearance of Jesse's eldest son Eliab (meaning "My God is father") Samuel felt certain that here was God's next anointed king. But the Lord at once rebuked Samuel saying, "Do not look at his appearance, or at how tall he is, for I have rejected him; for it's not what man sees. People look at the outward appearance, but the LORD looks at the heart" (7). King Saul, their present king, was a

---

1. It appears as a verb in vv. 1, 17, to "see" or "look at" in vv. 6, 7, as nouns in vv. 7, 12, and three times as "appearance" in v. 18.

full far above the height of all the people, but Samuel had incorrectly missed God's real indicator for selecting a leader approved by God. Eliab was not that man!

Next, Jesse introduced his second and third sons, named Abinadab and Shammah to Samuel, but they too were not the men God was looking for either (8-9). As the process went on, Jesse introduces seven of his sons to the prophet, but none of the seven men were acceptable to the Lord (10). Naturally, Samuel was baffled as to what was going on here, so he asked Jesse, "Are these all the sons you have?" (11). To Samuel's great relief, he answered, "No." "There is still the youngest, but he is tending the sheep." Samuel replied, "Send for him; we will not sit down [to eat] until he arrives" (11d). The Hebrew word "youngest" can also be understood as "smallest," in a deliberate contrast to David's oldest brother Eliab and to King Saul. In fact, a Hebrew pseudo-Davidic and non-canonical Psalm from Qumran (11QPsa Ps. 151) has David say:

> Smallest was I than my brothers, the youngest of my father's sons. So, he made me shepherd of his flock .... He sent his prophet to anoint me, Samuel to make me great. My brothers went out to meet him, handsome of figure and of appearance. Though they were tall of stature, [and] handsome because of their hair, the LORD chose them not.

Accordingly, when we had first meet Saul, in the previous search for a king, he was looking for his father's lost donkeys (9:2-3), but when we first meet David in this new search, he is looking after his father's sheep, which metaphor of shepherding is much more conducive to learning how to rule over a people.

David is numbered the "eighth" child in 1 Samuel 17:12-14; however, 1 Chronicles 2:13-15 lists Jesse's sons and calls David the "seventh," a position in the family order of birth which Josephus also assigns to David. But the solution to this puzzle must be that one of David's older brothers had by that time died without offspring, so he was omitted from the genealogy of 1 Chronicles 2:13-15 and David was moved up in the birth-order.

When David was finally brought to Samuel, he was seen as "ruddy" (Hebrew, *'admoni*) and a man of "fine appearance" with "handsome features" (12). Then the LORD said to Samuel, "Rise and anoint him; he is the one" (12b). So, Samuel took the "horn of oil" he had brought along and anointed David in the presence of his brothers. From that very day forward, "the Spirit of the LORD came upon (Hebrew, *salach*, "seized") David in power,"[2] then Samuel left for his home at Ramah (13).

David Arrives in The Court of Saul – 16:14-23

From this point onwards it seemed as if King Saul was beginning to lose his ability to govern. The Spirit of the LORD departed from Saul and an evil spirit from Yahweh "terrified" or "terrorized" him (14). It may well have involved a serious mental disturbance that appeared in Saul's mental health, but the fact that it came right after the departure of the Lord's Spirit from Saul cannot be discounted as an incidental incident. Was this disturbance the work of a demon or was it more of a spirit of distress and calamity?

Saul's attendants asked king Saul if they could search for someone to play the harp for the king, for when this evil spirit settled over him, this would make him feel better (15). When they were given permission for such a search, one of the servants volunteered that he knew someone who could really play the harp well; he was good looking and: the LORD was with him!" (18). Saul gave the approval to send for this man, who turned out to be none other than David, the son of Jesse (19). Notice how the providence of our Lord was at work in all that was taking place, for this would position David for his future work even without that fact being told to Saul.

At the request of King Saul, David was summoned to the king's quarters. Jesse loaded a donkey for David full of bread, a skin of wine, and a young goat, for David to take them to Saul (20). When David arrived and began to play his "harp" (Hebrew, *kinnor*)[3] for Saul, "Saul liked him very much" (21). David became one of Saul's armor-bearers, a member of his "secret service." Saul sent word to Jesse asking permission for him to allow David to remain in his royal service, which was granted (22). Thus, periodically, when the Spirit of God would come over Saul, David would quickly take his harp in hand and play in Saul's presence, and relief would come to Saul (23). No wonder, then, that David gained the reputation of being "Israel's singer of songs" (2 Sam. 23:1).

---

2. See David H. Howard, Jr., "The Transfer of Power from Saul to David in 1 Samuel 16:13-14," JETS, 32/4 (1989):1989: 473-83, especially 477.
3. "What Did David's Lyre Look like?" BAR 8/1 (1982): 34. Of the 15 occurrences of Hebrew *niggen*, "Play an Instrument," 7 appear in this section (1 Sam. 16:16 [bis], 17, 18, 23; 18:10; 19:9).

The fact that God himself is said to have used an alien spirit to serve his divine purposes is seen elsewhere in the Old Testament, for on such occasions, we can affirm, that God's people:

> "We're not that concerned with determining secondary causes and properly attributing them to the exact causes. Under divine providence everything ultimately was attributed to him; [so,] why not say he did it in the first place?"[4]

David Faces the Philistine Champion Goliath – 17:1-25

If King Saul's installation as king was followed quite quickly with his defeat of the Ammonite Nahash (11:1-11), so David's anointing was likewise quickly followed by David's defeat of the Philistine Goliath (17:1-25). Surely such victories coming so soon after both king's inaugurations were demonstrations of the help God would give to each new leader of courage and military ability.

The Philistines had gathered their forces for battle between the cities of Socoh and Azekah in Judah, where they pitched their tents on one hill and the Israelites had pitched their tents on the other side with the Valley of Elah that was spread out between them. This site was fourteen miles southwest of Bethlehem and nineteen miles southwest of Jerusalem. Here the battle lines were stalled for almost six weeks (16) as a Philistine warrior named Goliath from the town of Gath in Philistia (five miles due west of Azekah) would come out every morning and evening, and challenge to fight a representative warrior for Israel.

Goliath was over nine feet tall (4); he wore a bronze helmet on his head and wore a coat of armor weighing around 125 to 139 pounds. On his legs he wore bronze greaves (6), and he carried a bronze javelin slung over his back. He also had a spear whose iron head weighted sixteen- and one-half pounds. The man was a "champion" (Hebrew, *'ish habbenayim*, meaning "the man between two [armies]")[5] and quite impressive in appearance to say the least, for it is the most detailed description of anyone found in Scripture!

Goliath stood and shouted to Israel's army, which was lined up on the other side of the Elah Valley (8) with these words:

---

4. Walter C. Kaiser, Jr., *Hard Sayings of the Old Testament,* Downers Grove, IL., InterVarsity Press, 1988, p. 131.

5. This unusual name "champion" appears at Qumran meaning "infantryman," and in Ugaritic meaning "middleman" or "intermediary."

> "Why do you come out and line up for battle? ... Choose a man and have him come down to me. If he is able to fight and kill me, we will become your subjects; but if I overcome him and kill him, you will become our subjects and serve us." (17:8b-9)

Then Goliath added:

> This day I defy the ranks of Israel! Give me a man and let us fight each other" (10).

Goliath thought he is defying the army of Israel, but David had a bigger picture of what was going on: Goliath was defying "the armies of the Living God" (26, 36). But Goliath had no idea of how large a task or what he was taking on: he was casting himself in the role of opposing the God of gods and Lord of lords; this God was not like one of his dumb idols; he was alive and mightily powerful such as Goliath had never seen!

As part of Saul's army, we again meet up with three of David's brothers: Eliab, the firstborn, along with Abinadab, and Shammah (12-15). David is explained as being the youngest of Jesse's family and the one charged with going back and forth from Saul's encampment to tend to his father's sheep (14-15).

David's job involved three tasks during those days of running back and forth: (1)he was to take food preparations to his three brothers and their commander, (2) he was to get any news from the three brothers as to how things were going, and (3) he was to bring back assurance that the three boys were ok. (17-18). David made this trip to the battle line early in the morning (20), reaching the camp one day at the precise moment as the two armies were assuming their battle positions facing each other on either side of the Elah Valley (21). David rapidly unloaded his supplies consisting of an ephah of roasted grain, ten loaves of bread, and ten cheeses (17-18) with the keeper of supplies (22), as he raced and got there in time to hear Goliath shout out his usual arrogant defiance to the troops of Israel (23). When the Israel army saw and heard Goliath pompously spout off his propaganda of defiance, the Israelite army ran from him in great fear (24). Who did Goliath think he was anyway, and how dare he mock the Lord God of Israel's hosts!

David Faces Fearful Israelites: Angry Eliab, Indecisive Saul - 17:26-39

We now hear David speak for the first time in the Bible:

> "What will be done for the man who strikes down this Philistine and shall turn away disgrace from Israel? Who is this uncircumcised Philistine that he should defy the armies of the Living God? (26)

Here David begins to show what a man who is owned by the Holy Spirt can say and do in a critical moment. David bluntly asked: Isn't the fact that we serve a Living God meant to make an enormous difference in times like these? That guy out there is mocking the God we all love and serve, and we should just stand here and melt away in fear as he burst his guts falsely claiming the opposite to what we know is true? The troops however didn't get it, for they repeated once again what Saul had promised to do for the man and his family if he should kill Goliath (27). But David had no interest in the presumed reward!

Typical of the poor responses David would get to his profoundly serious question was the one that came from his oldest brother, Eliab. When he heard his little brother talking with the men, he burned with anger and let him have a good tongue lashing at full force. He rebuked him saying,

> "Why have you come down here? And with whom did you leave those few sheep in the desert? I know how conceited you are and how wicked your heart is: you came down only to watch the battle" (28).

David's response was typical little brother reply for such situations, for he asked: "Now what have I done? Can't I even speak?" (29). However, what David was saying to the men got reported to King Saul, so the king sent for David. But he too was more than just a little skeptical:

> "You are not able to go out against this Philistine and fight him; you are only a boy, and he has been a fighting man from his youth" (33).

David is not slow to respond to the king's questions, for he explains even though he may not have had any fighting experience in the army, nevertheless, his occupation as a shepherd involved his being involved oftentimes in hand-to-hand combat with lions or bears who would attack the sheep he had to watch over. When that occurred, he had to go after the lion or bear and rescue the sheep from its mouth. If it turned on David, he would seize it by its hair, strike it, and kill the filcher of his flock (34-35). Likewise, O king, I want to tell you that:

> This uncircumcised Philistine will be like one of them, because he has defied the armies of the Living God. The LORD who delivered me from the paw of the lion and the paw of the bear will deliver me from the hand of this Philistine" (36b-37).

Saul had to concede, for David had scored convincing points in his graphic depiction of his lion and bear encounters. Anyway, Saul had no other options, for neither he, nor his son Jonathan, or any other Israelite was willing to take on the challenge of Goliath. "Go," urged Saul with a reluctant consent, "and the LORD be with you." (37c). Then Saul dressed David in his battle armor, but David complained, "I cannot go in these, because I am not used to them," so he took them off (39c).

David Meets Saul's Challenge – 17:40 – 58

David, armed merely with his staff and sling, approached Goliath, stopping to pick up five smooth stones from the brook in the Valley of Elah, which he tucked into his shepherd's bag (40). Goliath and his shield bearer also kept coming closer to David, whom when he saw that he was only a boy, the Philistine man despised him saying, "Am I a dog, that you come to me with sticks?" He cursed David and added, "Come here, and I'll give your flesh to the birds of the air and the beasts of the field" (43-44).

David was unimpressed by Goliath's bravado. Instead, he warned, "I come to you in the name of the LORD Almighty, the God of the armies of Israel whom you have defied" (45). Moreover, it is not my flesh that will go to the birds, but it will be your flesh and the flesh of all the carcasses of the Philistine army (46). Moreover, mister,

> "The whole world will know that there is a God in Israel. All those gathered here will know that it is not by sword or spear that the LORD saves; for the battle is the LORD's and he will give all of you into our hands" (46b-47).

David reached into his bag and took out a stone, put it in his sling, and let it fly from his slingshot. It struck Goliath on his forehead and sunk into his skull as I assume Goliath yelled in an unrecorded observation: "That was an idea that never struck me in just that manner." "In fact, it has made a real impression on my thinking!" The giant then fell face down as David raced to stand on top of him as he snatched his huge sword from his scabbard to kill him and then to cut off his head with a sword (51).

When the watching Philistine army saw what had happened to their champion, they turned and ran. But the army of Israel charged after them with a shout and chased them the next five miles to the very gates of Gath and Ekron in Philistia, leaving the dead corpses strewn all along the five miles of the roadway (52). Israel returned to plunder the Philistine camp (53), but David took Goliath's head to Jerusalem and his weapons he put in his own tent (54).

Saul's ignorance of David's name, in which on three separate occasions he asks, "Who is he?" (55, 56, 58) may show that he was beginning to lose his memory. Hadn't David played the harp for him? Or was it a way of reporting Saul's haughty and snobbish way being overcome by his envy of the "boy" that he no longer could put things straight in line as he should have been able to do so? Or was this question by the king only a leadoff inquiry in which he wanted to know more things about this "boy," for a boy with this sort of talent surely would soon be a direct challenge to him and his throne!

Conclusions

1. David did not take his clues from the disdain and repudiation he received from Eliab, his oldest brother. Instead, he put his trust in the name of the Lord. Proverbs 18:10 – "The name of the LORD is a strong tower and the righteous run into it."

2. It is a serious offense to heaven to defy and defame the Living God, for there is no one or anything that even comes close to comparing with him.

3. As Hudson Taylor taught, it does not matter how great the pressure is when we are in a leadership position; instead, it only matters where the pressure lies.

4. David's help with Goliath was "in the name of the LORD, who made the heaven and the earth" – Psalm 124:8

Questions for Thought or Discussion

1. Discuss the statement: "Fear makes cowards of all of us." Discuss this in connection with King Saul, his army, and in relation to us in the work of our Lord.
2. How do David's actions in 1 Samuel 16-17 show what it means to live by faith and not by presumption?
3. Can you trace the providence of God in bringing David forward as king and then compare it as to how God has worked in your own life?
4. How is a reproach of God a reproach also on his people?
5. How would the Philistines and Goliath know that the Living God was present in helping a young man like David overthrow their champion and army? (cf. Deut. 5:26; Josh. 3:10; 2 Kings 19:4; Ps. 42:2; 84:2; Jer. 10:10)

Lesson 2

David's Deliverances and Saul's Legacy of Envy and Hate

1 Samuel 18:1-30; 19:1-24; Psalm 59:1-17

At first, Saul and his oldest son, Jonathan, were both one in heart and spirit with their new friend David (18:1). However, up to this point, as far as we can tell, Saul had no idea that David had been anointed as king by the prophet Samuel prior to this. Now Saul wanted to keep David on a permanent basis in his household and therefore Saul did not let him return to his father's house (18:2).

In the meantime, Jonathan made a covenant with David, for the two of them became attached[1] to each other (18:3). In fact, Jonathan took off the robe he was wearing and gave it to David to wear, along with his tunic, sword, bow, and belt (4). David continued to enjoy success in every task Saul sent him to do (5). So, Saul promoted David to an especially high rank in the army, which act caught the attention and pleasure of Saul's officers and all the people (5b), for they too were impressed with this young man.

But things suddenly went sour in vv. 6-9, symptomatic of Saul's progressive disintegration signaled by his loss of the Holy Spirit in the gift of leading the nation. This became especially troublesome for Saul when the women started greeting Saul's returning army with singing and dancing that included, at least from Saul's perspective, these outrageous words:

> "Saul has slain his thousands,
> and David his tens of thousands." (7).

---

1. The Hebrew verb that described this relationship was literally that they "loved" one another, so Tom Horner, in his article entitled *Jonathan Loved David: Homosexuality in Biblical Times,* Philadelphia: Westminster, 1978, declared Jonathan and David had a homosexual relationship. But the Hebrew verb *'aheb,* "love," is never used in the Old Testament to express homosexual activity or desire.

That did not strike Saul the right way at all; in fact, it "galled" him (8). Why was David being credited with ten times the success as he, the king of the nation had enjoyed, in the joyful view of the people (8). What else was this young buck going to strip from me, lamented Saul – would it be my kingdom — which was not a bad guess on his part! It is time to look at chapters 18 and 19 in more detail to see how this all developed.

The Outbreak of Anger and Envy Against David – 18:1-11

Saul, by now, was surely aware of facts that he could not avoid any longer. First, the Spirit of God had distinctly left him, and he was now on his own to govern the country. Second, the Lord was "with David" in a major way, so that everything he touched was at once turning out to be successful. Third, the people realized that David was the one favored by the Lord, and not Saul or his family – and that made him mad as hops! Moreover, despite the suspicious eye he kept on David, he had to promote him in his regular army by popular demand, for he had unusual success of the battlefield.

From all sources, David was a man who had physical prowess, courage, stamina, and personality, and it was this that easily captured the hearts of the officers of Saul's army, not to mention the nation. Saul was no longer the people's favorite.

Goliath had challenged Saul long before David arrived on the scene, but Saul did not rise to the occasion. But now when everyone was extolling the virtues of David, this high praise aroused a smoldering anger in Saul as his pride was given a mortal blow! Saul felt guilty for his abdicating his position and responsibility to set an example in front of his troops when Goliath came out every day calling for a challenger. Now, however, he was left with a deep depression and a troubling evil spirit from the LORD.

So severe were these spells of depression, that one day as David was playing his harp to relieve Saul of his mental discomfort, Saul took the spear, which for some reason was ready in his hand, and hurled it at David as he muttered something about "I'll pin David to the wall." Obviously, Saul was not interested in making out of David a permanent wall-portrait as his musician pasted on his wall; no, he wanted to kill him (10-11). Fortunately, David was quick enough to dodge the king's close aim, and thus he escaped being a fatality. But this was enough to show David that Saul was now vacillating between his anger and his fear. Saul had come unglued! What Saul had been building up inside a body of emotions was beginning to be unleashed in death-threats on David's life. However, in the providence of God, despite Saul's proximity to the king while he was playing his instrument for him, the Lord delivered David, for God had larger plans and a greater purpose for him and his life.

A Mounting Up of Anger and Secret Vengeance Against David – 18:12-30.

Saul knew full well by now that the LORD was obviously with David and not with him, so he began to be afraid of him (12). David was experiencing enormous success in everything he did, and that only increased Saul's fears (14-15). Therefore, Saul realizing things were getting out of hand, as far as the popularity polls in the nation were concerned, that Saul now started scheming and calculating various plans that might bring him relief from this young buck. Under the guise of congeniality, he thought promising his eldest daughter Merab to David in marriage would make an ideal plan, but only if he would prove his valiant self on the battlefield (17). If something tragic happened to David during his fighting, it would not be Saul's fault, for those things happen in battles, reasoned Saul! Saul could leave the dirty work of killing his enemy David to the Philistines and he would at last be free of this Mister Goody-Two-shoes! (17d). David however did not fall for such a gift, for he objected to Saul's largess by, saying:

> "Who am I, and what is my family or my father's clan in Israel that I should become the king's son-in-law? (18).

But when the time came for Merab to be given to David in marriage as Saul had promised, Merab was given instead to Adriel of Meholah (19). But then new word came that Saul had another daughter named Michal, who said she loved David. Saul was delighted with this news, for he thought, "I will give her to him so that she may be a snare to him, and so the hand of the Philistines may be against him" (21). Ruthlessly, Saul cozied up to David and pretended to be happy by saying these words:

"Now you have a second opportunity to become my son-in-law" (21d). What was Saul counting on? Did he think his daughter Michal would rob David of his strength and so he would be less effective in battle?

Saul began a whispering campaign among his attendants to the effect that the king was pleased with him, just as they too were pleased with David. However, David did not buy their foolish rumors, for he continued to depict himself as a poor man, one who was little known and unworthy to be the king's son-in-law (23). When Saul realized that neither he, nor his attendants, were going to be successful in their staged rumor-mill, his strategy took another direction. He instructed his attendants to say the king does not want any other bride-price for his daughter Michal other than 100 Philistine foreskins (25). Saul's devious plan was to have David fall into the hands of his enemy the Philistines (25b). Such samples would require close and personal fighting!

However, David felt this was a more sensible plan from his point of view; in lieu of the traditional bride-price, if the king was willing to accept 100 Philistine foreskins, which made more sense to him, for it would look like David had earned it in place of a bride-price (26). So, David and his men went out, and he doubled the price Saul had demanded as he brought back 200 Philistine foreskins (27). Saul's plan failed, leaving David alive and Saul frustrated. This kid was sticking to him like chewing gum; it seemed he would never be rid of him! Saul's fear of David only increased (29). In fact, David was experiencing so much more success against these annoying Philistines than the entirety of the rest of Saul's officers so that David's name became well known all over the place (30).

Anger That Turns into Violence Against David – 19:1-17

The more David enjoyed success the more infuriated Saul became (19:1). So, Saul gave the order to his son Jonathan and to the king's attendants to "kill David" (1). Saul's jealousy, animosity, and belligerence now knew no bounds. The greater the success God handed to David, the more David's reputation grew among the people; but simultaneously, the darker and more hideous did Saul's determination rise to kill and so away with David. Thus, in blind fury he ordered that his son Jonathan and his staff should put a target on David's back. He simply had to do away with his rival by murdering him, so he was rid of him and his reputation finally.

Jonathan alerted David to flee into the nearby fields and to go into hiding until he had had time to talk to his father. Jonathan knew something of his father's irrational fury, for he had faced it as well. Nevertheless, Jonathan would not be intimidated by his father's wrath, even if at times he acted like a deranged man.

Jonathan's plan for David was this:

> "Tomorrow morning …. I will go out and stand with my father in the field where you are [hiding]. I'll speak to him about you and will tell you what I find out" (3).

Jonathan, as could be expected from such a close friend, plead the case for David well. His point was that David had not wronged his father; instead, all he had done really helped his rule and kingdom quite a bit (4). If truth be told, David had oftentimes taken his very own life in his hands for Saul and the kingdom, as when he killed the giant, or won victory after victory for Israel over the Philistines. David was an innocent man (5).

Surprisingly, Saul listened to the counsel of his son Jonathan, as this son of his spoke both respectfully, yet forcefully. Jonathan summarized his case this way:

> "Why then do you want to sin against this innocent man like David, by killing him for no reason? (5) .

At least for the moment, Jonathan's defense of his friend David seemed to sink into Saul's darkened mind; unexpectedly he sensed the solemnity of his bitter hostility. Therefore, in a sudden reversal of his earlier position, he made a complete turn around and swore that David would be spared (6). But tragic as it became, Saul could not keep to his vow.

Jonathan's courage in respectfully confronting his father is a wonderful guideline for us when we meet similar situations. Jonathan spoke at risk to himself as he tried calmly and respectfully to challenge his father's conduct. Saul could in that moment have banished his son forever from his presence, for he saw him as colluding with his enemy. But Jonathan's stern and careful description of what his father was doing was a credit to him and to all who will follow his example.

All too often, the typical response in a tight situation as this is to say, "I am not to judge others." But what is forgotten in such a situation is that while we are not to condemn others, we are called upon at times to pass judgment on evil actions and incorrect behavior. God's word will supply us with the guidance we need when we try to figure out what is right and what is wrong.

Once more war broke out and David went out and hit the Philistines with such force that they took off and fled before him (8). But that brought back an evil spirit over Saul so that David had to play the harp for him to get relief (9). However, as David was playing his harp, Saul was sitting in his house with his spear in his hand once again (9). But as the first few chords flowed into the royal chamber, Saul suddenly let his spear go flying towards his harp player as he tried one more time to pin David to the wall. Fortunately, David again ducked in time. That night David made his escape, for he was not comfortable being a target for Saul's spear throwing game! (10). As darkness set in, David made his way to his home with Michal. But his wife knew as well as he that his home was not a place of safety, for Saul also sent his men to David's house to watch for him and to kill him as the morning light appeared (11).

Michal, David's wife, knew as well as her brother Jonathan also knew, that Saul's melancholy mood was not to be fooled with. So, she let David down through a window (just as Rahab let Israel's spies down through a window from her house on the wall) and he escaped (12). Then Michal took an idol (but what was an idol doing in David's house?) and she laid it in the bed covered over with a garment and put some goat's hair on the head of the idol to give the impression a person was sleeping in bed (13).In this way she was prepared to double-cross her father. Did the daughter deceive both Saul's men and her father, a skill she learned from watching him?

David Composes a Psalm for the Occasion: Psalm 59:1-17

There are eight "Fugitive Psalms" (7, 34, 52, 54, 56, 57, 59, 142) that David composed during this period of trying to avoid the lethal intent of King Saul on his life. These Psalms grant us a good insight into what was going on in David's heart and mind while he waits for the deliverance that came from God and the kingdom of Israel for which Samuel had already anointed him.

To gain a little insight into this, we turn to Psalm 59, whose heading[2] informs us that this psalm was written "when Saul had sent men to watch David's house in order to kill him." This matches the precise time mentioned in 1 Samuel 19. We are given David's prayer as he faced the wrath of Saul and his men. David prayed:

> Deliver me from my enemies, O God.
> be my fortress against those who are attacking me.
> Deliver me from evildoers
> and save me from those who are after my blood.
> See how they lie in wait for me!
> Powerful people conspire against me
> for no offense or sin of mine, LORD. (Ps 59:1-3)

David shows us in this psalm, composed as we noted, at the very time he was under a death-threat from Saul, that he was not a bit overwhelmed by his enemies, for even though his enemies "return at evening snarling like dogs [that] prowl about the city" (Ps. 59:6), David called on God to deliver him. Notice, David refused to be overcome by such enemies that currently were surrounding his house waiting to kill him. In his view, the Lord "laughed at them" and he "scoff[ed] at all those nations" (Ps. 59:8) that would try the very same trick. For David affirmed "You [LORD] are my strength. I watch for you; you, my God, are my fortress, my God on whom I can rely" (Ps. 59:8).

The difference between God being our strength itself and our very own stronghold or defense, as opposed to his being the one from whom we derive these gifts, is that our Lord does not merely give us these helps, but instead the point is that in him we find the fullness of his strength. He not only gives us a defense, but he is our defense. Thus, David and we are to be strong in the Lord and in the power of his might.

This 59th Psalm comes to a climax in vv. 16-17. The Psalmist of Israel concludes by saying:

---

2. The headings of Psalms often go back to the times of their original composition. Hebrew terms were untranslatable by the time the Septuagint was written in the third century B.C.E.

> But I will sing of your strength,
> in the morning, I will sing of your love,
> for you are my fortress,
> my refuge in times of trouble.
> You are my strength; I sing praise to you.
> You, God, are my fortress,
> my God on whom I can rely. (Ps. 59:16-17)

David had learned how to pray when he was surrounded by his enemies; he prayed when he was in a panic, when he had doubts, and when he had no idea what the future held for him. But David had learned how to sing as well. He could praise the Lord even when he had not yet seen his deliverance from God's hand.

Saul sent his men to capture David at his home, but Michal lied to them, saying he was sick in bed. When Saul got this report, he sent the men back again with orders to bring David, the man, his bed, and all, to him at Gibeah at once (15). But when the men entered the house, Michal's disguise of the idol in bed disgusted Saul when he later learned what Michal had done. Saul griped: "Why do you deceive me like this and send my enemy away so that he escaped" (17). Saul declaring David to be his mortal "enemy" barred David from ever returning to Saul's court in Gibeah.

Saul And His Men Captured by the Prophesying Spirit of God - 19:18-24

David fled from his house as Michal had recommended. He then went to the prophet Samuel's hometown of Ramah, which was far in the northwest of Gibeah (18). Samuel and David, in turn, went to Naioth (meaning "habitations"), signifying a compound of dwellings where a "group of prophets" lived (20, cf. 2 Kings 6:1-2). Saul sent men to Naioth three times to capture David, but each time God protected him. Eventually, Saul went himself, stopping at Secu to ask about Samuel and David's whereabouts. But he too was overcome by the Holy Spirit as he went on his way, and so he began to prophesy as well. However, as the Spirit of God overcame him, Saul stripped off his robes (the symbols of his rule) and he prophesied in Samuel's presence as had the earlier delegations done before he arrived (24). Hence, there arose a proverb in Israel, "Is Saul also among the prophets? (24b).

Conclusions

1. It is impossible to miss the four references to the success of David in chapter 18: 5, 14, 15, 30. The God who called God to be king was the same Lord who promised to grant him success, which he did.
2. To back up David's success, the Lord promised to be "with him" three times in this chapter – 1 Samuel 18:12, 14, 28. The presence of the Lord with David must have comforted him to no end.
3. David was also loved by all he met and worked with, for this is what the text affirmed six times – 1 Samuel 18:1, 3, 16, 20, 22, 28. However, despite all this love shown to David, three times Saul is said to fear David and stand in awe of him – 1 Samuel 18:12, 15, 20 which did not lead him to loving David..
4. The Lord protected and delivered David, for 1 Samuel 19 gave four such "deliverances" as a gift from God (1-7, 8-10, 11-17, 18-24).
5. The Holy Spirit of God is no respecter of persons, for he overcame three sets of messengers that Saul sent to capture David, as he also overtook Saul himself.

Lesson 3

Learning to Depend on the Lord

1 Samuel 20:1-42; 21:1-15; Psalm 56:1-13; Psalm 34:1-22

David fled from Naioth at Ramah where he had been with Samuel and suddenly went to be with Jonathan. His question of Jonathan was this: "What have I done? What is my crime? How have I wronged your father, that he is trying to take my life?" Now no case can be made for David that claims that he was perfect and without sin; however, surely David had not deserved all that he was facing with Jonathan's father. In fact, according to Polzin,[1] the language of the first half of 1 Samuel 20 is filled with words that were emotionally charged, and words that were definite, forceful, and strident as David inquired as to what was happening to him.

Jonathan received David's charge that his father was trying to take his life as being wrong. "Never" (20:2), Jonathan replied, for he was both a loyal friend of David's and a trusting son of his father. In fact, Jonathan was so sure his father would not do anything without confiding in him that he found David's charge unbelievable (2b).

David responded with an oath that Saul surely knew his sons' favorable attachment to David, so there would be no way he would let Jonathan know the full facts of his attitude to David. So, David affirmed in an oath the following: As the Lord lives and as Jonathan lived, "there [was] only a step between me and my death" (3). Jonathan promised he would investigate the matter for David (4), but he was still unconvinced that David's story was correct.

David prompted Jonathan to lie on his behalf (6-8), for on the next day the Festival of the New Moon took place when David was supposed to dine with the king. However, David would go and hide in a field during the first day of the feast. If the king missed David, then Jonathan was to say on David's behalf that he had earnestly asked him permission to hurry

1. Robert Polzin, *Samuel and the Deuteronomist*, San Francisco, Harper, 1989, p. 191, 264, nn. 10-13. He meant that the verbs were strengthened by having a preceding Hebrew infinitive absolute of the same stem verb seven times in vv. 1-21.

to Bethlehem for an annual sacrifice made for his whole clan, which was not correct. If Saul reacted badly, then he was to bring word to David, which of course is exactly what happened. These two chapters, therefore, need to be examined more in detail.

Trusting in the Lord's Steadfast Love Instead of Trusting Men – 20:1-42

It is to David's credit that despite the horrendous attacks that Saul was hurling at David that he did not seek revenge on Saul, nor did he look to drive a wedge between father and son! David was committed to honoring the integrity of Jonathan's home. This became an outstanding feature in David's life, for he consistently refused to create a breach between Saul and Jonathan even amid the worst provocation. Moreover, David respected the sanctity of the crown, for Saul's kingship was under the rule and reign of a Sovereign Lord who had appointed Saul and anointed him.

David was prepared to die, if he must; however, he preferred it would be from the hands of Jonathan, for their friendship was formalized with a covenant (18:1-5). It was because of such sterling love between the two men that they could air out those things that either of them thought was fracturing their friendship. David expected Jonathan to act with "kindness" (Hebrew, *hesed*[2]) toward him because of the covenant they had jointly made. In this light, then, David was determined to find out what Saul's intentions towards him were. So, he decided to purposely be absent on the special feast day of the New Moon. If Saul missed him, which most certainly would, Jonathan was to offer the excuse that David invented; he had been suddenly called by his brother to return home to Bethlehem for a family reunion.

The signal the men set up is that Jonathan will come out in the field where David is hiding in the evening of the n day after tomorrow. There he will shoot three arrows (20), and he will send a boy to recover the arrows. If Jonathan will say to the boy, "Look, the arrows are on this side of you; bring them to me," then come for you are safe (21). But if I say to the boy, "Look, the arrows are beyond you, then you must go because the

2. The English versions render this Hebrew word *hesed* in ways including "to deal kindly," "to show faithful love." This term occurs 248 times in the Old Testament. It carries the idea of "love," "affection," "compassion," "loyalty."

LORD has sent you away (22). And as for the matter we discussed earlier, Behold, the LORD is between you and me forever (24).

In the morning, Jonathan went out into the field with the young boy to send the signal to David (34-40). After Jonathan had dismissed the young boy, David came out of his hiding place and bowed to Jonathan three times with his face to the ground. They kissed each other good-bye as they reaffirmed their sworn friendship by saying, "The LORD is witness between you and me, and between your descendants and my descendants forever (42).

Calling on The Lord's Help Instead of Speaking Lies -21:1-9

David went to Nob, which was a mere one and half miles northeast of Jerusalem and a mere two and half miles southeast of Saul's fortress in Gibeah (21:1). It was at this spot that the tabernacle rested, without the Ark of the Covenant for a brief period of time.

The priest at Nob at that time was Ahimelech, meaning "the King [i.e., God] is my brother." When he saw David, Ahimelech "trembled," for he explained with two questions why he was so shaken: "Why are you alone?" and "Why is no one with you?"

David responded to both questions by alleging that the "king" had sent him on a secret mission that he wished to discuss with the priest (2a), and his men were not with him because they were to meet him later (2c). Did David mean that Saul had sent him on this mission, which could not be true at all, or was he referring to the Lord as the King? This sounds as if David was using the convenience of a lie to get out of a jam, for there is no evidence to back up his story. David assured Ahimelech that women had been kept from the men (5), for the word "holy" was the opposite of the Hebrew word for "common."

David followed that up with two more questions: "What do you have on hand?" (3) "Don't you have a spear or a sword here? (8). The priest Ahimelech answered each question: "I don't have ordinary bread on hand; however, there is some consecrated bread here – provided the men have kept themselves from women" (4). "The sword of Goliath the Philistine, whom you killed in the valley of Elah, is here; it is wrapped in a cloth behind the ephod. If you want it, take it; there is no sword here but that one" (9). David was pleased with the priest's response, for he replied: "There is none like it; give it to me" (9d).

There was one huge problem to the story David told Ahimelech; one of Saul's servants, his "head shepherd" named Doeg the Edomite, had been detained at Nob that very same day David arrived there (7). Why he was there, the text does not say. He may have sought religious communion with Israel either for ceremonial purposes or as a proselyte. That incident would lead to a tragic ending.

Fleeing to God for Refuge Instead of Taking Shelter from the Godless – 21:10-15

On that very day David left Abimelech at Nob and went in sequence from Gath in Philistia (21:10-15) to Adullam in Judah (22:1-2), then on to Mizpah in Moab (22:3-5) in his flight from King Saul, he became a fugitive.

What caused him to leave the first place he had stopped in, Gath in Philistia, was no doubt the fact that the servants of King Achish of Gath recognized who David was right away. They began to ask, "Isn't this David, the king of the land? Isn't he the one they sing about at their dances: 'Saul has slain his thousands, and David his tens of thousands'" (21:11). It is most noteworthy that the Philistines recognized David as the real king of "the land," even though Saul was still the titular head of Israel!

What drove David to go to Gath, especially carrying the legendary sword of Goliath, the heroic former champion of Gath, is beyond our imagination. Or had David gone to Gath seeking employment as a mercenary soldier? Whatever reason he had, it sure seemed suicidal, at the very least!

David recognized the danger he was in and thus he became very much afraid of Achish king of Gath (12). He quickly decided he needed to escape that situation as smoothly and as quickly as possible, so he began to pretend like he was insane. He acted like a madman as he began to let saliva run down his beard as he started to make mark or scratch on the doors of the city gates. This performance must have been a convincing one, for Achish, king of Gath had seen enough. He denounced David in a sarcastic voice, saying: "Look at the man! He is insane! Why bring him to me? Am I so short of madmen that you must bring this fellow here to continue like this in front of me? Must this man come into my house? (14-15).

Depending on the Lord for Escape Instead of Depending on Godless Men – Psalm 56:1-13

The ancient title given to this Psalm includes the note that this psalm is "Of [or from] David." It is also called a *miktam* (meaning a "golden oldie"), and it was composed, claimed the heading in the Psalter, "when the Philistines had seized him in Gath." Although no "seizure" is mentioned in 1 Samuel 21, it is very conceivable that such did take place once David's identity became known in Gath. What was this man up to? Did he have any ulterior motives for storming into the enemy's camp?

This psalm is one of the most beautiful among all the Psalms. This prayer of lament begins without the usual build up call for "mercy." David paints his adversity in rapid strokes of a man who is being "hotly pursued … all day long" (1). It raises the question whether David had been seized and taken as a prisoner by the Philistines in this incident in Gath, for the lords of the Philistines were indeed "many," and all of them surely opposed David (2). However, David's testimony was that at "What time [he was] afraid, [he put his] trust in the [LORD]" (3). No matter how difficult the times proved to be, David decided he would put his trust in the LORD rather than feed his fears or stare at his problems. After all, concluded David, "What can mortal man do to me?" (4c).

The thoughts of the Achish court were fixed on a plot to harm David, for what they desired was his life (5-6). They lurked in hiding to catch David in an unguarded moment (6). Therefore, David plead with God in prayer, "Do not let them escape;" let them face what the other nations will face in your anger (7). Indeed, David prayed that God would keep record of his tears and store them up in his memory (8). In this way David would know that God would turn his enemies back on themselves and that God was for him (9).

Again, David repeats that his affirmation was this: "In God I trust; I will not be afraid What can man do to me?" (4d, 11b). The reason David was so confident was he had put his solid trust in the LORD and his word (10).

Instead of concluding with more of the lament or petition to God to intervene, instead he gives a ringing thanksgiving and praise to God for his victory (12-13). David made a vow to present a thank offering to the LORD for his deliverance; he his Lord had been true to his promises.

Calling on the Lord Instead of Trying to Save Ourselves from All Evil – Psalm 34:1-22

Psalm 56 was written when David visited the king of Gath while fleeing from Saul. Psalm 34 is also attributed to David and believed to have been composed during the same period. Another way to put it is to say that in Psalm 56 we have David's prayer offered in his time of deep trouble and in Psalm 34 we have his thanksgiving for being delivered.

The title for Psalm 34 reads: "Of/by David. When he pretended to be insane in front of Abimelech, who drove him away from Gath and he left." David's authorship of this Psalm is disputed since 1 Samuel 21 names "King Achish," while the Psalm refers to "Abimelech." This so-called contradiction, however, disappears when we realize that "Abimelech" is the title given to all Philistine kings just as all Egyptian monarchs are called "Pharaohs," or the kings of Hazor are called "Jabin."

Therefore, in this Psalm, David gives thanks to God for his safe escape from the pending disaster he had walked into. David exhorted all who know the LORD to give thanks with him for God's deliverance, for our LORD always manifests himself as equally ready to help all who are his just as he had helped David.

This Psalm is also an alphabetic Psalm that has two equal parts with the first part coming in vv.1-10 and the second part coming in vv. 11-21, using v. 22 as a summing up verse, while leaving no verse for the Hebrew letter *vav,* which is omitted in this Psalm.

The Present Occasion of David's Deliverance – 34:1-10

The psalmist began in vv. 1-3 showing his desire to praise God for his narrow deliverance from the Philistines in the city of Gath. David, then, used the basis of the help he received from God to exhort all who were godly to join in with him in praise the LORD. Therefore, the "afflicted" hear and likewise "boast in the LORD" (2). Thus, all who know the LORD are urged to make the name of the LORD great and to exalt his name forever. (3).

David sought the LORD, when it was discovered in that town that he was the David who had slain so many Philistines in battle. Therefore, David pretended he had gone crazy, so the king ordered him out of his town (4). Just as a child who is seriously ill looks to his parents for help (5), so David looked to the LORD, and he delivered him. So, what was true of the general principle, it could also be applied to his case in v. 6. In fact, "the Angel of the LORD encamps around those who fear [the LORD]" (7). This Angel is the same as the Lord Jesus, who is called "the Captain of the LORD's army" in Joshua 5:14. The imperatives of vv. 8-9 are promises of God's goodness – so, do "taste and see, fear the LORD." Meanwhile, "the lions," who in this case are the powerful and violent men, are reduced to poverty so they lack everything (10).

The Future Times of Leading a Quiet Life in the Fear of the Lord -34:11-22

In this second strophe of Psalm 34, all are invited to enjoy the safety that is to be found in the fear of the LORD. So, David urged his listeners to "come… and listen" to him, for he would "teach [them] the fear of the LORD" (11). David will show these God-fearers not only what the fear of the LORD is, but he will also give them the strongest and best reasons for following that path.

Those who seek lasting contentment and wish to enjoy such days are recommended to refrain from malicious speech and avoid dishonesty in their communications (13). This can be done by "turn[ing] from evil and do[ing] good; seek[ing] peace and pursu[ing] it" (14). The LORD has his eyes on the righteous and his ears are alert to their cry (15). But those who do evil can expect to have "face of the LORD" oppose them (16). However, when the righteous cry, the LORD hears them, and he delivers them (just as he delivered me out of Gath) (17). So, all who are "brokenhearted" and "crushed in spirit," can expect God's deliverance (18). In fact, the righteous may face troubles, but the LORD delivers them from all of them (19). Not a bone in their bodies will be broken, for (now David summarizes the whole Psalm), the LORD redeems and delivers all who take refuge in him (22). Those who oppose us in wickedness will be judged, especially in times of adversity.

Conclusions

1. Loving kindness is an expression of deep-seated loyalty of love and generosity to members of the covenant community.
2. We should never be convinced of a bad report against others unless we gain the evidence for such from our own inquires. Johnathan did not believe his father was guilty of David's charges until he evaluated them himself.
3. Saul lost his ability to rule and reign because he lost the gifting of the Holy Spirit in his life. Without that gift he was unable to perform the duties of his office.
4. In emergency situations and under certain restrictions, what was holy and sacred to the LORD, such as the twelve loves of consecrated bread, could be used to help in common or secular situations.
5. When David pretended to have gone insane, he was able to escape being captured and locked up without outside help. Did he break any divine rule in doing so?

Questions for Thought or Discussion

1. How can individuals who are in the same tight straits that Jonathan was between loyalty to his father and loyalty to his friend David make a godly decision in that situation? What would you suggest?
2. Why do you think David suddenly left the protection of the prophet Samuel and went off on his own? What other choices did he have?
3. Was what Jonathan said, at the insistence of David about his excuse for not attending the New Moon Festival, a lie or was it excusable in God's sight?
4. Was David responsible for the death of Abimelech and his family because he lied, or did he have a reason for doing so?
5. Why would David take refuge with Achish king of Gath while also carrying a war trophy along with him? What do you think he was trying to do? Why did he go to Gath in Philistia?

Lesson 4

Waiting for God's Deliverance

I Samuel 22:1-23; Psalm 57:1-11; Psalm 52:1-9

David fortunately escaped the tight situation he found himself in the Philistine city of Gath and took refuge in a cave in Adullam, a town found in the low hills of Judah, called the Shephelah, about twelve miles east of Gath. David's brothers and family went down from Bethlehem to join David in Adullam, for they no longer felt safe. They were afraid that they would be subject to Saul's royal reprisal if they stayed in Bethlehem (22:1).

However, his family was not the only people who came to be with David, for a rather motley crew of all sorts of riffraff and malcontents in society of all sorts, including folks in debt, others in one type of distress or another began filtering down to the cave where David was to join him. Eventually the number of those who "gathered" around David was 400, a formidable group of potential fighters, but what a crew of discontents. They were attracted to David as their leader because they figured he too was a social misfit and now a malcontent given the treatment he had received from King Saul (2).

Uppermost in David's mind, however, was the fact that he needed to make some arrangements for the safety of his parents, since he had brought this tragedy upon them by being anointed a king first of all, and then by his being taken into Saul's court, he only added more trouble to his family because of a huge case of jealousy and envy that was growing in the king's lunacy (3-4). Moreover, David's parents now were well-up in years (17:12), so they were not up to the rigors of bouncing from place to place with a fugitive to avoid the wrath of Saul. Therefore, David went to "Mizpah" (meaning "watchtower," located on one of the heights of the tableland east of the Dead Sea) in Moab, from which country David's great grandmother Ruth the Moabitess had come (Ruth 4:18-22), to arrange for a place of refuge for his parents. Surely David and his folks were reminded of the words of that great Psalm 46 –

> "God is our refuge and strength, an ever-present help in [a time of] trouble. Therefore, we will not fear though the earth give way, and the mountains fall into the heart of the sea, though its waters roar and foam and the mountains quake with their surging .... The LORD Almighty is with us; the God of Jacob is our fortress." (Ps. 46:1-3, 11)

David's request of the foreign king of Moab was this: "Would you let my father and mother come and stay with you until I learn what God will do for me?" (3b). In doing so, David was putting into practice the fifth commandment, the way to treat one's parents (Exod. 20:12; Deut. 5:16), as well as employing a customary practice of caring and honoring one's parents (Josh. 2:13). Since David had Moabite blood in him, he hoped it would count for mercy from the king of Moab. This did influence the Moabite, for asylum was granted to his parents. His parents remained in Moab for the whole period that David fled from one place to another as a fugitive from Saul. But for now, David had taken refuge in the stronghold (4-5; 24:22), the Rock, the Lord God himself.

Just as the prophet Samuel had in his earlier days counseled Saul, God had now raised up the prophet Gad (5) to advise and counsel David. In fact, in 2 Samuel 24: 11, Gad is called "David's seer," which is the ancient name for "prophet." It was the usual way that God mediated his word to the leaders of Israel in the days of the prophets, as well as seeing that these prophets were simultaneously the ones who also recorded the events of those royal reigns (1 Chron. 29:29). Gad instructed David not to remain in that stronghold, but he should go into the land of Judah. At Gad's word, David left the stronghold, which may have been in En-Gedi, west of the Dead Sea, and went to the "Forest of Hereth," whose location is also unknown to us (5b).

Let us review what we have learned this far:

We have already covered the first two "situations" of points I and II in the brief texts already examined in the material above; viz., in 1 Samuel 22:1-2 and 22:3-5. However, another one of the Eight Fugitive Psalms, Psalm 57, includes in its historical heading these words: "Of David. A Michtam: when he fled from Saul into the cave," which is exactly where we are now. So let us go to this Psalm 57 to catch what David learned from God in that situation and what the Lord wishes us to also learn.

A Psalm of Mercy to David and Rebuke to Saul – Psalm 57:1-11

Psalm 57 is called a "twin Psalm" to Psalm 56; however, it distinctly says that it was written "in a cave," which matches what I Samuel 22:1 said. But even more importantly, Psalm 57 is divided perfectly in half by the refrains in vv. 5, 11:

> Be exalted, O God, above the heavens,
> Let your glory be over all the earth.

Psalm 57 represents the enemies of David's soul as mortals who are crafty, strong, and merciless. But there is a difference between the ungodly and the godly, for the ungodly seek deliverance by their own devices and with self-help; however, the godly seek deliverance from God alone.

The theme of this fugitive psalm is found in vv. 3 and 10 where God will send forth his love to those who have felt hounded and hunted like animals. However, God will show his faithfulness to all those who counted on him to make an enormous difference when it seemed as if no one else cared for them or bothered about them. So, v. 3 strongly rebukes those who hotly pursue their victims for no good reason. If David and all who are pursued cannot find a shelter or refuge in the Lord, there is no other place that such protection can be found. In fact, all the caves in Adullam are utterly useless if "our souls [cannot] take refuge …. In the shadow of [God's] wings."

That last phrase is reminiscent of the story of Ruth who had left her family and homeland of Moab and confessed to Naomi in Ruth 1:16, "Where you go, I will go and where you stay, I will stay. Your people will be my people and your God my God." Her future husband, Boaz, responded to her in Ruth 2:12, "May the LORD repay you. ….. The God of Israel, under whose wings you have come to take refuge. Those words must have been shared among the family over the years since the days when David's great-grandmother spoke to them in Moab! Thus, David, and we too, take refuge under those same "protecting wings" until the disaster has passed (1), for there is a purpose in all of this and it is God himself who will fulfill it (2). Even if our enemies act like ravenous beasts (4) with teeth like spears and arrows (4b) and tongues as sharp as swords (4c), God will send help from heaven and save both David and us if we call on him. God will rebuke those who hotly pursue such individuals as David, and of course he will save us if we also call upon him.

David intersperses his complaint and prayer to God with a doxology that declares: "Be exalted, O God, above the heavens; let your glory be over all the earth." (5, 11, cf. Hab. 2:14). What a resounding offering of praise to our God!

God's faithfulness will bubby trap those who had planned on trapping David and any of his saints (6-11). Moreover, even though the net is spread and the pit has been dug for our ensnarement, it will actually catch the very ones who built it for their enemies and for those who were like such brutes (6). Such awesome divine deliverance calls for the music of praise to God and results in his steadfast heart fixed on us for our good (7-8). No wonder, then, that David will praise the LORD even if it is offered in front of all the Gentile nations (9). For God's love reaches all the way to the heavens and his faithfulness reaches up to the skies (10). Once, again, therefore, it is time to sing the same doxology sounded in v. 5j and now repeated in v. 11.

But now we turn to the third SITUATION.

When Evil Seems to be in Control -22:6-23

King Saul has developed a severe case of paranoia (22:7-8), for we find him seated with a spear in his hand, under a tamarisk tree on the hill of Gibeah lecturing his officials about the evil paths of the son of Jesse. In his paranoia, he depicted to his staff of officials who might have been siding with David, in hopes of gaining receiving fields and vineyards, a very dismal picture. (7). Saul is convinced that all his staff members were in a conspiracy against him, for no one had told him previously that his son Jonathan had made as covenant with David or that his son had incited David to lie in wait to harm him (8).

Suddenly, Doeg the Edomite and king's herdsman, must have been moved by Saul's speech, for he decided to speak up and say, "I saw the son of Jesse come to Ahimelech son of Ahitub at Nob .... Give him provisions and the sword of Goliath the Philistine" (9-10; 21:7-9). There it was, just what Saul wanted: a solid case for collusion between David and the priests of God. So, the priests were also colluding with David – imagine what that meant!

Saul at once sent for the priest Ahimelech, along with all his men and family (11). When they arrived at Gibeah, Saul demanded they tell him why they had conspired and colluded against him and his government (13). He charged Ahimelech with giving bread and a sword to David, therefore, David, in his view, was lying in wait for Saul that very day (13d). This was nothing but high treason against the crown in Saul's mind.

Saul ordered his men to "kill the priests of the LORD because they have sided with David" (17), but they had the good sense not to do anything like that (17 c, d). So, the king ordered the foreigner Doeg to do the job (18). And that is what he did; he killed "85 priests who wore the linen ephod," including the priest's family, the town of Nob, all the priests, with all the men, women, children, infants, cattle, donkeys, and sheep (18b-19). What a carnage and vast amount of destruction, and what a blot on the name of King Saul and his henchman who would dare to lay their unrighteous hands-on God's anointed! Only one son escaped to report to David what had happened, a priest named Abiathar who served David during his whole term as king, but whom King Solomon later told him to go back to Anathoth, even though he was worthy of death instead of mercy, for he committed treason as he sided with his son's rebellion against the crown owned by David. Thus, the final person in the house of Eli was last to receive the fulfillment of Samuel's prophecy against Eli (1 Kings 2:26).

The Evil Use of the Tongue: Lying – Psalm 52:1-9 [1]

In another one of the eight fugitive psalms, the ancient heading of Psalm 52 has in part: "A maskil of David, when Doeg the Edomite had gone to Saul and told him: David has gone to the house of Ahimelech." This psalm treats the problem of the tongue as an evil weapon being used as a more dangerous affair than any military arsenal of weapons known to man. It was Charles Haddon Spurgeon who said, "A lie can go around the world while truth is just putting its boots on." The prophet Jeremiah (9:8) agreed, for he said, "The tongue is an arrow shot out; it speaks with deceit." The New Testament book of James (3:6) added, "The tongue also is a fire, a world of evil among the parts of the body. It corrupts the whole person; sets the whole course of events of one's life on fire and is itself set on fire by hell." Samuel Cox[2] also added this: "It is hardly an exaggeration to say that half of the miseries of human life spring from the reckless and malignant use of the tongue."

---

1. Walter C. Kaiser, Jr., "When They Spread Lies About You: Slander During the Journey," in *The Journey Isn't Over: The Pilgrim Psalms for Life's Challenges and Joys,* Eugene, OR., Wipf and Stock, 2018, pp. 21-30.
2. Samuel Cox, The Pilgrim Psalms: An Exposition of the Songs of Degrees, London: R. D. Dickinson, 1885, p. 17.

Psalm 52 shows there can be no doubt that the tongue can be unwisely used to:

Boast of evil (52:1)
Boast all day long (52:1)
Be a disgrace to God (52:1)
Plot destruction (52:2)
Practice deceit (52:2)
Speak falsehood (52:3)
Love words that harm others (52:4)

The charges that Doeg made against Ahimelech were well-timed to ingratiate Doeg the Edomite to King Saul, who was complaining that he was without friends, who would otherwise keep him informed. But David was perfectly clear when he condemned Doeg in v. 4, "Surely God will bring you down into everlasting ruin. He will snatch you up and pluck you from your tent; He will uproot you from the land of the living." Doeg had no business sticking his nose into a foreign affair he had no understanding of or responsibility.

On the other hand, all who are righteous will both see what is going on and thus they will be afraid of such risky use of the tongue, but they will also laugh at those who falsely use the tongue as they say, "Here now is one who did not make God his stronghold" (6-7). You would have thought that Doeg would have known enough to regard this situation as one that was an awesome and fearful situation; but in the end, the righteous would rightly mark this as the loathsome conclusion of all such who lie and trust in themselves rather than resorting to God as their stronghold. Instead, these liars make prevarications and outright lies their place of refuge. They make wealth, which they have gained by deceit, cheating, lying, and falsehood, to be what they are counting on to rescue them (7b).

David, however, will continue to flourish like and olive tree in the house of God, for his confidence will rest in *God's hesed*, i.e., his "unfailing love" (8). David's hope did not rest in himself; instead, it was fixed on the name of the Lord, i.e. in God's character, his doctrine, his ethics, and his person (9). And for all that God has done and continues to do for David, he will continually praise him even in the presence of all his people (9a).

Conclusions

1. This text calls on all of us to wait "until [we] learn what God will do for [us]" instead of going ahead on our own and creating mischief for others.
2. There is real safety under the wings of the Lord, for he is our Refuge and Strength.
3. Our tongues must be used instead to trumpet forth the word of God; they must not be used to practice deceit and lying against others.
4. David had a responsibility to tell the truth as well Doeg. He should have told Abimelech what the real problem was. He did finally realize this, "I am responsible for the death of your father's whole family" (1 Sam. 22:22).

Questions for Thought or Discussion

1. People argue that David was in a hostile situation, therefore the story he concocted about not having enough time to get his weapons or food was divinely approved in this situation. Do you agree and if so, why?
2. Did David do the right thing in placing his parents under the protection of the king of Moab? Is the doctrine of "separation" from the world applicable here?
3. What right did an "Edomite" have in being in an Israelite army? Was this a violation of the Law of God?
4. What do we learn from David's theological ponderings of the two fugitive psalms written on these occasions?

Lesson 5

Following God's Directions

1 Samuel 23:1-29; Psalm 54:1-7

Thc prophet Gad had urged David to return to Judah from the heights of Moab, where he had gone to make provision for the safe keeping of his parents (22:5). David was responsive to Gad's instructions from the Lord and so he heeded that word from God. But it must be clearly noted that with David's restoration back to the land of Israel once again after caring for the security of his parents, there came a new period of usefulness for David, along with a new test.

David, in his new guidance from the Lord, was being asked to deliver the Judean town of Keilah from the attack by the Philistines, who were also looting the Israelites threshing floors, which were the storage places where Israel saved her grain, after thrashing the harvests. However, the Philistines would let the Israelites do all the work of raising the grain and then after they had harvested it and removed the husks from the grain, these raiders would descent on the farmers of Keilah and steal all that they had stored on their threshing floors (23:1).

David, having taken note of this grave injustice, asked the LORD if he and his motley crew should go and attack the Philistines for this outrage (2) One would have thought that King Saul, as the authorized protector of the people, would have been attacking this problem and trying to solve it for the nation under his care, but no, he was too busy trying to save the kingdom from a usurper named David. Therefore, the real affairs and needs of state often had to go in abeyance, for the David-issue was of far greater concern and demanded priority –especially to Saul. This sets up the discussion for this chapter.

Seeking Directions for Ourselves – I Samuel 23:1-2

When There Was a Need

Saul had become so distracted by his hate and envy for David that he had neglected his role as the One who assured the land of public safety from all sorts of hostilities. Meanwhile, the Philistines had made it a routine practice to pilfer the threshing floors of Keilah (a site 18 miles southwest of Jerusalem and 3 miles southeast of Adullam), for in various sorties and raids the Philistines engaged in on the Judean territory resulted in the Jewish feeling that their work seemed to be all-for-nothing by the time these thieves were finished with their sorties. The threshing floors were located just outside the city, which made their attack even easier (Judg. 6:11; Ruth 3:2, 15).

In such a circumstance, God called David back into his homeland because he had work for him to do. God would never leave Israel defenseless and without a source of help, for after all, that was why he had already planned for Saul's removal. So, David returned to Judah with his 600 rag-tag team of fighters.

When We are Confused as What to Do

David began by inquiring of the LORD: "Shall I go and attack these Philistines? (2). The answer of the LORD was clear and had no ambiguities, for he said: "Go, attack the Philistines and save Keilah" (2b). David made repeated inquiries of the Lord about whether he should go to Keilah and attach the Philistines, for he wanted to be sure he was going to do the right thing. God's answer was always the same!

Seeking Assurances for Others – 23:3-5

David's men were not as convinced as David was about going to save Keilah. They complained in this manner: "Here in Judah we are afraid. How much more, then, if we go to Keilah against the Philistine forces!" (3). Now David had just received assurance from the Lord God that he would experience success if he went up to Keilah, but the men were no ready to agree. So, to make sure, David asked the Lord once again if he was to go fight the Philistines at Keilah (4a). Word came back again from the LORD that he had not made a mistake; he was to go down to Keilah in full confidence, for the LORD added, "I am going to give the Philistines into your hand" (4b). So, David and his men went off to Keilah and as the LORD predicted, they "inflicted heavy losses on the Philistines and carried off their livestock" (5). Thus, he saved the people of Keilah (5c). Even though all the verbs in v. 5 are in the singular number, as if it was only David who personally pulled off this victory, this may just be another occasion in the Tanakh (OT) where what is attributed to the leader also involved the men who fought with him.

Seeking Discernment in Difficult Situations – 23:6-13

This section begins with a parenthetical note for those who may have been wondering just how David got such usable information. The answer is this: When Doeg slaughtered the eighty-five priests of the house of Ahimelech, Abiathar was the only priest that had escaped the massacre and thus he was able on an earlier occasion to bring the priestly ephod to David as he fled him after leaving Nob (21:9; 22:20). Thus, v. 6 is a central verse in the structure of vv. 1-13, for Abiathar's ephod gave specific directions to David both on going in to save Keilah and on getting out of Keilah to avoid capture.

This passage teaches a real contrast between David's means of obtaining guidance and direction in life versus the method used by Saul. Saul was by this time reliant on human espionage and reports (cf. vv. 7, 13, 19, 25, 27), which only often increased his frustration and failure. Interesting as a side note also is the fact that the Hebrew verb "inquired, asked" in vv. 2 and 4 is a wordplay on Saul's name, the Hebrew word *sha'al*, which means "to ask." Saul then relied on an informal sort of spy network to keep him informed and to direct and guide his steps in this contest for the next kingship.

Saul's pursuit of David traces a path from Keilah (vv. 7-13) to the Desert of Ziph (14-24a), to the Desert of Maon (24b-28) and concludes as David enters the stronghold of En Gedi (29).

We are given in this text one of the closest looks at just how the guidance procedure worked when it was used with the priestly ephod. David asked two questions in v. 11a.

> "O LORD God of Israel, your servant has heard that Saul will come to Keilah and destroy the town on account of me. Will the citizens of Keilah surrender me to him? Will Saul come down, as your servant has heard? O LORD God of Israel, t]ell your servant."

David received a direct answer to his first question: "He will [come down] to Keilah" (11b). But that led to a second Davidic question:

> "Will the citizens of Keilah surrender me and my men to Saul? (12a)

Again, the LORD clearly answered in a single Hebrew word, "They will." (12b). Herein is an important piece of theology that should help us when are seeking guidance from the Lord. Many people have read the book by my good evangelical friend Gary Friesen entitled *Decision-Making and the Will of God.* Gary stated that God has a general will for believers, but not a specific one like who to marry. The text shows that David sought guidance by asking both general and specific questions about what actions to take, according to Scripture. Saul, on his part, had wrongly concluded that "God has handed [David] over to me, for David has imprisoned himself by entering a town with gates and bars" (7). While Saul's reasoning might in other situations have proven to be realistic, in this case it was not true because God was with David, and he would instruct him on when and how he should get out of the city that had walls. Also, Saul was not paying close attention to what was going on, for by now it had to be abundantly clear that God was now with David, and therefore Saul was up against the highest odds there are in the universe by taking a contrary stand to God. Moreover, it is not clear what made David suspect the very people he had just graciously delivered from the Philistines' attack, i.e., the men and women of Keilah. These ungrateful people would be the ones who would deliver David and hand him over to Saul -- except for the fact that God was helping David!

Ingratitude is particularly difficult to bear when you have just risked your life and all your being to save the people of Keilah that are now of a mindset to favor the one who is your enemy! Such an action showed hardly any ties of honor, gratitude, or even patriotic affection for one's own countryman; but God was with David to protect him and to guide him.

Notice especially that God knows both what would have happened if Saul came down to Keilah and what will take place if David is obedient to his will. Therefore, Obedience and a quick action on David's part to leave Keilah is much better than his remaining in that city with the false security of the walls of Keilah. One should never trust blind fate or a passive attitude that says whatever will be will be (13).

Modern believers have reacted differently. They have said in effect: "This was all good and well for David, but he is a hero in the Bible and therefore gets special help. But this is not the kind of direct and precise guidance that I get when I pray for help in my decision-making; it is simply different from it was for David. He had a priest Abiathar who had an ephod, but I do not have access to those sorts of tools in my day and world.

Dale Ralph Davis, however, responded to this question very nicely by claiming, "Yes, you do." In fact, he argued, "You enjoy one who is even greater than Abiathar. Davis pointed to Hebrews 4:14-16,[1] which says, "Since we have a great high priest," our Lord Yeshua/Jesus the Messiah, it is possible for us to come to his very throne of grace and find "help at just the right time." It doesn't get any better than that!

Seeking Deliverance from Harm to Ourselves – 23:14-29

The site of Ziph is about four miles southeast of Hebron with a height of 2900 feet above sea level. So, the quest of Saul to find David continued. David escaped Saul's reach once more, but David did not escape the shelter of the Most High. Interesting enough, while Saul was unable to root out where David was hiding, Jonathan had no trouble in finding him at Horesh (16). Jonathan was able to help David find strength in God (16b). Moreover, Jonathan encouraged David with these words:

> "Don't be afraid. My father Saul will not lay a hand on you. You will be king over Israel, and I will be second to you. Even my father knows this. (17).

David and Jonathan therefore made a covenant before the LORD and Jonathan left for his home, but David continued to remain in Horesh. Jonathan was pleased to be second in David's government, which tells us something more about his character. Though neither man knew it at the time, this would be the last time they would ever see each other alive on this earth. Another pastor has longed, in the tough spots of ministry, to have a friend like Jonathan visit him at their place that also could be called Horesh.

In another case, where Saul had not particularly sought out David, the men of Ziph voluntarily journeyed up to Saul in Gibeah with news that David was hiding among them in Horesh, on the hill of Hakilah, south of Jeshimon (19). Saul had approached them for such information, but they had sought Saul out. The action of the Ziphites, therefore seemed to be as treacherous as that of the citizens of Keilah. It seems probable that both the citizens of Keilah and of Ziph had by now heard what had happened to the whole family of priests at Nob under Saul's leadership. Even if they

---

1. Dale Ralph David, *Looking on the Heart: Expositions of 1 Samuel 15-31,* Vol 2, Grand Rapids, MI., Baker Books, 1994, p. 96.

were not fully informed about all the details of what Saul had ordered Doeg to do there, both places of Keilah and Ziph seem to reek of spinelessness and ungratefulness to one such as David who would risk his life to deliver a city. Why would such fellow compatriots of Judah so easily turn in one of their own? Who can a person trust anymore? What does faithfulness mean among citizens of the same tribe? David's people grew distant after a split in the kingdom, caused by a leader envious of a competing claimant to the throne.

It was Charles Haddon Spurgeon who said: "As long as God has an open ear, we cannot be shut up to trouble. All other weapons are useless, but all-prayer is evermore available – no enemy can spike this gun."

Saul blessed the man of Ziph for their fresh and voluntary intelligence report. He encouraged them to find out where David usually goes and who it is who has seen in one place or the other (22-23). He noted that from the reports he had, David had the reputation of being very "crafty." Come back and tell me what you have learned, then Saul said he would go and if that rascal David was in the area, he would track him down (23b).

The men of Ziph went ahead of Saul and they discovered that David had moved to the "Desert of Maon" in the Arabah south of Jeshimon, a site four miles south of Ziph and eight miles south of Hebron. Saul trailed after David and really came as close to closing the net on his nemesis as he ever had thus far or ever will. However, in the providence of God, suddenly, just as "Saul was going along one side of the mountain and David and his men were on the other side, hurrying to get away from Saul, ... A messenger came to Saul saying, "Come quickly! The Philistines were once again raiding the land" (26-27). Some think that this was just a case of luck, but the eyes of faith can never read situations like this and claim it was just a coincidence or a chance happening. Is not God in charge of the universe? What, then, goes on without his knowledge or direction? God used the distraction of the invasion of the Philistines into Israel to save David instead of the aid of the Judahite men of Ziph. But the work was his and a freak happening in life. What would have happened if that messenger had been delayed say for ten minutes. David might have been captured and brought to Saul who just might have turned to his son Jonathan and ordered him to slay David! If he had ten obeyed his father, what would have become of God's Messianic plan for David and Israel? This was not the work of luck; it was the strong work of our Sovereign God!

Saul had to break off his hot pursuit of David. They took a new name for that place because of what happened there: they called it "Sela Hammahlekott," which may have meant "smooth/slippery Rock," but by popular usage it came to mean "Rock of Parting" (28). Incidentally, the same Hebrew root was used for David's five "smooth stones," which he used against Goliath.

Seeking Relief from Friendly Betrayers – Psalm 54:1-7

David wrote Psalm 54, like Psalm 52, while he was fleeing from King Saul after hearing news from the Ziphites. The ancient historical heading of Psalm 54 reads: "A maskil of David. When the Ziphites had gone to Saul and said, 'Is not David hiding among us?'" The references to the Ziphites are important, for here David finds himself distressingly rejected by the men of his own tribe of Judah in the very passage we are examining. In such a circumstance, where can David go and what are his options? (23:19-29; 26:1).

David began his prayerful lament in this Psalm by appealing to God's name to vindicate him in the narrow straits of his situation. The Ziphites who were willing to betray him were opportunists who showed no regard for holding on to principles or the cause of justice and the cause of what was right. Those who had ganged up against David with King Saul had not taken the time to find out what the problems were, therefore, they all too easily slurred David and his character. The question David had put to Saul must also be put to them as well: "What have I done? What guilt am I being accused of?

Those who attack David are "arrogant" and "ruthless" in the way they are seeking David's life (3). Moreover, these accusers are "men without regard for God."

Suddenly the psalmist shifts from worry about what the arrogant are doing to a triumphant note of finding his "help" in the Lord. He calls God "the One who sustains me" and the One who upholds his life (4). Therefore, David is willing to leave any needed requital or pay-back in the hands of God (5). As for his part, David will "sacrifice A freewill offering," "praise" the LORD's name, for the LORD is the One who has delivered him from all his troubles (6-7). Others have tried to defame David, but this warrior's eyes will look with triumph on his foes (7b).

Conclusions

1. Is our Lord open to being asked for help in the manner David did when we are trying to make decisions, or to decide what his will is for our lives?
2. God can give us both general guidance as well as particular and special guidance to questions we ask of him in prayer.
3. Our Lord often uses the gift of friendships, such as the way Jonathan gave comfort and help to sustain David, in our times of crisis and perplexity.
4. Nowhere in the Bible is the doctrine of Providence more dramatically exercised that the time when God send a messenger for Saul to come fight the Philistines at the very moment when he was about to seize David and end his run for the headship of the government.
5. When David finds himself rejected by his own countrymen and tribe, he composes a Psalm that praises God for being his Helper and the upholder of his life.

Questions for Thought or Discussion

1. Is there a difference between the general and special providence of God? Does 1Samuel 23 help us to see how each function in our prayers to our Lord?
2. Is it fair to protest the fact that David had the distinct advantage over us in the incident where he had the priest Abiathar and the priestly ephod for David to make decisions, whereas we do not have such tools when we ask God to help us make decisions, so we must use our best instincts? What do you think about Davids' answer to that objection?
3. Was David's decision to leave his parents in the care of the King of Moab a good one, or was that an example of not being separated from the world and the culture of that day?
4. Was Jonathan being precipitous in claiming he would be second to David in ruling in Israel or did he have good grounds for saying so?
5. Were the Ziphites taking the proper action by reporting to Saul that David was in their midst?

Lesson 6

David: Offering Forgiveness to Those Hurting Him

1 Samuel 24:1-22; Psalm 7:1-17; Psalm 142:1-7

The link[1] between 1 Samuel 24 and 1 Samuel 23 is clear in that chapter 24 begins just where chapter 23 ended with David in the strongholds of the desert of En Gedi. Therefore, the relentless pursuit of David continues into chapter 24 without any letup. But while this close connection between chapters 23 and 24 can be noted, it can be just as convincingly argued that chapter 24 is also practically a mirror image of chapter 26, with each reporting David's latest hiding place (24:1 and 26:1), and David's refusal to lift his hand against the "LORD's anointed" (24:6; 26:11). Saul's return home from chasing after David is found also in both texts (24:17-22; 26:21, 25). Chapters 24 and 26 frame chapter 25, highlighting its pivotal role in the narrative and presenting Nabal as a churlish figure who mirrors Saul's alter ego. On an even more prominent note, all three chapters 24-26 stress the fact that God had mercifully kept David from working his own revenge and shedding blood he was not authorized to shed.

Refuse to Take Matters into Our Own Hands - Especially with the Lord's Anointed -24:1-7

David was a man who was willing to wait patiently for God to give to him the kingship at the proper moment. He was not one who would seize that kingship whenever he felt he was ready to do so, and that is what chapters 24-26 show repeatedly.

Once again, as Saul returned from "pursuing the Philistines" (24:1), he was told where David was found – in the desert west of En Gedi. Saul had

1. The material in the paragraph was gathered from Ronald F. Youngblood, "I Samuel" in *The Expositor's Bible Commentary,* Revised Edition, Eds., Tremper Longman III & David E. Garland, Grand Rapids: Zondervan, 2009, p. 231.

no other aim in mind than to capture and kill David, so he chose 3,000 men (2), who were more than enough to match David's 600. Saul's men were also men who had been trained, but David's men came with merely their own native gifts for fighting. So, the search by Saul was on again as he headed for the "Crags of the Wild Goats" – an inaccessible area near En Gedi.

Saul and his men came to the "sheep pens" at these Crags (3), which no doubt consisted of low stone walls than appeared at the entrance of a cave. Saul passed through the sheep pens to get into the cave that lay behind these pens. His purpose was to "cover his feet," a standard euphemism (cf. Judg. 3:20) for "relieving oneself." Saul entered the cave to deal with personal needs, unaware that David and his men were positioned further inside the same cave.

What Saul did not realize at that time, as we have already mentioned, was that David and his men were "far back in" the very same cave. David's men were pleased to no end to realize that David's enemy was being handed to them on a silver platter, as it were, for Saul and his army were completely without any knowledge of what they had walked into (4). In the providence of God, this day, claimed David's troops, was the very day God had in mind when he had said "I will give your enemy into your hands for you to deal with as you wish" (4). That surely sounded convincing and downright proper, given their present situation in the cave. David made no reply to the men, but instead he "crept up unnoticed and cut off a corner of Saul's robe" (4b).

Insignificant as it may seem, David's cutting off a corner of Saul's robe" caused this man of God to be "conscience-stricken." He recognized that even this, which may have seemed so small and so innocent, was a sin against God! There is only one other occurrence of this expression, with the use of conscience in the Old Testament, and that is in connection with the Nabal story, where at the arrival of Abigail, David suddenly realized that what he was about to do to Nabal also struck his conscience full force as a sin (1 Sam. 25:31).

David continued to instruct his men that what he had done was wrong (cf. 26:11). David had a high respect for the LORD's anointed, for the word appears seven times in this context and in chapter 26 (24:6 [bis], 10;

26:9, 11, 16, 23). Saul was king, not by his choice, but by divine appointment. Moreover, by his taking such a high stand on the divine anointing of a king, David was setting a precedent for his own later administration. David had decided he would never lay his hand on Saul as the anointed man of God. Thus, David strongly rebuked his men for even using that the type of thinking they were engaging in, as if it were even possible or permissible for a believer. That same type of thinking should be part of the thinking of the Believers and citizens of nations. All too many persons sin against heaven by assuming that such a choice is open to them, but it is not! Hebrews 13:17 advises individuals to respect and comply with their leaders, recognizing that these leaders are responsible for their welfare and will be accountable to the Lord. We must obey them so that their work will be a joy to them and not a burden, for if the work became a burden to them, that would be no advantage to us!

As a result, then, to continue our narrative, Saul left the cave and went on his way having not a single clue of the possible harm that could have come upon him in that cave, had he been dealing with another type of person than conscientious David.

Arise Lord in Your Anger and Judge Our Enemies – Psalm 7:1-17

In this Psalm, David set his case before the LORD whom he called his "righteous judge" (7:11). David began by addressing "Yahweh my God" (1) as the One in whom he was now taking refuge in and the One who would deliver him from all who pursued him (1b).

The heading for this seventh Psalm was "A shiggaion of David, which he sang to the LORD concerning Cush, a Benjaminite." Nowhere else does the Bible mention "Cush, a Benjaminite," thus, interpreters are divided on whether this Psalm refers to the pursuit of David by King Saul the Benjaminite, or does it instead refer to the time of Absalom's rebellion. In fact, David declared how he would be ripped to pieces by Saul and his pursuing men if the Lord did not help him.

David went on to plead to the Lord in Psalm 7:4-5, that if he deserved this constant pursuit of his flesh, and if it was because of the guilt that was on his hands, he could understand why he must die at the hands of Saul (5). However, if he had not done anything wrong to Saul, and he was at peace with him, then he asked that in that case God would "rise up against the rage of [his] enemies and administer justice" (6).

Of course, the LORD knows our hearts and searches out our minds. He will judge our integrity and discern what we know of righteousness, for only in this way can he end the stupidity and violence that was so commonly seen amongst us on earth (8). In this manner, our Lord saves all who are upright in heart (9). Our Lord, on the other hand, is upset with the wicked every day (11). Moreover, the wicked very often fall into the trap they have set for others.

After focusing on the Lord's righteous rule, David develops the theme of God's judgment of his enemies. The same Lord who knows the character of his people is now called on to judge them along with the rest of the nations. The faith found in the righteous looks up to God "who searches minds and hearts" (9) and therefore is our "shield" and Savior (10). But God is indignant as he "expresses his wrath" against those he has examined and found wanting (11). Meanwhile the "upright in heart" (10) are those who are loyal to God and ask him to judge them and search their hearts (8-9).

Burt David is convinced that God will deal with evil, for he also is a warrior who is equipped with a sword, bow, and arrows (12-13). His lightnings are like "flaming arrows," which refers to the practice of that day of dipping the arrows in the flammable materials of oil or pitch before they were released from the bow. As such, the metaphors of his sharp sword and flaming arrows speak of the fact that God's judgments are inescapable and hit their marks.

David depicted evil metaphorically in this psalm as a "lion (2), an army (5) and now like a "pregnant woman" who is about to give birth to evil (14). But if evil is prevalent (14-15), then so is the certainty of God's judgment. For God's judgment is like a boomerang that "recoils on [itself]" and comes right back on "[the enemy's] own head" (16). David is sure that the wicked will be judged (14-16). Because God is just and fair in his dealings with the righteous and the wicked, David "will sing praise to the name of the LORD Most High" (17). The name of God is Yahweh/LORD, but he is also "El Elyon," "the Creator of Heaven and

Earth" (Gen. 14:18-20, 22). This title El Elyon describes the universal rule of God, who is the One who will finally remove evil.

Insist on Leaving the Avenging of Wrongs to God – 24:8-15

After Saul left the cave, David appeared from the same cave a short period of time after Saul, and he called out to Saul, "My lord the King!" (8). That must have startled the life out of Saul, for where had his nemesis come from? Had he been in that cave as well? As Saul turned around, sure enough, there was David with his face to the ground. David, however, gave no time for Saul to reply, but launched into his *apologia* in which he argued the case for his innocence (9-11) and made his case for the LORD's justice (12-15).

David began his defense of himself by asking "Why?" first (9). Why was Saul listening to what men were saying about him, i.e., they claimed that David was determined to harm Saul? (9). If Saul needed any further proof, then what he had just seen that day should have convinced him of the opposite truth, for the LORD had delivered Saul into his hands in that very cave, but David did not make the choice to kill him. Although David was encouraged to kill Saul, he chose not to. David had decided long ago that he would not lift his hand against his master, for he was the LORD's anointed (10). To do so would be to resist God!

As further proof of his "no harm policy," David, calling Saul his "father," urged him to examine his robe and note the piece that David had torn from it (11). Could not Saul recognize from this act of mercy that David was not guilty of wrongdoing, or of rebellion (11). So why was Saul hunting him down and trying to take his life? (11b. Moreover, David's use of the term for Saul of "My father" may have been more than a term of respect, for after all, he was his "father-in-law." But the "piece of the corner of Saul's robe" was central to this dialogue, for it is mentioned four times in this chapter (4-5, 11 [bis], and now by David in v. 11).

But David was not expecting any change of heart from Saul or even a new promise that he would never more hunt down David; David cast his whole case on the LORD instead (12a). Nevertheless, despite what Saul might or might not do, David pledged to him that he would "never lay a hand on [him]" (12-13). David had committed his case to the LORD, who would be his judge and the adjudicator who would make the decision between the two of them (15). After all, who did Saul think he was chasing anyway: He who was only "a dead dog?" or merely "a flee?" Surely, God would vindicate David and deliver him from Saul's hand. God is the real judge, and we must leave in his hands the execution of all vengeance and retribution. The ungodly, however, presume they are the ones who are in charge and that they therefore can take over the operation or outcome of all things into their hands.

Rescue Us from Those Wrongly Dogging Our Footsteps -Psalm 142:1-7

The Psalmist here gives the theology for leaving the avenging up to the Lord, instead of our taking charge to vindicate ourselves. The metaphor of David being in "prison," as used here, is either an expression for his being oppressed or a figure of speech for his being in a cave when Saul pursued him at En Gedi (1 Sam. 24:1-22) or in the cave at Adullam (1 Sam. 22:1,4). The historical heading reads: "A maskil of David when he was in the cave. A Prayer."

David began his lament by voicing three expressions of bitter anguish:

> I cry aloud to the LORD.
> I lift up my voice to the LORD for mercy.
> I pour out my complaint before him.
> before him I tell my trouble (142:1-2).

Even though David may well have been at the point of complete despondency and total spiritual depression, he refused to give up his trust and full dependency on the LORD. Nevertheless, just at the point where his spirit was the weakest within him, he claimed no one other than the LORD as his all, who alone knew the way he had taken, and the course of his life (3).

Still, despite such bold adherence to the LORD, David still had a complaint which he must now make to the LORD. In the very path he had chosen to walk, men have laid snares and traps for David (4). It seemed as if no one was concerned for him, no one cared for his life, and he had no refuge (4). So, what could David do?

He would cry out to the LORD and affirm, "You are my refuge," "my portion in the land of the living" (5). David felt his situation was one where he was "in desperate need," and he needed to be rescued from those who were too strong for him (6). His conclusion, therefore, was this: "Set me free from my prison, that I might praise your name." (7).

Accept the Request for Forgiveness from Our Enemies – 24:16-22

When David had finished his speech to Saul, Saul asked David in a contrite voice, "Is that your voice, David my son?" (16). Saul wept aloud, the Scripture reported, but we are not sure what that meant. Was Saul asking for forgiveness? Did not Saul go on to concede,

> "You are more righteous than I. You have treated me well, but I have treated you badly. You have just now told me of the good you did to me; The LORD delivered me into your hands, but you did not kill me" (17-18).

Saul was not finished yet, for he also conceded amazingly that he knew David would certainly be king one day and that the kingdom of Israel would be established in his hands (20). It is for that reason Saul wanted an oath from David that he would not cut off any of his descendants or wipe out his name from his father's family (21). David willingly gave Saul that promise in an oath after which Saul went home, a chastened man, one who was fortunate to still be alive. But had he repented? David, however, went with his men up to the stronghold, meaning he still did not trust Saul.

Conclusions

1. The whole point of this chapter is this: Once again David is told that the kingdom will come to him, only this time he is told this by his enemy. That however did not make the promise of God any more correct.
2. Those we work hardest to help may abandon us when we face our own crises.
3. The providence of God involves not just the major generalities of life, but it may and does involve at times extremely specific and special areas of guidance in our decision-making.
4. Sometimes what may appear to be the providence of God, such as Saul accidentally choosing to occupy the same cave where we are hiding, is not an indication of an approval from God that he has been delivered into our hands, for our Lord had explicitly put an interdiction against slaying God's anointed leader.
5. A leader who is working outside the Word of God is a danger to himself and the people he is pretending to lead.

Questions for Thought or Discussion

1. If we today do not have the advantage of the presence of a Levitical priest or an ephod, can we expect that God would also give to us specific and special guidance, as well as general and overall direction for life?
2. Why would God call David to deliver the men and women at Keilah and then tell him that these people will hand him over to the Philistines? How far can gratefulness reach and how easily can it be jettisoned?
3. What is the difference between accidental happenings (such as Saul dropping by in the same cave where David was hiding?) and the doctrine of divine providence? Can you give illustrations of each?
4. When God has given over the government to another party, but the current occupant does not wish to yield power, is it right for the newly named or elected party to force the issue in any means available, since this new appointment has come from God? Does this apply to present day dictatorships such as Venezuela?

Lesson 7

David: Learning to Cope with Impatience

1 Samuel 25:1-44

Up to this point in David's life, the thorn in his side had always been the king of Israel, King Saul. It seems, David could bear the active assaults of a king and the apathetic responses of a nation that failed to be fully informed of the true nation of things. But when it came to the deportment of others, enough was enough. It was clear when Nabal, a ranch owner, refused David's request for supplies for his 600 men during a time when such generosity was customary.

Of course, in general, rebuke and slander from dignified and honorable enemies with a great reputation was one thing, but it is a different matter when one was reproached and treated shabbily by the likes of such a despicable person as the churlish rancher named Nabal. David decided he was not going to take it any longer. It was enough that he had to take it from King Saul, but when every other person, regardless of their station in life, began to pile on and lambast David, he decided that this must stop somewhere and that place was right at this point.

Despite how David viewed what was happening, the God of David and of Israel remained faithful, for, as the New Testament would later teach, he would not allow his follower to be tempted beyond what he was able to bear, but he would provide a way of escape (1 Cor. 10:13). And that is what this chapter is about! In ways Nabal seems to act as King Saul's surrogate, for Nabal's cocky attitude replicated King Saul's demeanor. Moreover, Nabal's sudden death likewise prefigured Saul's premature death as well.

By Exposing Us to Different Types of Tests – 25:1-13

The Loss of a Key Friend – 25:1

Samuel, the prophet who had anointed David and had been his counselor on an occasion, died, and David felt alone in an even more dramatic way. Israel, however, assembled and came to mourn over Samuel's death (25:1). They buried Samuel at his home in Ramah (1b). Local traditions, however, place Samuel's tomb in Nebi Samwil, a site northwest of Jerusalem, but that identification depends on equating Ramah with Nebi Samwil. We cannot be sure of this equation. Obviously, one point was true, this was a huge loss for David, for now he had to find other avenues of support, since Samuel was David's chief supporter.

Israel, naturally, mourned for Samuel, now that he was dead, but such an attitude of respect for Samuel had not always been true during the prophet's lifetime. The nation preferred to follow King Saul rather than a prophet Samuel, which meant the nation was usually the greater loser.

The Insults of a Churlish Fool Named Nabal

If Samuel's death was David's first test of his patience, then his second test came in the form of a confrontation with that an irascible rancher named Nabal. David and his men moved from the funeral site of Ramah back down to the "Desert of Maon" where he had been previously (1b). David feared what would happen now more than ever, since Samuel was gone, for he headed back to the area where he clearly felt more comfortable.

But it was in Maon that he ran into a wealthy man, who had property in the town of Carmel whose name was Nabal. He owned 1000 goats and 3000 sheep. However, it was also a festive time, which always involved "sheep-shearing." Usually, the sheep were sheared either by plucking the wool with one's hands or more typically by using bronze combs, until later in the Iron Age, following the days of Nabal, iron shears replaced the bronze ones. Nabal, whose name meant "fool" was known for his "surliness," "meanness" and downright "evil" (3b). He was also called a "Calebite," which may mean he was "doglike" in disposition. Nabal could be compared to the contemporary Clint Eastwood, recent mayor of another Carmel, but this one was in California. Eastwood was famous for saying, "Go ahead and make my day," as he threatened quick reprisals to all who crossed him or dared to challenge him. Contrary to this awry character, his lovely wife was named Abigail, meaning "My [divine] father is Joy." She was an intelligent (lit. "good in understanding") and a woman who was "beautiful (lit. "Lovely in form") (3). What a contrast to the uncultured person she had married!

Sheepshearing in ancient Israel was a time for significant celebration and a time of sharing gifts, for after the summer grazing period had ended, it was now a time when profits could be distributed (2 Sam. 13:28). So, David sent a ten-man party, no doubt, officers in his small army, to extend kind greetings and salutations to Nabal and to remind him that the 600 men had voluntarily provided free of charge protection for Nabal's men and their herds and had not taken one of his flocks. Since David and his small retinue of followers had not mistreated Nabal, the delegation from David continued by asking would this sheep owner be of a mind to give a gift to David and his men, following the usual events at this time of festivity? (5-8).

The ten men gave the message and "waited" (9). Nabal was not at all impressed, nor was he going to yield to such a bold request for a gift (10-11). Instead, he tried to pull the wool over David's eyes, being a man who was not known for having sheepish ways, by claiming he did not know David. Despite the fact that the request of the ten men was tactful, respectful, and full of filial regard for Nabal (whom David addressed through his men as "your son"), Nabal shot back at the ten men these sassy questions: "Who is this David?" and "Who is this son of Jesse?" There are all sorts of servants who are breaking away from their masters in these times, so "Why should I take my bread and water and the meat I have slaughtered for my shearers and give it to men coming from who knows where? (10-11). The answer was a clear rejection!

David took Nabal's rebuke hard, for often ingratitude, from those you have helped, is harder to bear than most other kinds of response. But we readers are bound to respond on David's behalf in a sympathetic way, for we sympathetically ask, hasn't David been in the school of affliction long enough? Why did he need another problem? Hadn't Samuel just died? How much more could he take? This was the time to answer a fool according to his folly (Prov. 26:4) – or did that text in Proverbs mean something different?

By Sending to Us Sensible Individuals to Stop Wrong Actions - 25:14-25.

David's men returned to him and reported what they had run into with Nabal (14). With that, David had had enough. He ordered his men, "Put on your swords," and so 400 of the 600 men went off to Carmel to take care of Nabal and to teach him a lesson or two. True, the steps of a good man are ordered by the LORD, but in this case, God had not ordered David to take matters into his own hands (Ps. 37:23-24). That psalm, however, went on to say, "though [that good man should] fall, he shall not be utterly cast down, for the LORD upholds his hand."

And that is what happened, for an alert employee of Nabal decided he had better do something and do it quickly. Therefore, he went directly to Nabal's wife Abigail, and reported what had just happened, begging her to intervene. Although this unnamed employee may have acted out of self-preservation, he still fulfilled God's larger purpose regardless of his motivation.

Abigail, eloquent woman that she was, "did not tell her husband" (19), who was stone drunk at the time anyhow, but sensing the danger her husband and household was in, she swung quickly into action. She took 200 loaves of bread, two skins of wine, five dressed sheep, seven seahs of roasted grain, 100 cakes of raisins, 200 cakes of pressed figs, and loaded them all on donkeys and headed out with her servants to intercept David and his men, who by now were on their way to demolish Nabal and his household (18-19).

Abigail met David and his 400 men near a mountain ravine, reminding us of the out of the way place where this hunted fugitive named David continued to inhabit. Abigail bowed before David with deep respect (23), and then the interview began as she raised the themes of bloodguilt and revenge with David. She gave one magnificent speech that was excellent both in its use of reason and in appealing to David's emotions (24-31). Abigail began by showing submission to David, calling him "my lord/master" (24). To save her husband's life, Abigail assumed his guilt, which also avoided showing any disloyalty to her husband. However, she does admit that Nabal was a "wicked man" and a "fool" (25). Nevertheless, she urged that David should deal with her rather than with Nabal, for even though she did not see the ten men who had visited her husband, she wanted to take the blame for what had ensued, therefore she begged David to forgive her for the offense (28).

By Reminding Us of Our High Calling – 25:26-31

Abigail wisely warned David not to let wrongdoing grab hold of him, for she added, "the LORD has kept you, my master, from bloodshed and from avenging yourself with your own hands" (26). Let your enemies and all who intend to harm you be like Nabal, she instructed (26b), for you should "Let no wrongdoing be found in you as long as you live" (28). She went on to affirm that "even though someone is pursuing you to take your life .... The life of my master will be bound securely in the bundle of the living by the LORD your God" (29). But as the lives of your enemies, Abigail noted that God "will hurl [them] away from the pocket of a sling" (29b). This was a very proper metaphor given the instrument David had used to defeat Goliath. Abigail must have known about that story as well! We wonder how far the story had traveled!

Abigail added to this beautiful statement, one that obviously must have won David's thinking and heart over, because of the profound common sense and great theology it enfolded. She argued that David should not feel guilty for another man's death or pursue revenge, as vengeance is God's domain (31). David would be forever thankful if he took this preferred path for divine justice, especially when he was finally given the kingdom of Israel he had been installed to take. And one more thing David, she coyly added, "remember [me] your servant" when this is all over (31b). Was she making an obvious advance for her future?

By Preventing Us From Doing Something Foolish – 25:32-35

How gracious and merciful our Lord is in his dealings with us, even when we are deeply stirred to anger by the way we have been treated. Everyone can recall times when they were crossed, delayed, hindered, deterred and were about to work our own private vengeance! But then, God stepped in, at what seemed like the last minute, and delivered us from what would have been both foolish and tragic.

David thanked Abigail saying, "Praise be to the LORD, the God of Israel, who sent you today to meet me. May you be blessed for your good judgment and for keeping me from bloodshed this day and from avenging myself with my own hands" (33). Had Abigail not come along with the donkeys loaded with gifts and with the good sense and godly wisdom God gave her, David would have ended up harming her and everyone belonging to Nabal and his household (34). No one would have been left living by daybreak (34d). The fact that David suddenly realized this fact was a mark of his spirituality, one that saw the Lord's hand in such deliverances and in his protecting providence.

Often our LORD has interposed his hand to prevent mortals from an evil course of action. For example, our God intervened as the Angel of the

LORD halted his actions three times as the prophet Balaam rode on his way to curse Israel, when they had already been blessed. Our Lord did the same to Pilate’s wife with a dream that made her warn her husband not to be involved in crucifying Jesus. When the Man of God from Judah confronted King Jeroboam about his pagan altar, Jeroboam's arm became paralyzed after he ordered, "Seize him." He asked the prophet to pray for him, and his arm was healed.

By Letting God Avenge the Insults Hurled at Us – 25:36-44

Abigail left David and she and her servants headed back home to Carmel where Nabal was holding forth at a banquet, acting like he was a king (36). Abigail did not say anything to him at the time, but when Nabal had sobered up next morning from his drunkenness the night before, she told him what she had done to allay David’s wrath. When Nabal heard this, he suffered a stroke and died ten days later, possibly due to shock from the danger he faced or feeling undermined by his wife's actions.

When David heard that Nabal was dead, he rejoiced saying, “Praise be to the LORD, who has upheld my cause against Nabal for treating me with contempt (39). The LORD “has kept his servant from doing wrong and has brought Nabal’s wrongdoing down on his own head” (39c).

David then sent word to Abigail, asking her to become his wife. He must have been really impressed by the way she presented herself and her case to him! David, however, did not go to her himself, but he sent his servants to ask her to be his wife (40).

When she gave her answer, which came in quick order, she bowed her face to the ground and spoke of herself as their “maidservant,” “ready to serve [them] and wash the feet of [her] master’s servants” (41). Talk about getting on the good side of the household, she was as a master of the whole episode. Abigail “quickly got on a donkey, with little or no delay, and attended by her five maids, went with David’s messengers and became [David’s] wife” (42).

David had already married Saul’s daughter Michal, but Saul, as usual jumping the gun, and had given Michal to Paltiel son of Laish, who was from Gallim (44). David had already married Ahinoam of Jezreel, so she and Abigail became his two wives (43).

Conclusions

1. Too often, those who lavishly spend on themselves begrudge giving relief to those who are destitute and without support.
2. God has preserved his saints from avenging themselves when they would otherwise have brought grief and wrongdoing on themselves.
3. The death of God's choicest leaders leaves a huge gap in the spiritual and wise growth of his people, until God sends new leaders.
4. Thank God for his gift of wise and discerning women who can give excellent guidance to his people even though they are rarely credited for doing so!

Questions for Thought or Discussion

1. What sorts of tests that you know about illustrate how God often has called his leaders to go through such trials or tests to prepare them for the task of guiding his people?
2. Do you find it easier to bear the hurts and insults of people who have standing and position in the community, but you cannot stand it when persons of lower rank criticize and attack you? Why is that? What are examples you can share?
3. What do you make of the proverb in Proverbs 26:3-4 about answering a fool according to his folly or not answering him? Is this contradictory advice?
4. Was Abigail wrong for acting on her own and the wrong for not telling her husband what she had done when she got home? Did she cause his death?
5. Is Abigail the sort of woman you would have wanted to marry, or does she resent too many problems for potential husbands and for other women?

Lesson 8

David Spares Saul's Life Once Again

1 Samuel 26:1-25; Psalm 54:1-7

The Ziphites have returned once again to Saul's residence in Gibeah to report that David was back in their territory and they were again available to help King Saul in corralling this fellow if he wished their help (26:1). The Ziphites gave their new intelligence to Saul by asking a question: "Is not David hiding on the hills of Hakilah, which faces Jeshimon?" (1b). So, true to form, Saul, despite promises of giving protection to David to the contrary, returned to stalking David as he went down to the "Desert of Ziph" with his 3000 men to search for David (2). This whole encounter is reminiscent of Saul's earlier foray into the same places that the Ziphites had pointed out in an earlier occasion to Saul where David might be hiding (23:19).

Contemporary critical scholars see significant parallels between chapters 24 and 26, often referring to them as "doublets" or simply viewing them as different versions of the same event. Is this approach truly the most effective way to address partial similarities between the two chapters, given that such cases happen in real history? The point that needs to be raised instead, is the fact that the Ziphites, who opposed David's investiture of king, were adamant in their desire to block him from gaining the throne and sustaining Saul's rule over them.

Saul left his home in Gibeah and continued to search for David in the very spots where the Ziphites directed him to look. Saul set up his evening camp beside the road on the hill of Hakilah facing Jeshimon, but David had sent out scouts who correctly informed him as where Saul had bivouacked for the night, so he was keeping a close watch on all of Saul's movements. David had learned that Saul had come looking him one more time, so he used his scouts to mark where Saul had gone and those times when he decided to move (3-4).

It is time we examined this chapter more closely, so let us post our outline first.

Refusing to Lay a Hand on the Lord's Anointed – 26:6-12

Ahimelech the Hittite, not to be confused with the priest in chapter 21 by the same name, is mentioned here in v. 6 along with Abishai, son of Zeruiah, David's sister, as two of the men who had joined David's spontaneous army. David asked if either one was willing to volunteer to go with him by night (7) into Saul's encampment? (6). Abishai was the first to volunteer, with visions of being the man who personally would take out Saul, perhaps as David had victoriously taken out Goliath!

In the meantime, the Lord had caused a "deep sleep" (12) to overtake Saul and his army that night, so David and Abishai had a good deal of freedom as they moved about the camp of Saul and quietly talked in quiet voices between themselves. David and Abishai found Saul, and his top man Abner, accompanied by all the men, lying asleep with Saul's spear "stuck in the ground near his head" (7b).

This was altogether too tempting for Abishai, who whispered to David, "Today God has delivered your enemy into your hands. Now let me pin him to the ground with one thrust of [the] spear; I won't strike him twice" (8). Abishai wanted to assassinate Saul with Saul's own sword, thus making Saul's hallmark, his ever-close companion of his "spear," the means of climaxing and concluding his life. That surely would be a way of making a major point with Saul! Was Abishai deliberately mirroring the words David had used when he had confronted Goliath ("This day/today the LORD will hand you over to me," 17:46). Abishai must have envisioned himself as God's instrument of divine deliverance (8). David rebuked Abishai with words he used in three of his Fugitive Psalms, "Do not destroy him! (9, titles in Psalm 57, 58, and 59). If he did lay a hand on Saul as God's anointed, however, Abishai would not be guiltless (9).

David, however, would not allow Abishai, or anyone else, including himself, to take advantage of the one who was the LORD's anointed (9, cf. 24:6). Moreover, David gave a solemn oath, "As surely as the LORD lives, the LORD himself will strike [Saul]; either his time will come and he will die, or he will go into battle and perish. But the LORD forbid that I should lay a hand on the LORD's anointed" (10-11). With that, David took the spear and water jug that were near Saul's head and left Saul, with Abner and their troops, to sleep on (12).

Praying for God to Vindicate His Hunted Man – Psalm 54:1-7

The authorship of this Fugitive Psalm is uncertain, as it is not clear whether David wrote it during the first or second occasion when the Ziphites informed Saul of his presence in their territory (1 Sam.).

David's restraint at this crucial moment highlights not only his respect for the LORD's authority but also his deep understanding of justice and timing. Rather than seizing the opportunity for revenge or personal gain, David chose to wait on God's providence, trusting that the outcome would be determined by divine will rather than human intervention. This choice sets David apart as a leader who valued righteousness over expedience, and whose faith was steadfast even in the face of ongoing danger and provocation (23:19-29; 26:1). The ancient historical heading in the Psalm could fit either or both situations—"A Maskil of David: When the Ziphites had gone to Saul and said, 'Is not David hiding among us?'" for they acted the same way twice.

Nonetheless, one cannot doubt that David prayed a similar prayer on both occasions. His plea once again was this, "Save me, O God by your name; vindicate me by your might" (Ps. 54:1). Once more, David cried out to the LORD that "strangers are attacking me; ruthless men seek my life – men without regard for God. Selah" (Ps. 54:3). But David switched from his prayer of lament, half-way through this Psalm, to a note of triumph, for he knew he could count on God to help and sustain him (Ps. 54:4). David knew he also could count of the LORD's pay-back of such slanders. Therefore, David would not try to work his own vindication; instead, he would sacrifice a "free-will offering" to the LORD, for he was sure his LORD would deliver him from all his troubles (Ps. 54:6-7). Soon, David expected that he would be able to look on his foes, meaning the likes of King Saul, with triumph and relief, for God would have given him the victory.

Awaking the Enemy to the Danger He Was In – 1 Samuel 26:13-16

David and Abishai crossed over to the other side of the hill and took their stand on top of the hill, leaving a good distance between Saul and his troops and these two men. By now King Saul must realize that he was one helpless man in that the Holy Spirit had left him, and he was now on his own. Therefore, David boldly and loudly called up in the middle of the night to the sleeping enemy. David especially singled out Abner, Saul's personal bodyguard, "Aren't you going to answer me, Abner?" (26:14).

Abner called back, "Who are you who calls to the king?" (14c). David answered,

> "You're the man, aren't you?" "Why didn't you guard your lord the King?" Someone came to destroy your lord the king. What you have done is not good.... You and your men deserve to die, because you did not guard your master, the LORD's anointed. Look around you. Where are the king's spear and water jug that were near his head?" (15-16).

David and his man Abishai had effortlessly stolen the king's spear and water bottle without stirring even one man from his deep sleep. As such, David had in one quiet moment disarmed Saul from all his future ambitions of subduing his enemies, including even of David himself! Had Saul been more alert, he should have seen that there was nothing that would stop David from inheriting the kingdom. Both the fact and the irony of the whole affair should have been clear to King Saul by now.

Choosing the Point David Preferred to Make – 26:17-25

I imagine that Saul could hardly believe his ears, for the voice sounded familiar, but could that really be David's voce? (17). Saul must have asked himself, "Where in the world did he come from?" But it turned out that really was David calling out to him in the dark night.

Moreover, David asked Saul pointedly about his dogged pursuit of his life, "Why is my lord pursuing his servant?" (18). David further inquired of Saul, "What have I done and what wrong am I guilty of?" While David had Saul's attention, he offered advice, and the king could choose his perspective. Therefore, he began with this proposition: It is one thing if the LORD himself had incited Saul to rise up against him, for in that case David would offer a sacrifice and surely the LORD would accept it and that would be the end of this seek and destroy game. On the other hand, the other proposition was this: if the trouble the nation was in was merely one where men who had stirred all this trouble, then David asked that they would be cursed, for in this undeserved mischief they had raised against David, they had driven David away from his share in the LORD's inheritance and said in effect, "Go serve other gods" (19). David is explaining that his exile forced him away from his homeland and prevented him from participating in its tabernacle, sacrifices, priests, and festivals due to the king's anger. David went on to request from Saul his affirmation that his blood would not fall to the ground too far away from the presence of God's land and people (20). He continued by liking the pursuit of the king after his life like going out to look for a flea or looking like one hunting down a partridge in the mountains (20b).

David's point was that here was the most powerful man in Israel chasing down something as trivial and so undeserving of his time and effort as a single flea – viz. David. David had used the "flea" reference in 1 Samuel 24:14 in the form of a question, but here he used it as being like tracking down a "partridge" (Hebrew, *qore'*, "caller"). The partridge is the sand partridge of the desert due west of the Dead Sea, noted for its ability to run when chased until it becomes exhausted and then it can be easily taken.

Saul's response to David's impassioned speech began first with a speech, "I have sinned. Come back David my son" (21). Saul will call David his "son" three times in this concluding passage of vv. 17, 21, and 25. Moreover, Saul knows by now what he has been told previously, namely that David will be his successor and he will sit on the throne of Israel.

David urged Saul to send one of his young men to come up the hill to pick up the "spear" stuck in the ground near Saul's head, but there was no mention of the "water jug." Did David keep that jug as a symbol of his control over life-giving waters, but the symbol of death, Saul's "spear" he would return to his owner!

David reminded Saul that the LORD rewards every person for their righteousness and faithfulness (23). So, once again David would not lay his hands on Saul, for he was the LORD's anointed (23b). Amazingly, even though David valued Saul's life, he did not request Saul to reciprocate and pledge to do the same for his own life (24).

The writer closes this episode by simply saying that Saul returned to his place and David went his way (25). It was all so matter of fact and so seemingly heartless way to end these tragic days, for David and Saul never saw each other again. What A great loss for Saul; he and his government would have benefitted immensely from David's skills, but he was left to go it on his own. David, however, still had the assurance of the near and continued presence of the Holy Spirit to walk with him and the promise of ruling over Israel.

Conclusions

1. The theology of this passage can be found in the four speeches of David: 1 Samuel 26:9-11, 15-16, 17b-20, 23-24.
2. The Ziphites are examples of those who want to do what is right, but they are without the facts and so they end up complicating the situation.
3. Abishai is anxious to be the hero who knocks off King Saul, but he lacks spiritual information that helps him sort out the complexities of the situation.
4. Abner, Saul's bodyguard, is loyal to the crown, but he has no understanding of the working of the divine mystery in calling or rejecting individuals for leadership.
5. Saul prays that David might be blessed and do remarkable things as he triumphs, but it is doubtful how sincere and true he was to his own feelings at that point.

Questions for Thought or Discussion

1. If God had called you to be a leader of a congregation or organization, would you put up with all the delay and outright attack against your person that David for all the years he had to wait until that was fulfilled?
2. How can we discern what is the providential working of God versus what is an unusual coincidence – such as finding Saul's sleeping in his night quarters, especially when his whole army has fallen into a deep sleep?
3. Since Saul has already thrown his spear at David at least twice, would you blame David for keeping it as a souvenir? Why should he do so or why should he not do so?
4. What made David so full of courage that he walked right into the enemy's camp without prior knowledge of the enemy's state of sleep? Did this boldness have anything to do with the anointing of the Holy Spirit? Or was this tied to his days of wrestling stolen sheep from the mouths of predators like lions and bears?

Lesson 9

David Escapes from Saul Among the Philistines

I Samuel 27:1 – 28:2; 29:1-11

The narrative that tells the story of David's rise to power, complicated though it is, is embodied between 1 Samuel 16:1 and 28:2. Most sense that 1 Samuel 28:3 begins the story of Saul's final days in office and the end of this life that goes to the end of the book of 1 Samuel (31:13). The amazing point to be raised in connection with 1 Samuel 27:1- 28:2, however, is that God's name is never mentioned in this chapter. Therefore, we are left with a question that haunts the interpreter: What can a text in which God does not appear teach us either positively or negatively?

To be sure, David has by this time felt exhausted and betrayed by his government, for he has been on the run to escape King Saul's murderous and envious attempt to kill him. The chapter opens with David expressing his anxiety about Saul in 1 Samuel 27:1, and closes with Achish, the Philistine king of Gath, revealing his own thoughts in verse 12.

David has concluded by this time that his only security now lies in the low-lying Philistine hills of Canaan, called the Shephelah (27:1). Could it be that neither he, not any of his 600 troops, had not up to this point enjoyed one full night's sleep ever since he began playing the fugitive from Saul and his army of 3000. Moreover, if he stayed in the land of Israel, soon Saul was going to be successful in killing him and he would be "swept away" from this earth! David's use of the "swept away" is very noticeable, for David had used that very same word in 26:10 when he told Abishai that the Lord God would "sweep away" King Saul one of these days as he went into battle. But now David reverses his judgment and in his inner self he feels that Saul may "sweep away" David if he does not get out of Israel.

We want to question David and ask him what has happened to his theology and his confidence in the LORD? Where has the power of the Lord and the certainty that sent him courageously into battle with Goliath gone by now? Has God failed David on any occasion yet? Has the LORD ever left him trapped with no way of escape? What has happened to David's trust in the LORD? Now David's only thought is he must escape Saul's range of administration, so David is willing to live with Israel's major enemy, the Philistines! We need to examine this chapter more minutely, for something has gone very wrong.

Placing One's Trust in a Former Enemy – 27:1-3

Rev Dale Ralph Davis[1] called to our attention an incident that took place in the first year of the ministry of the famous Charles Haddon Spurgeon, which was the year of 1854. This was the year the cholera had struck England, and so one family after another called on their new pastor Charles Haddon Spurgeon to come to the bedside of their loved ones or to lead daily in a graveside service for those who had succumbed to the disease. At first, the young Spurgeon threw himself into the visitation of the sick and giving comfort to the heartbroken wherever he could. But after a sustained period, with little or no relief, even this youthful pastor began to fold a bit under the pressure. One day, as he was on the Great Dover Road, wearily dragging himself home from another funeral, he suddenly noticed a poster in a shoemaker's window that caught his attention. Written in the center of a large sheet in handwriting were these words from Psalm 91:9-10 –

> "Because thou hast made the LORD, which is my refuge, even the Most High, thy habitation; there shall no evil befall thee, neither shall any plague come nigh thy dwelling."

Spurgeon said that the words had an immediate effect on his weary body, for suddenly, he felt refreshed and secure. He would lean on the Lord for his strength and support. David also could have used a good teaching like that at this very time, but he showed no dependence of the Lord or his word. He seems to have concluded that he must keep on going to try make it on his own. Yet the question is this: Does he want to end up like Saul? Come on David, Think and get back into the word of God, or you will be in a heap more trouble than you are right now with Saul.

David was convinced that his only support and real security now lay with his residing among the Philistines, the very people he had fought so valiantly against in the days he followed King Saul. Moreover, Gath was

1. Dale Ralph Davis, *Looking on the Heart: Expositions on the Book of 1 Samuel,* vol 2, Grand Rapids: Baker Books, 1994, pp. 141-42.

the same town from which the all-time Philistine champion named Goliath had come, but this now was the very town to which David was planning to take refuge and cover. What possessed David that he befriended King Achish, son of Maoch, the king of Gath, Philistia?

Not only did David go to Achish for refuge, but so did the 600 men, their wives and families that were with them (2-3). David himself brought along his two wives, Ahinoam of Jezreel and Abigail of Carmel, the widow of Nabal (3). I wonder if his wives, not to mention any of his 600 men, asked David what he was doing? Had David suddenly switched sides? Had he given up all hopes of ever becoming the king of Israel, even though Samuel the prophet had anointed him to be such and had conferred on him that blessing?

Leading A Double-Life of a Friend and A Destroyer of Others – 27:4-12

One thing was for sure: when Saul was told that David had fled to Gath, he stopped searching for him (4). That part of his strategy was working! This was the second time David had fled to the city of Gath (21:10). Gath is almost thirty miles northwest of the Desert of Ziph, where David had hidden most recently (36:1-2).

Surely David had good reasons to question in his own mind whether his residing in Gath with King Achish was a good decision, for we just might recall that David had to pretend to be insane to get out of the jam he found himself in when he was trapped inside the Philistine city of Gath (21:11-12). But David's hopes were pinned on his finding favor in the eyes of Achish and also that Achish would allow David and the families of his men to live in a country town far from Gath, rather than reside with Achish in a "royal city: where his movements could be watched and guarded more closely. Fortunately, Achish gave David and his men the town of Ziklag, a country town about 20 miles southeast of Gaza. There David stayed in Ziklag for a year and 4 months (27:7).

Just as David successfully deceived Achish the first time by pretending to have gone insane (21:12-15), so he was able to deceive Achish once again as he continued his raiding operations a distance from Achish's view (27:8-12). No doubt, this became the way David was able to find food, clothing, and livestock to keep paying his men and to support their families. David chose to raid the Geshurites, a southern people noted in the Bible only here and in Joshua 13:2, the Girzites who are otherwise unknown, unless they are related to those who from the town of Gezer, along with the Amalekites, whom Israel met in Exodus 17:8-16 made up the list of those David and his men used to raid.

David's practice was to make sure that he did not "leave a man or woman alive" (27:11) to inform Achish, or anyone else, what he had been doing. Moreover, he continued to deceive Achish by telling him that the Judahites hostility towards David was mounting. Records show that the tribe of Judah continued to support David, as he had effectively dealt with raiding parties from neighboring regions to the south, reducing their impact on Judah.

While David built up this deceitful report to Achish about how odious he was becoming to his own people of Israel, he continued to deceive the Philistine king and to give him the wrong impression about who he was and what he was doing.

Joining the Enemy to Fight Israel – 28:1-2

Once again, the Philistines declared war on Israel and so they gathered their forces to fight against the nation of Israel (28:1). It was now pay-back time for David to his Philistine benefactor, so Achish, king of Philistine Gath informed David, "You must understand that you and your men will accompany me in the army" (28:1b). David does not act in protest or show any surprise at his announcement; instead, he merely seemed to say that this challenge would provide a real opportunity for David to show Achish what he could do for him in battle, for he said, "Then you will see for yourself what your servant can do: (28:2). That was the end of what we would have guessed would have been a tough situation. Achish replied, "Very well, I will make you my bodyguard for life." (2b).

Protesting Being Dismissing the Philistine Forces -29:1-11

This 29th chapter of 1 Samuel really completes the action that was started in 1 Samuel 27:1-28:2, so we are going to jump ahead in the text of Scripture and complete that part of the story before we undertake the tragic and astonishing end that came to Saul's reign. In effect, the 29th chapter frames the story of Saul and his encounter with the witch of Endor (28:3-25). Added to this set of preliminary notes to this chapter 29 is the fact that this will now make it the third time that David deceived Achish, the king of Gath (21:12-15; 27:8-12; 29:1-11).

This chapter also introduces the fact that David would later defeat the Amalekites. This highlights the difference between King Saul, who was unsuccessful in defeating the Amalekites years earlier, and David (15). This group of chapters will also show the sad failure of Saul and the army of Israel to defeat the Philistines (31), a battle in which Saul commits suicide to avoid being abused by his nemesis, the Philistines. David's position was undeniably complex. On one hand, he needed to maintain loyalty to Achish to ensure the safety and stability of his people, while on the other hand, he had to navigate the delicate tension of not directly harming his fellow Israelites. His actions reveal a calculated balancing act, where survival and diplomacy were prioritized over open confrontation or outright allegiance. This duality showcases David's strategic mindset and his ability to adapt to challenging circumstances without abandoning his long-term goals.

The narrative in chapter 29 began by repeating the muster to battle for the Philistines and Israelites as was posted already in 1 Samuel 28:4. Thus, all the Philistine forces and the five Lords of the five Philistine cities have by now arrived and assembled their troops at the town of Aphek, at the sources of the Yarkon River, in the Plain of Sharon (29:1), as preparation to march on to meet Israel at the Spring of Jezreel (29:11). So, later that evening the two armies were set for battle, the Israelis were spread out on Mount Gilboa with the Philistines making camp to the north of them at the town of Shunem (28:4).

What is different about the lineup of the armies this time, however, is the fact that the Philistines were marching in their units of hundreds and thousands, and here was David with his men marching at the rear of the line of march with King Achish (29:2). If we do not see anything curious about such an arrangement, the commanders of the Philistines did, for that is why they asked, "What about these Hebrews?" (29:3).

Achish instantly came to the defense of David and Jewish contingency, not just once, but on three times (29:3, 6, 9). Achish had made David his personal bodyguard for life (28:2). Poor deceived Achish rose magnificently to argue the case for David's presence as part of the Philistine army. For instance, Achish acknowledged that at one time David had been an "officer" of Saul, but from the day he left (lit. "fell away from") Saul, he has now been with me, the king of Gath enthused, for "over a year." (29:3). Moreover, all this time he has been with me, I can tell you that "I have found no fault (lit. "nothing .... not anything") in him." (29:3).

Achish was not successful in convincing any of the Philistine commanders, for they were angry with King Achish and ordered him to "Send the man back to the place you assigned him (i.e., Ziklag). He must not go with us into battle, or he will turn against (Lit. "become and adversary against," where the word "adversary" Hebrew, *satan,* namely "Satan") us during the fighting. How much better could he regain his master's favor than by taking the heads of our own men? (29:4)

These same Philistine commanders reminded Achish of one of the popular hit-tunes of the day that was being sung in Israeli dances:

> "Saul has slain his thousands,
> And David his tens of thousands." (29:5b; cf. 18:7-8; 21:11).

The Philistine commanders won this argument, for Achish could no longer oppose his peers. So, he called David to tell him the sad news. But once more Achish declared his total trust and confidence in David, for he affirms, "You have been reliable" (29:6) and "I would be pleased to have you serve with me in the army" (6b). Once more he tells David, "I have found no fault (using a different word this time, one meaning "evil") in you, but the rulers do not approve of you" (6c). So, that was that!

David took the position that he was disappointed, but how did he think he was going to manage the battle situation against his own people? David, however, protested, for he wanted to know, "But what have I done?" – the same question he had put to his oldest brother Eliab (17:29), also to his friend Jonathan (20:1) and later to King Saul (26:18). Is David just pretending he wants to fight against his own people, or does he really mean it? Surprisingly enough, David never mentions the name of the Lord, nor does he show at any point that he has inquired if the action he now wishes to take was following the action God wanted him to take. In fact, the name of Yahweh or God is mentioned only twice in this chapter (Yahweh, 29:6; "God" in v. 9), but these names come from the mouth of a pagan king, not from the anointed David. Achish becomes even more lavish in his praise of David, for he brags. "You have been as pleasing in my eyes as an angel of God" (9).

Nevertheless, Achish instructed David and his men to rise early the next morning and leave the camp as soon as it is light (10). So, that is what happened as David and his men got up early and began to travel back to Philistia. The Philistines, however in the meantime made their way up to Jezreel to meet Saul and his army.

Conclusions

1. 1 Samuel 27 begins with David thinking to himself internally, instead of his seeking instructions from the Lord as to how he was to act. Is this the best place to draw a line?
2. David went to a pagan king for refuge among the enemies of the people of God instead of making the Lord his refuge. See Psalm 91:9-10 in KJV. Is this effective advice in times of a pan endemic?
3. Why is the pagan king Achish the only one in this chapter who uses or refers to the name of God? Does this tell us something about David's spiritual condition at the time?
4. What would David have done if he went into that battle and it was the battle, as it was, where Saul and a sizable number of Israel's army ended their lives?
5. Is there any sign that God approved of David's deceitfulness with Achish?

Questions for Thought or Discussion

1. Do you think God approved of David's raids on the southern part of the Negev, especially since they were a real help to Judah who suffered from raiding parties from these same people?
2. Is it ever proper and right for a believer to practice deceiving others if it is in a worthy cause? Or there situations where conceivable it might be OK to do so?
3. Does the Biblical injunction to "Be separate" from the world have any place in discussing this narrative?
4. Why do you think King Achish was so familiar with the name of "Yahweh" as Israel's God? Had he been taught who he was in an earlier contact with Israel?

Lesson 10

Saul and the Witch at Endor

1 Samuel 28:3-25

This indeed is a very strange chapter, for it recounts how Saul in his desperation to get a word from the supernatural world, especially when God refused to answer him by any of the traditional ways, Saul went to a "witch," also called a "medium," or a "necromancer," where he learned he would die in his last battle with the Philistines (28:19). What is going on here?

This chapter in the life of Saul (as it affected David) clearly traced the current problem Saul faced (28:4-6), Saul's conversation with the necromancer (7-14), then his amazing conversation with the prophet Samuel, who had just been called back from the dead (15-19), along with the story of his final meal before his death (20-25). Let us go to this text and see if we can understand what is going on.

Tormented By No Answers from God – 28:4-6

This text begins by reminding us that the prophet Samuel had since died, and he was buried in his hometown of Ramah (28:3; cf. 25:1). In the meantime, Saul had expelled all mediums and spiritists from the land following the teaching Moses and others had given on this topic in Leviticus 19:31; 20:6-7; Deuteronomy 18:9-22; Isaiah 8:19-20. What had so suddenly prompted this action, we are not told. Might it have been a desire on Saul's part to suddenly appear to be super religious, after a period that showed an absence of his desire to follow the teaching of Scripture, or was there another motivation?

Once again, the Philistines assembled their men for war and set up camp at the town Shunem (4). This town of Shunem (modern name, Solem), was found on the southern base of Mount Moreh, nine miles east-northeast of Megiddo. It appears two other times in the Biblical record, (1) as the town from which Abishag came, she who was the virgin that functioned as a warming pad for shivering King David in his old age (1 Kings 1:3), and (2) the home of the well-to-do woman who built a prophet's chamber on her roof, for whenever the prophet Elisha passed through the area (2 Kings 4:8, 12). Over against these pagan Philistine forces ten miles south-southeast Saul's army encamped at Gilboa, the site where Saul, his son Jonathan, and a large part of his army would lose their lives.

When Saul "saw" the size and preparedness of the Philistine army, he became "afraid" (which may involve a wordplay, for both words, "to see" and "to be afraid," are spelled in Hebrew as *wyr'* 28:5), and "terror filled his heart." Saul decided he had better ask of the LORD what to do, but no matter how he tried to get an answer, whether by dreams, by the Urim (the sacred lots stored in the priestly ephod), or by a word through the prophets, the LORD would not answer him. This must have been a huge clue to him that not only something was going to be terribly wrong, but that the LORD had abandoned him just as he had said he would.

Helped by a Necromancer – 28:7-14.

Although Saul had removed all mediums, spiritists, and necromancers from the land, he asked his men to find a woman with those abilities so he could consult the netherworld (28:7). Interesting enough, Saul's men knew just where to turn to find such a woman – there was one at Endor (7b). That is how this chapter came about in the history of Israel. What a tell-tale sign of how low Israel had gone in her falling away from the LORD God who loved them and had rescued them from Egypt. It may be saying too much to say Saul inquired of the LORD for an answer, for by now he had long lived without contact with the Lord ever since Samuel gave up on him. In fact, Saul simply "asks" of the LORD, but the verb used in the parallel passage in 1 Chronicles 10:14 is the Hebrew verb *drsh,* "to seek."

This passage raises the question, "Does this Scripture permit Believers today to try to contact the dead by means of mediums or necromancers?" The answer is "Absolutely not!" But a second question follows, "Did this chapter involve, then, a piece of fakery with no contact with reality?" Probably not," for when the woman sees Samuel, she cries out and screams at the top of her lungs for two reasons: (1) she probably was not in the habit of seeing such a trick as "calling up" of Samuel from the dead to work (12a), and (2) she realized all of a sudden that her disguised client was none other than Saul himself and therefore she was doomed, for Saul had previously ordered all such persons killed (13).

It is easy to see that the questions about this chapter are legion in number. For example: Was this woman and her craft able to raise people from the dead? Was her ability due to Satanic power, or was she simply mistaken in believing she could perform such a feat? Did Samuel appear, if he did at all, not because the necromancer was able to do so, but because God intervened and raised Samuel himself?

Early Church Fathers were fearful of what doctrinal aberrations this text would produce in the Church, and so they argued either that (1) the sorcery involved here was simply demonic, for Samuel had not been reduced to a "shade" in Sheol, in which a medium could act as an intermediary between two worlds in summoning him forth , or (2) Samuel was not in Hades, but had been sent by God to announce Saul's fate. The Church Father Origen gave another approach, treating the whole matter typologically. He saw the whole calling forth of Samuel standing for Messiah, who voluntarily descended into hell, prophesied to the souls there, and has the power to bring inhabitants back from Hades! Wow! That was off the mark! On the other hand, another Church Father, Gregory of Nazianzus said, Samuel was raised, or so it seemed, said Gregory, by a woman having a familiar spirit, so he left the ambiguity in the text.

Saul wrongly thought that he could disguise himself from the medium (8), but that thought turned out to be wrong (12). And if Saul was hoping for good news for all his trouble, he too was mistaken, for his cover and desires were completely exploded. The two men who went with Saul (8) asked the medium on Saul's behalf to "consult" a "spirit." The Hebrew word for "to consult" is *qsm,* elsewhere translated "diviners," or "divination." But that word brings back to the event that came at the start of Samuel's days of instruction for King Saul. In 1 Samuel 15:23, Saul's rebellion in refusing to leave neither man nor beast standing decided to bring back a sizable number of animals as an offering to the LORD, to which Samuel compared this act to the "sin of rebellion."

When the woman reminded Saul of his threat to "cut off" all those of her craft (9), he promised her that she would not be punished or put to death as the others had, by taking a solemn oath in the Lord's name (10). Whether she saw Samuel in a real apparition or not, we do not know. But whatever she saw was enough to shock the liver out of her and to blow Saul's cover (12). Saul urged her not to be afraid but instead asked her what she saw. She retorted, "a spirit," which in this case used the Hebrew word *'elohim.* In the apparition, Samuel is seen coming up out of "the ground," (Hebrew, *ha'arets*).

Saul was unable to see the "spirit," but he asked the woman to describe what she saw (14). She said he looked like "an old man wearing a robe," which Saul assumed was Samuel (14). Saul never saw Samuel himself.

Rebuked by the Prophet Samuel – 28:15-19

The apparition that appeared to be Samuel complained to Saul, "Why have you disturbed me by bringing me up?" (15), for Saul by now has arrived at the medium's place of business. Endor was found two or three miles northeast of the town of Shunem on the northern slope of the same Mount Moreh, while the Philistines were at Shunem on the southern slope of Mount Moreh. This meant, therefore, that Saul, risky as it was, had to skirt around the camp of the Philistines undetected to get to the witch at Endor.

Saul answered Samuel (or the apparition) with this sorrowful explanation,

> "I am in great distress. The Philistines are fighting against me, and God has turned away from me. He no longer answers me, either by prophets or by dreams. So, I have called on you to tell me what to do (15b).

Saul was in desperate straits, for he fully realized that God had abandoned him. Saul uses the general word, "God" (Hebrew, *'elohim*), while Samuel consistently used the covenantal term for God, *Yahweh*. Moreover, the fate that Saul was confronting was the same one that had been announced years before by Samuel (16:14; 18:12). Why had Saul not acted in that interim to get his heart right with God if he accepted the truth of those divine revelations?

The LORD had done as he had predicted back in 15:28 to tear the kingdom of Israel from Saul's hands and to give it to another "one of his neighbors," i.e., to David (17b). Verse 18 lists two reasons why the LORD wrenched out of Saul's hands the kingdom: (1) Saul had disobeyed the command of Samuel (chap. 13), and (2) he had refused to fully carry out God's command against Amalek (chap. 15). It is true, of course, that over the years God had delivered the Philistines to Israel (7:3, 14), but now he would "hand over" Israel to the enemy (19). Samuel told Saul in as polite terms as possible, "Tomorrow you and your sons will be with me" (in the realm of the dead, 19).

With his final appearance in v. 20 of the two books of the Bible in his name, Samuel does not appear again in these books. But he surely must be recognized as one of the greatest leaders Israel had in her early years of development. Scripture labels him as the head of the prophets (Acts 3:24; 13:20); he is also called both "prophet" and "Seer" (1 Chron. 9:22; 26:28; cf. 1 Sam. 9:9, 19), yet he also functioned as priest, judge, counselor, and anointer of Israel's first two kings.

Sustained by Eating a Final Meal – 28:20-25

Saul was overcome by the message Samuel, or the apparition, now delivered to him, for "immediately [he] fell full length on the ground, filled with fear because of Samuel's words. His strength was gone, for he had eaten nothing all that day and night" (20).

The woman, like Saul, was deeply shaken by all that was happening. But she also saw how distraught, fearful, and overcome Saul was, for he had not taken nourishment all that day and he suffered from total exhaustion. So, she begged Saul to listen to her advice to eat something she would prepare. At first Saul refused everything, but she and the men with Saul persisted in this point of view (23).

The medium quickly got together a meal fit for a king, for she butchered a calf and baked unleavened bread, in what could be labelled a typical eastern sumptuous feast (24-25). Saul and his men sat down and ate. However, the chapter ends with the mournful note that "Then they got up and went away that night" (25b). Yes, the writer wanted us to know not only the late hour this was coming to, but there was more than the time that was in his mind, for what had begun so hopefully perhaps forty years ago filled with such promise of a new king named Saul, ruling over Israel, had now ended with darkness and the prospect of a military calamity of epic proportions.

Conclusions

1. What a grim chapter, for it begins with the death of the prophet Samuel and ends with the prediction of the tragic death of Israel's first king along with his sons and his army.
2. It is a choice that is dead wrong: viz., to choose to ask the forces of death and hell for advice when one has for so many years resisted the loving advice of a Heavenly Father in the Scriptures.
3. The focus of this chapter is not on the geography and resources of the netherworld, but on the Lord, who has given us his revelation to inform us as to how we should live to please him.
4. What God has predicted in the past holds firm and true for all times past and present. God does not revise or change his mind about what he has said will take place in the days to come.
5. It is improper for believers to think that they are in Saul's shoes when they wrongly conclude they have been cut off from the presence of God. When we feel abandoned by God, like Saul did, remember that as believers we can call out to God, our light in dark times (Psalm 13:1).
6. Never doubt in the darkness what God has promised to do in the light!

Questions for Thought or Discussion

1. Why was Saul so unsuccessful in the latter half of his reign while in his earlier days he seemed to thrive and enjoy the power and presence of the Lord?
2. 2.What would David and his priest Abiathar have done if they had still been in the Philistine battle that took place on Mount Gilboa? What side would they have taken? What explanation could they have given to God?
3. God's saints, like the hymnist William Cowper, have often felt like they were reprobate? How would you have offered help to them from the Gospel?
4. What word from the Scriptures would you have for all who use the arts or the occult world to guide others?

Lesson 11

David Defeats the Amalekites at Ziklag

1 Samuel 30:1-31

David arrives back at his home base of Ziklag and finds it destroyed along with thc fact that all his wives and the wives of his men were gone, taken captive by the Amalekites. He had just been delivered three days ago from the trap of having to fight against his own people Israel in the mercy and providence of God, so, in many ways, therefore, in some ways, it actually must have felt good to be booted out of Achish's line of march and headed home to Ziklag again. However, the sixty-mile, three-day, journey from Aphek to Ziklag came to an abrupt halt when he arrived in Ziklag, for it had been burnt to the ground, only to find no town, no wives, and no families! Just when it seemed that things could not get any worse, they did! It is time, then, to examine this chapter in detail.

Life's Trials May at Times Seem to be Too Much – 30:1-6a

After a three-day trek from the Philistine gathering point in Aphek of their military machine, from which David and his 600 men had just been summarily dismissed, the weary men arrived home at Ziklag only to find it had been "raided" (lit. "stripped", cf. 31:9 of the Philistine treatment of slain Saul) and burnt to the ground with fire (30:1). This destruction, they would soon learn (13) was done by the Amalekites, Israel's long-time enemies (cf. Exod. 17:8-16), who inhabited rather large tracts of land southwest of the Dead Sea. True, David had previously raided the Amalekites (27:8), therefore, in retaliation they struck Ziklag just when David's men had left their town to join with the Philistines in their battle against Israel. The Amalekites had "taken captive" all who lived in the town (30:2-3). Despite David's own policy of leaving nobody alive when raiding sites, no one was killed in this raid. They would be offered for sale as slaves, instead.

The men in David's retinue wept aloud until they had no more strength to weep over their losses (30:4). The situation seemed hopeless, for they had no clue as who had done this act of treachery or where they had come from or gone.

God's Strength is More Than Enough – 30:6b-8

Finding the destruction of his town Ziklag and the disappearance of all the wives, children, and cattle, the grief of the men and of David was unbounded. Added to that grief was the fact that David was "greatly distressed" because his men blamed him for what had happened (6a) – they wanted to stone him! Under such heavy pressure, it was at that point that David "found strength in the LORD" (6b).

But what did that mean? Surely it was not some kind of magic, nor was it a quick fix, or deciding that the LORD was a type of genie that one could massage to help one to feel better. The tears and weeping were poured out copiously, but strengthening oneself in the LORD was an altogether different matter. Instead of these humanly devised antidotes for the relief of all the grief that had overcome all of them, David found that strengthening oneself in the LORD implied recalling the promises of God and affirming what God had said in his word! Another way of strengthening ourselves in the LORD was by using our access to the LORD's presence.

> "Then David said to Abiathar the priest, the son of Ahimelech, 'Bring me the ephod.' Abiathar brought it to him, and David inquired of the LORD, 'Shall I pursue this raiding party? Will I overtake them?' "Pursue them," he answered. "You will certainly overtake them and succeed in the rescue" (7-8).

It has been a good while since David had asked for the use of the ephod (23:9) and David had not been showing any instances of speaking to the LORD since chapter 26. But now David has once again strengthened himself in the LORD by using the sacred lots connected to the ephod.

Believers may take umbrage at this exhortation by saying that we as believers do not have access to a priest like Abiathar or the sacred ephod, so how could this passage apply to us? However, that is just the point we need to make, for we have a great high priest who has passed through the heavens, Jesus, God's son (Heb. 4:14). Since we have such a great high priest, let us receive mercy and find grace to help in time of need (Heb 4:16). Even when our questions are not answered directly, we are given grace to help, which we sometimes need more definitely than the direct answer.

Finding God's Providential, Dehydrated, Discarded Slave Was Essential – 30:9-20

David and his men, weary from the sixty-mile trek of the previous three days went off right away to catch up to the raiders. They came to Wadi Besor (9), which some identify with Wadi Ghazzeh, about twelve to fifteen miles south of Ziklag. The Wadi Besor empties into the Mediterranean Sea about four miles south of Gaza. There at Besor David had to leave 200 of his men as a staging area, for these men were too tired and worn out to continue the march southward, so David pressed on with the remaining 400 (10).

Immediately David and his 400 men came across a starving, dehydrated Egyptian slave (11), to whom David gave him food and water, consisting especially cakes of raisins and cakes of pressed figs, the stuff that is most suited for armies on the march. When David questioned him about to whom he belonged, and where he was from, he gave an answer David was looking for. Up to this point, David had no idea who it was he had been chasing after, but this man providentially gave David the key he needed. The slave answered,

> "I am an Egyptian, the slave of an Amalekite. My master abandoned me when I became sick three days ago [lit. "today is day three"]. We raided the Negeb of the Kerethites and the territory belonging to Judah and the Negev of Caleb. And we burned Ziklag" (13-14).

This statement is important for two reasons. First, it used the idiom for a three-day-period, but it clearly shows that talking about "three days," or "three days and three nights," is comparable to the same phrase used at the time Jesus was in the grave, for it can also apply when just a part of the full period was intended, for this phrase ended with the explicit statement that today was "day three," just as "three days and three nights" might in our usage of such a phase indicate a full period of 72 hours, but in the case of our Lord's entombment, it was much less, lasting from about 3 p.m. on Friday, all day Saturday and until about 5:00 a.m. on Sunday – a period of merely 38 hours!

The second piece of information we gain from this slave's report is that he belonged to a hated Amalekite overlord who had burnt Ziklag along with their pillaging the Negev of the Kerethites and an undefined part of Judahite territory.

The Egyptian agreed to show David where this Amalekite army had gone if David agreed not to kill him or to hand him over to his former master (15-16). Thus, the Egyptian led David to where he discovered the Amalekite bivouac (16). When David came upon the Amalekites, he found them "eating and drinking and dancing/reveling," given here as further marks of a degenerate people who cared little for the rights of others, but only for the excesses of their own appetites (16). After a full night and another full day of fighting, large numbers of Amalekites fell dead with none getting away except 400 who took off on camels (17).

David's rout of the Amalekites was so extensive that he not only got back his two wives who had been captured (18), but he retrieved everything that had been taken so that "nothing was missing" (19). The retrieved plunder is specifically referred to as "David's plunder" (20). This will play an interesting role in the rest of the chapter.

God's Grace Provides the New Norm – 30:21-25

The triumphantly successful army of David's 400 men returned to the 200 men he had left behind at the Besor Ravine (21). These men came out to greet the returning party, but when David's followers approached the greeters, trouble broke out among David's victorious army against the 200, whom he had been left at the staging area. These troublemakers were of one opinion: "Because [these 200 men] did not go out with us, we will not share with them the plunder we recovered. However, each man may take his wife and children and go," was how they reflected on the whole situation (22).

But David was quick to reply, for he said,

> "No, my brothers, you must not do that with what the LORD has given us. He has protected us and handed over to us the forces that came against us. Who will listen to what you say? The share of a man who stayed with the supplies is to be the same as that of him who went down to the battle. All will share alike." (23-24).

David refused to let those who had remined behind to be regarded as inferior to those who went to fight the battle. David boldly and magnanimously called the troublemakers “brothers” (23). Moreover, he clearly taught that all the plunder had been given to them from the LORD himself, therefore the men were to be especially careful in how they managed and disposed of it (23). This then became a “statute and ordinance in Israel from that day forward!”

Distribution of the Victorious Booty Wins Friends – 30:26-31

David returns to Ziklag (26), sending part of the plunder to Judah's elders, his friends from his time in Ziklag. With the plunder he sent this note along to 12 cities of Israel: “Here is a present for you from the plunder of the LORD’s enemies” (26b). This list included: Bethel (but not the Bethel in Benjamin, but the Judahite Kesil), Ramoth Negev (mentioned in the Arad ostrasca), Jettir (thirteen miles south-southwest of Hebron), Aroer (about fifteen miles south of Jattir), Siphmoth (an unknown site), Eshtemoa (nine miles south-southwest of Hebron, Racal (perhaps a scribal error for Carmel, Hormah (the site of Israel’s earliest loss in a battle, Num. 14:45), Bor Ashan (twelve miles southwest of Hebron), and Athach (unknown site), those in the towns of the Jerahmeelites, and other places where David and his men may have roamed. Surely David meant kindness by all these actions, but he nonetheless was ingratiating himself to all those in Judah as well. David and his men distributed part of the spoils to others who had experienced attacks from the same enemy.

Conclusions

1. It is a mystery why David would have sided with the Philistines in a battle that finally killed Saul, but David was spared at the last moment.
2. Mercifully none of the wives of David or the men or any of their children were slain by the raiding Amalekites.
3. Just when David was close to being stoned but his embittered men over what they thought were their losses, David found strength in the Lord.
4. God's counsel given though the ephod of Abiathar was that he should pursue the raiders and he and his men would be successful.
5. The booty David gained from his attack on the Amalekites had been given to them from the LORD, so no person was to claim it was owed to him as his personal reward. Since it came from the LORD, it was to be shared with all including those who stayed with the supplies.

Questions for Thought or Discussion

1. In your view, should David have taken refuge among the Philistines to get away from Saul?
2. How would David ever have been crowned king by Israel if he had been a participant in the battle of Mount Gilboa in which King Saul and his son Jonathan died?
3. What are the avenues in our day for finding "strength" in the Lord?
4. What lesson was David teaching his men by distributing the battle booty to those in Judah? Could he also have had underlying motives of gaining favor with the people of Judah?

Lesson 12

David's Lament Over Saul's and Jonathan's Deaths

1 Samuel 31:1-13; 2 Samuel 1:1-27

The battle on Mount Gilboa, that David providentially missed by being sent home by the Philistines, went on up north (1 Sam. 29-30), while David was tracking down the raiding Amalekites down south. The verbs in 1 Samuel 31:1-3 carry the sad impact of the story, for the Israelites "fled" rather than face the advance of Philistines (1) as the enemy "killed" Saul and his three sons, Jonathan, Abinadad and Malki-Shua (2). The archers had pressed hard the battle that surrounded Saul in its fiercest form, so that they wounded him most critically and he was at the point of dying (3).

We, the readers, are especially moved in sympathy over the loss of Jonathan, who had played such a major part in David's life up to this point (1 Sam. 14, 18-20 and 23). However, long ago Jonathan had acknowledged that the kingship belonging to David in one of their conversations (1 Sam. 18:1-4). But Jonathan also remained loyal to his father Saul as well, despite his full knowledge of his father's shortcomings and his mean sins. This chapter 31 can be divided in half, with vv. 1-7 describing the battle on Gilboa and vv. 8-13 picking up what took place after this.

Divine Prediction of the End to Saul's Life – 31:1-7

The Battle of Mount Gilboa is strikingly different in how the battle progressed from the way David's forays with the Philistines progressed. Instead of the army of Israel going in "hot pursuit" of the Philistines and defeating them (14:22), the tables had been turned against Israel with the Philistines taking the upper hand. Three of Saul's sons had been killed before Saul committed suicide (31:2, 6, 8).

Israel had sustained an awful loss, for three sons had died, his armor-bearer, his bodyguard and Saul himself, including Saul's crack troops, were among the slain. One after another the men of Saul "fell" in death, just as Saul had fallen on his sword; however, there was no falling of the word of God, for it never will fall nor has it ever fallen or failed. Its word always happened, and it did not fail to be fulfilled or pass away!

Although this period was characterized by hardship and setbacks for the kingdom of God, it stayed within the scope of God's plan and was not beyond His providence. Ronald F. Youngblood[1] has called our attention to three of the stanzas of "Song of Saul before his Last Battle" by George Gordon (Lord Byron) where he imaginatively reconstructed Saul's last words to his men, his armor-bearer, and his son Jonathan.

> Warriors and chiefs! Should the shaft or the sword
> pierce me in leading the host of the Lord,
> Heed not the course, though a king's in your path.
> Bury your steel in the bosoms of Gath!
>
> Thou who art bearing my buckler and bow,
> Should the soldiers of Saul look away from the foe,
> Stretch me that moment in blood at my feet!
> Mine be the doom which they dared not to meet.
>
> Farewell to others, but never we part,
> Heir to my royalty, son of my heart!
> Bright is the diadem, boundless the sway,
> Or kingly the death, which awaits us to-day!

The Problem of Yahweh's Honor -31:8-13

The next day, the Philistines returned to the battlefield to "strip the dead," but in doing so, they discovered that there was Saul's corpse (which they could find by his height and his distinctive armor) along with others who had died along with him (31:8). The armor of Saul would soon be put on display in the temple of their goddesses Ashtoreth (Astarte). Obviously, they broadcasted the news of Saul's defeat all over Philistia. The Philistines mangled Saul's body (9a) and chopped off his head, along with stripping his armor.

The Philistines sent back word (9-10) via messengers to proclaim their victory -- no doubt along with Saul's head. Meanwhile, the corpses of Saul and his sons were spiked to the walls of Bethshan (10b).

---

1. Ronald F. Youngblood, *The Expositor's Bible Commentary,* vol 3, Grand Rapids, Zondervan, 2009, p. 290.

Thus, it looked like the gods Dagan and Astarte had won the day; Yahweh for the moment had been defeated. In that day, once the people suffered a major defeat, then so did their god suffer the same defeat. For believers in all generations, the sadness of our hearts is not merely in the fact that Israel had been trounced, but the LORD God of the whole universe had also been simultaneously mocked and defied. There was the real basis of the tragedy.

When those who were living "on the other side of the valley" (7a), i.e., the people north of Mount Gilboa, but who were living on the east side of the Jordan River, saw what was happening, they suddenly abandoned their towns leaving them open to the Philistine incursion, who rapidly occupied the newly provided site.

When the residents of Jabesh-gilead heard how the Philistines had abused Saul's corpse, they had not forgotten how Saul had so dramatically come to their aid at the beginning of his reign (11:2). The people of Jabesh-gilead had faced another mutilator of men captured in battle named King Nahash, the Ammonite (11:6), but Saul had settled that score in favor of the people of Jabesh-gilead. A group of their strongest men traveled overnight to Beth-shan and took Saul's and his sons' bodies down from the city walls. These men quickly returned to Jabesh-gilead, which was about ten miles southeast of Beth-shan, making a round trip in less than twenty-four hours of a twenty mile-rescue.

Very few things in the Bible look as desperate as the massacre on Mount Gilboa, for it appeared as if both Yahweh and the kingdom of God had been set back in time by years and had suffered unbearable stigma. Yet, all this time God had been preparing a young shepherd boy, who knew how to care for scattered sheep, for our Lord was looking not on the outward appearances of defeat, but on the heart of young David.

An Amalekite Claims to Have Killed Saul -2 Samuel 1:1-16

2 Samuel begins exactly where 1 Samuel had concluded by saying: "After the death of Saul" (2 Sam. 1:1) .... That is the identical way that the books of Joshua and Judges began, "After the death of Moses" (Josh. 1:1) and "After the death of Joshua" (Judg. 1:1). Moreover, beginning with the lists of the sons born to David in 2 Samuel 3:2-5, a good part of 2 Samuel is replicated in 1 Chronicles as well. In addition to the paralleling of the same information in 2 Samuel, mention should also be made of Psalm 18, which is replicated from 2 Samuel 22.

So, the narrative about David's final arrival and years of experience, first as the king of Judah, then of all Israel, can be found in 2 Samuel. The words of 2 Samuel 1:1 parallel 2 Samuel 1:15-16 that frame this literary unit that had as its subject the "striking down" of the Amalekite(s) by David. Another inclusion can be seen between 2 Samuel 1:1 and 8:13, which section precedes the court history of David in 2 Samuel 9-20, while the section in front of this court history takes us to the time David "returned from striking down" the Edomites (8:13).

2 Samuel began by talking about the Amalekite fugitive, who arrived at David's camp in Ziklag from the terrible battle scene on Mount Gilboa, eighty miles, a full three-day trip. The Amalekite fugitive arrived with torn clothes and dust on his head (1:2). The dust on the individual's head showed distress, which is consistent with someone who had seen significant destruction and loss of life. Seeing the man's appearance, naturally David wanted to know where he had come from. His response was that he had just escaped from the Israelite camp on Mount Gilboa where he along with the other Israelites had fled from the battle on Mount Gilboa, led by the victorious Philistines 1:3-4). Then this fugitive blurted out the awful news that King Saul and his sons were dead. This news fell like a ton of bricks even to the battle-weary troops of David.

There is one major problem, however, with the Amalekite's report of what happened at the battle on Mount Gilboa. It did not match all the established facts. Some of the more obvious differences would include the following: (1) in 1 Samuel 31, King Saul committed suicide, but in the Amalekite's report, he was the man who actually killed Saul as he was in the throes of dying, (2) in 1 Samuel 31, Saul was wounded by the archers, but in this new account by the Amalekite, his enemies were the charioteers, (3) in 1 Samuel 31, the Philistines took Saul's armor, but here the Amalekite brought Saul's crown and armlet to David.[2] Now, given this disparity, which one was telling the truth? Scholars contend that the Bible has two conflicting accounts; however, this interpretation does not align with the evangelical perspective about the doctrine of inerrancy. Others contend that the Amalekite's story was the correct one, but then that makes the Bible's report in 1 Samuel 31 false, which earns the same rebuke as the preceding view. Another view set forth by the ancient historian, Josephus, contends that the armor-bearer refused to finish off

2. See Bill T. Arnold, "The Amalekite's Report of Saul's Death: Political Intrigue or Incompatible Sources?" *JETS*, 32/3 (1989): p. 290.

Saul, when he requested it, and therefore Saul fell on his own sword; however, he was too weak to do so completely, so Saul turned and spied the Amalekite nearby and at the king's request, he killed Saul. After he had killed Saul, he picked up the king's crown and armband and fled.[3]

Josephus has come up with the best conflation of the events that are in tension in this story, however, his basic error is in the assumption that the Amalekite was telling the truth. The way the Amalekite told his story, he "just happened" to be on Mount Gilboa when he met wounded Saul "leaning on his spear" as the "chariots and riders were almost upon him" (1:6). But what is this Amalekite doing leisurely wandering about a mountain when a battle is ongoing? (1:7)

Saul is said to have seen this Amalekite and asked him who he was. He answered, "I am an Amalekite" (1:8). That must have brought back to Saul a whole bunch of memories – his failure to obey orders a long time ago! Saul is supposed to have said, "Stand over me and kill me! I am in the throes of death, but I am still alive" (1:9) – like an earlier expression used by Goliath to David, "Stand over me and kill me. (cf. 1 Sam. 17:51). The Amalekite was happy to oblige Saul (1:10). That is what happened! Wow!

Neither David nor his men were impressed by this young man's story, for all of them took hold of their clothes and tore them and wept and fasted for the rest of the day until evening came (1:11-12). That evening David recommenced the interrogation of this curious visitor, asking him, "Where are you from?" (1:13). The lad, apparently not up on his current newscasts said, "I am the son of an alien, an Amalekite." (1:13b). Now it was time for David to speak, for he scolded him for not being afraid to destroy the LORD's anointed (1:14). With that, David called for one of his men to "strike him down," and he did so! That ended both the man and the story!

David's Lament for Saul and Jonathan – 1:17-27

David composed a powerfully compassionate poem that depicted his love and deep regard for Saul and especially his son Jonathan. This poem is dated about 1000 B.C.E. and is in the same style as another lament that David composed on the death of Abner (2 Sam. 3:33-34).

The lovely elegy could properly be given the title of "How the Mighty have Fallen" from its lead line at the beginning of the poem (2 Sam. 1:19) and in its closing line (2 Sam. 1:27), thus giving symmetry to the poem.

3. Flavius Josephus, *Antiquities of the Jews, 6.370*-72.

The Hebrew word for "mighty" (Hebrew, *gibborim*) is the most distinctive part of this poem, for it appears six times in a matter of nine verses (1:19, 21, 22, 23, 25, 27).

The first time I ever heard a sermon on this passage was in my young years I heard my father speak at the funeral at the request of his best friend, a past pastor in Philadelphia of a Reformed Church of America, named Rev. William Green, but who, more recently, had given up that position to take a key role as a representative of the Pocket Testament League. He and my father had been very close friends, so when the request came for my dad to give the message at the funeral, he who was only a lay leader in a small suburban church, my father choose this passage for 2 Samuel 1:18-27, as he too, along with the writer of this Scripture, repeatedly asked, "How the Mighty have Fallen!"

Just like Joshua's poetic address to the sun and moon (Josh. 10:12-13), so David's lament was likewise written down in "the book of Jashar" (1:18; cf. 1 Kings 8:13). David Noel Freedman[4] argued that the word translated "glory" (v. 19) should be rendered as "the gazelle," a nickname used as a metaphor for Jonathan, who also appears later in v. 25. Thus, the name stood for a "fleet-footed warrior." Later Saul and Jonathan are both compared to "eagles" and "lions" in v. 23, but the image of a deer is used in connection with the "heights" in 22:34. Accordingly, the use of the simile of a gazelle for Jonathan fits here quite well. Thus, the word "mighty" is parallel to the "gazelle" in our revised reading of this text following Freedman's suggestion. Notice that David does not slight King Saul even though Jonathan is given preference.

David warns that Saul and Jonathan's friends are not to "Tell" this news in the Philistine city of Gath, which is a city on the eastern edge of the Philistine territory, nor should they sing it out in a "proclamation" in the streets of Ashkelon, which is by the Mediterranean Sea, and therefore together both represent all of Philistia from east to west. So do not tell and do not proclaim this sad news, lest that pagan country rejoice over Israel's defeat and loss (1:20)!

The third stanza in this lament (vv. 21-22) pronounces a curse on the "mountains of Gilboa," where Israel was defeated. These mountains do not have a solitary peak, but they have a ridge that goes for eight miles in length and three-to-five miles wide, forming a watershed between the

4. David Noel Freedman, "The Refrain in David's Lament over Saul and Jonathan" in *Ex Orbe Religionum:* Studia Geo. Widengren, Part I, Leiden: Brill, 1972, p. 120.

plain of Esdraelon and the plain of Beth-shan. Because the shield of Saul and the bow of Jonathan were defiled on Mount Gilboa, David called for a withdrawal of dew and rain from the fields in the mountain, so that the soil would no longer yield its grain.

In the next stanza, the father and son, Saul, and Jonathan, who were both loved and were gracious, yet even in death they were not parted (23). In fact, they were "swifter than eagles" and "stronger than lions" (23d-e).

So, it is right that the "daughters of Israel" should weep for King Saul, for he is the one who clothed them "in scarlet and finery" (24c). Saul also "adorned them in garments with ornaments of gold" (24d). Interpreters refer to this stanza as the central section of David's lament. These daughters who were invited to weep and mourn over the sad happenings of this event may have been professional mourners, who also chanted a lament on behalf of these two dead heroes, as well as on the part of the nation (cf. Jer. 9:17; Ezek. 32:16). The words "scarlet" and "clothes" are linked in the acrostic poem about the Virtuous Woman in Proverbs 31:21-22.

In the next stanza of vv. 25-26, there is the only stanza where Jonathan appears alone and where David heaps praise on the man he calls "my brother," for he was "very dear to [David]" (26b). Moreover, David went on praising Jonathan by saying, "Your love to me was wonderful, more wonderful than that of a woman." Even though this expression of David's deep "love" for Jonathan has been perversely understood to be homosexual love for each other, this love was instead a "covenantal love" that spoke of a love in which they were bound by a treaty and by a deep appreciation for the devotion each man held for the other.

The lament closes as it began with the sorrowful words, "How the mighty have fallen," but it adds "the weapons of war have vanished" (27). The expression "weapons of war" seem to hide another metaphor for Saul and Jonathan. Yes, the two of them were used mightily as God's weapons to clear the land and make it habitable for Israel to dwell in the land.

Here then was a most fitting tribute to two of the real heroes in the building of the nation of Israel. Notably, David does not address his own experiences or discuss the challenges he faced during the period before his inauguration as king by the prophet Samuel in this lament. Instead, just as God commanded Moses to "teach" his song to Israel (Deut. 32:1-43), so David ordered that this lament be "taught" to Israel as well (2 Sam. 1:18). Indeed, "How the mighty have fallen."

Conclusions

1. Saul and Jonathan were both slain in battle on the same day on Mount Gilboa. It was a sad day for all Israel.
2. The Amalekite, who claimed to have given the final fatal blow to Saul, no doubt lied to David, but his story could not to be trusted, so David rebuked him for treating the Lord's anointed in that manner and had him killed.
3. Saul should have obeyed at an early event in his reign by polishing off the Amalekites, so none would have been left for David to fight at Ziklag or for a liar to pretend he had been the last man alive to see Saul still living. These Amalekites will infect the story of Israel all the way up to the life of Esther, who attached her people.
4. David's lament is framed by vv. 19 and 27 with five stanzas in between, viz., vv. 20, 21, 22-23, 24-25, and 26.

Questions for Thought or Discussion

1. In what ways was the lament of 2 Samuel 1:18-27 evidence of the character of David as a man after God's own heart?
2. What good characteristics do the men of Jabesh-gilead evidence as they come by night to Beth-shan to steal the bodies of Saul and his sons pined to the walls of that city?
3. Was Saul justified in falling on his own sword and committing suicide?
4. What was David to think about God's call to anoint him as king all those years Saul pursued him with a desire to kill him, and he was never so recognized? Did he still cling to the promise of God in the face of such dire circumstances? How did he do it?
5. How do you assess the personality of Jonathan, given the temperament of his father? Couldn't Jonathan see that if David lived, his chances of ever being king were zero.

PART II
David as King

2 Samuel 2—24

Lesson 1

David's Accession to Kingship over Judah

2 Samuel 2:1 – 3:5

Now that King Saul was dead and buried, the time had finally come when what had been done in private, such as the private anointing of David as king by the prophet Samuel (1 Sam. 16:13), could now be repeated in public – at least for the tribe of Judah! David's triumph over Saul was now complete and what had been delayed for eight years could now be done in public.

It was time for David to inquire of the LORD what he should do now. So, David asked the LORD, "Shall I go up to one of the towns of Judah?" (2 Sam. 2:1). The Lord's answer was, "Go up!" But that raised a further question, "Where shall I go?" Again, the LORD replied, "To Hebron" (2:1d). And that is why David left stopped roaming the desert in the southern Negev of Israel, and together with his two wives and the families of his men, he went to Hebron. David left Ziklag and journeyed twenty-seven miles northeast to the city of Hebron in the hills of Judah (2:2), the same city David had sent booty, after defeating the Amalekites (1 Sam 30:31). There in Hebron David was anointed "king," which was so significant as stated by the fact that he was made "king over the house of Judah," that is emphasized twice in 1 Samuel 2:4a and in 7b.

Word came to David that the men of Jabesh-Gilead had risked their lives to retract Saul and his sons from being nailed to the walls of Beth-Shan and that they had given him a dignified burial (2:4b). It is, therefore, significant that David twice blesses the men of Jabesh-Gilead for the kindnesses (Hebrew, *hesed*) they had shown to "Saul [their] master" (2:5, 7), for they were forever grateful for all he had done for them years ago, as he began his reign as king over Israel. Clearly, David was hoping that the men of Jabesh-Gilead would now show to him and his administration the same kind of love and kindness they had shown to Saul. Nevertheless,

David emphatically pledged to treat them the same way they had treated Saul! (2:6). However, in a not-too-subtle way, David reminded the men of Jabesh-Gilead that Saul was now dead, and the house of Judah had now made him king over the house of Judah! (2:7). David concluded his offer to enter a covenantal relationship with the Jebeshites by urging them to be "strong and brave" (2:7). This, then, sounds like an invitation from David to enter a mutual defense treaty with him! And this interaction with the men of Jabesh-Gilead is enough to set a new course for David in his call by God to lead the nation of Israel, the second part of his life.

David Anointed King Over Judah – 2:1-7

God called David to go to Hebron when he asked him what he should do next. The word "Hebron" is usually meant to indicate an "alliance" or "communion," where the city they had just left, Ziklag is said to mean, by way of contrast, "self-will." Thus, we are encouraged to know that David, after 8 hard years of fleeing from Saul, is even further allied with God and in communion with him. It is always best to act within the will of God, rather than to act out our own wills and desires, which fail and fall flat. In fact, Scripture teaches us in the New Testament passage of 2 Corinthians 3:5 that we are not sufficient in ourselves, but all sufficiency we have must originate from God.

David did not abandon his men when he moved from Ziklag, for they and their households moved with him. They had shared months and years of tribulation and stress; it was time for them to share in the blessings of his new communion with his Lord. So, it happened that the men from the tribe of Judah came and anointed him as king over Judah. True, God had not yet given to David his rule over all 12 tribes of Israel, but it was necessary that David build a bridge as he reached out to the other 11 tribes of the people of Israel. David had to first take over the throne of the tribe of Judah in Hebron before anything opened for the whole nation. This meant more waiting and more work for David. But there was no complaint or open dissatisfaction from this shepherd boy. He would follow God's bidding and God's timing, even if he may at times have wondered if anything like what the prophet Samuel had promised him would ever happen! This would mean another seven and one-half years in Hebron as king before the whole kingdom would be gathered under his regime (2:11).

Abner, Saul's Captain of His Army, Makes Saul's Son King - 2:8-11

While David was being installed as king over Judah, it did not mean that the old Saulide interests were dead and over with. Instead, the captain of Saul's army, Abner, son of Ner, had taken it upon himself to bring Ish-Bosheth, Saul's son forward as king and set him up as such in Mahanaim. There, Abner dictatorially pronounced Ish-Bosheth as king over Gilead, over the Ashurites and over the Jezreelites, as well as over Ephraim, Benjamin, and all Israel (2:9). Ish-Bosheth was 40 years old when he began to reign as king, but he reigned for only 2 years (2:10).

One might ask why David, after being anointed king by Samuel, did not simply overthrow the current ruler and claim the kingdom as promised. But typical of David, he waited to see what God would do on his behalf. All of this took not only lengthy periods of time, but it also involved a good sense of discernment on David's part. Surely, David must often have had lots of advice from his rogue army forces to end this spectacle of waiting, but David was more in tune with the small voice of God and not with the shrill voices of battle! There is little doubt that David's forces could have been victorious, but then what would he have from the men who had been won against their wills, and without the blessing of God? So, David decided not to "fret himself because of evildoers," for the wicked would "soon be cut down like the grass and wither like the green herb" (Ps. 37:1-2).

The Contest Between Abner's Men and Joab's – 2:12-3:1

Abner, son of Ner, commander of Saul's army, and cousin to Saul had somehow escaped the Battle on Mount Gilboa, the battle where Saul lost his life, but he was determined to see Saul's dynasty continue. So, in an action that showed he was still loyal to the deceased king, he took Saul's fourth son, Ish-Bosheth (meaning, "man of shame") and crossed over the Jordan River to a place about 7 miles east of the Jordan River, into the territory of Gad to a site called "Mahanaim (meaning "two camps") just north of the Jabbok River.

The name of Ish-Bosheth was used euphemistically to cover up his real name, which was "man of Baal." Did this mean, then, that Saul had intended to honor the Canaanite god Baal when he gave him the name of "Ish-Baal"? They could have been true!

Abner on his own plays the role of kingmaker, for he alone chooses Ish-Bosheth as king over a selected group of tribes, while "the house of Judah" came together to make David king of Judah. It could naturally be expected that David and Ish-Bosheth would sometime in the future attempt to bring the kingdom of Israel back under their own rule. So, Abner, along with the men of Ish-Bosheth, son of Saul, left Mahanaim and went to Gibeon (2:12). It was time for a showdown! But in the rules of warfare in those days, an all-out and out war was not the only way to do this. Rather than engaging all soldiers in a confrontation, each group might appoint representatives to compete on their behalf, like historical instances where one individual was chosen to face an opponent from the other side. Therefore, in this situation, instead of just one champion standing for each side of the conflict, two teams of twelve each were matched up at the pool of Gibeon.

Gibeon was known as one of the royal cities of Israel (Josh. 10:2), allotted to the tribe of Benjamin (Josh. 18:21, 25), which goes by the name of el-Jib to this day, which is an abbreviation that reflects the original name. Gibeon is six miles northwest of Jerusalem. Even though technically Gibeon was in Saul's territory of the tribe of Benjamin, it might be significant to recall that Saul had acted against the people in Gibeon in opposition to the treaty Joshua had made with them (Josh. 9; 2 Sam. 21).

This became, then, the Battle between the men of Joab (representing David and Judah) and the men of Abner (Saul's cousin representing Ish-Bosheth or what remained of Saul's kingdom). This confrontation not only reflected the deep divisions within Israel at the time but also highlighted the complex loyalties and political realities David faced as he assumed leadership over Judah. The standoff at Gibeon revealed that the path to unifying the nation under his rule would be fraught with further conflict and negotiation, requiring both wisdom and restraint.

Joab, son of Zeruiah, along with David's men, met Ish-Bosheth's men at a well-known pool in Gibeon. Twelve men from Abner's group positioned themselves on one side of the pool, while Joab's twelve men took their places on the opposite side (2:13). This pool was well-known in the past and still exists as an unused pool to this day (Jer. 41:12), but in that day it may have been used for storage of grain or a basin to hold the water needed in bottling wine.

In 1956 James B. Pritchard of the University of Pennsylvania excavated this pool, which he found to be a cylindrical shaft that was thirty-seven feet in diameter and thirty-five feet deep. It had a five-foot-wide spiral staircase that wound around the inside wall of the pool in a clockwise direction. The pool continued further below this staircase to make a total of 45 feet in depth. From this pool Pritchard found two jar handles bearing the name of "Gibeon" on them, written in the Hebrew script of that day.[1]

It was Abner who suggested the teams fight the battle by "fight[ing] hand to hand," which Joab accepted. Twelve from each group are counted off (2:15), with the number twelve standing for the twelve tribes of Israel on each side. This contest ended quickly as each man "seized" his opponent by his head and then thrust his dagger into his opponent's side. The twenty-four men fell together (2:16), so that from that day on this place in Gibeon was called "Helkath Hazzurim," which means "Field of Daggers," or "Field of Hostilities." Thus, the contest ended in a draw, with each of the twelve men being slain by his opponent's dagger and his slaying his adversary the same way (2:16). Apparently, not only was there a standoff and draw between the two sides, but it was followed with a fierce battle in which Abner and his men were soundly defeated by David's men (2:17). However, there was one casualty that was noteworthy, for David's sister had three sons: Joab, David's commander, Abishai, and Asahel. It happened that Asahel had a talent for being known as being fleet of foot. He, then, chased after Abner, staying right on his tail as Abner tried to dissuade him from pursuing him. But Asahel would not be deterred, for when Abner asked if he was Asahel, he answered "it is [me]." When Asahel held to his course of chasing right after Abner, "Abner thrust the butt of his spear into Asahel's stomach, and the spear came out through his back" (2:23). Asahel dropped dead in his tracks, and all of David's troops stopped when they came to the spot where he perished.

Asahel's brothers, Joab and Abishai, pursued Abner until the sun was setting on the hill of Ammah (2:24). There the men of Benjamin rallied behind Abner as they formed up for battle and took their stand on that hill. At that point Abner called out to Joab saying, "Must the sword devour forever? Don't you realize that this will end in bitterness? How long before you order your men to stop pursuing their brothers?" (2:26). It was Abner who had started these hostilities, but n ow it was he who now

---

1. James B. Pritchard, *Gibeon, Where the Sun Stood still: The Discovery of the Biblical City*, Princeton, NJ: Princeton University Press, 1962, pp. 64-74.

wanted this fighting to stop (2:26). Joab realized Abner made a valid point, so he ended the conflict by sounding the trumpet, halting the battle (2:27-28). The men of Abner marched on eastward through the night until they came to their home in Mahanaim while Joab's men likewise marched all night southward until daybreak, when they arrived back at the new capital of Judah in Hebron. It was clear, however, that Joab's men had the edge in this battle, for Joab had lost only nineteen men, in addition to Asahel, while Abner had lost 360 Benjaminites (2:30-31). Asahel's corpse was carried back home and buried in his father's tomb in Bethlehem. The war between the house of Saul and the house of David went on for quite a while. However, during all this time, David grew stronger, while the house of Saul grew weaker (3:1).

The Sons Born to David – 3:2-5

David settled down in Hebron for the next seven and one-half years with his two wives, Ahinoam and Abigail. They gave to David quite a family. The firstborn of his sons was Amnon (meaning "faithful"), son of Ahinoam, who was later killed by Absalom (13:28-29). Abigail born to David Kileab, but he must have died early on, for he does not appear in the confusion of who would succeed David as king. The third son was Absalom, meaning "my father is peace," who was born to him from the daughter of Talmai king of Geshur. David had married this princess from Geshur as part of a diplomatic agreement with King Talmai, who had a small kingdom northeast of the Sea of Galilee.

The fourth son of David was Adonijah, meaning "My lord is LORD," born to him by Haggith, meaning "Festal one." Adonijah tried to steal the government from Solomon, but he was assassinated in his attempt. The fifth son was Shephatiah, meaning "the LORD judges," born to him from Abital, meaning "My father is dew." The sixth, and last-named son of those born to David in Hebron, was Ithream, meaning "My kinsman is abundance," said to be "the sons of David's wife Eglah" (3:5). These all were born to David while he was in Hebron!

Conclusions

1. David showed great trust and patience in the Lord as he waited for another eight years to finally be called by just one of the twelve tribes to be the king at Hebron, the tribe of Judah.
2. David thanked the brave men of Jabesh-Gilead for their daring rescue of Saul and his sons' bodies from Beth-Shan and providing a dignified burial in their land. Their kindness and faithfulness were indeed praiseworthy.
3. After being installed as king at Hazor, Judah, David had to wait another 7½ years until all Israel provided a national coronation for him over the whole land of Israel.
4. Abner's proposal of having two teams of champions represent the entire armies of both Abner and Joab ended in a tie so that an ordinary battle ensued anyway.
5. There was constant warfare between the remnants of Saul's reign and David's forces all the time David was king in Hebron.

Questions for Thought or Discussion

1. Why did hostilities continue between the forces of David and the remnants of Saul's house? Since Saul and Jonathan had perished in the war with the Philistines, what was the basis for anyone claiming his line was still in charge of the kingship?
2. Did Ish-Bosheth was really in charge of the government or was it more like Abner was in charge?
3. Was there a good reason for David to compliment the men of Jabesh-Gilead, or was this only plain politics?
4. Do you think Abner was a "power-grabber" or do you think he was sincere in his efforts to revive the kingdom of Saul?

Lesson 2

David's Accession to the Kingship Over Israel

2 Samuel 3:6- 5:16

There is a sort of wonderful literary craftsmanship in how the author tells the story of David as he begins this new section. First, he tells how David became king over the Judahites (2:1-7), and then second of how he became king over all Israel (5:1-5). Both of the narratives have their origins in the story, first, of how an Amalekite tried to get David's favor by claiming that he was the one who killed King Saul, but he lied (1:1-13), and second, how Saul's army commander, Abner, planned to bring what was left of Saul's friends into David's camp (3:6-21). Both stories were followed by the murder of the Amalekite (1:14-16) and the murder of Abner (3:22-32). These tragedies were followed, in one case by the lament by David over "How the Mighty [Saul and Jonathan] have Fallen" (1:17-27), and in the other case of David's lament over Abner's death, whom he called "a prince and a great man" (3:33-34, 38). As part, if not the central feature, of this double mirrored picture of the two anointings of David as king can be found brief reports of David's investiture as king over Judah (2:1-7) and later as king over Israel (5:1-5). One more similarity can be seen in this balanced and carefully crafted introduction to David's kingship can be seen in the fact that both stories end with a list of sons born to David at each site that was his capital, the one in Hebron (3:2-5) and the one in Jerusalem (5:13-16). Thus, the narrative of the transition of leadership of Israel from the house of Saul to the house of David is brilliantly laid out in 2 Samuel 1:1-5:16.

Abner Defects as Ish-Bosheth's Commander of His Army – 3:6-21

It could well be that David's triumph over the forces of Ish-Bosheth's men at the Battle of Gibeon left a real impression on Saul's cousin Abner, for he had never faced in battle David's army commander up to this point in time, or had he faced Joab, and the way the men David had trained! Therefore, as a shrewd politician, he decided that there was little, or no, future in trying to back up the remnants of Saul's dynasty. Moreover, Abner surely had heard that the Lord had promised that he would hand the kingdom of Israel over to David (1 Sam. 22:12, 17) as well as hand the Philistines over to David as well. So, Abner must have decided it was time to get with the program!

Even though Abner had been strengthening his position in the house of Saul (3:6b), David did not allow him to become the sole power broker for uniting the kingdom into one nation. In the meantime, a heated controversy broke out between Abner and Ish-Bosheth over Abner's alleged sexual relations with Saul's concubine, named Rizpah, daughter of Aiah (3:7).

Abner got exceedingly angry with Ish-Bosheth for accusing him so forthrightly of such an act, but Abner never firmly denied he had done such in plain language and that he had, in fact, had (or not had) sexual relations with Saul's concubine. The reason for making so much out of this incident was because this was the usual way a person claimed the right to ascend to the royal throne. But Abner was not going to let this charge against him even be discussed. Instead, he asked, "Am I a dog's head?" (3:8) – a derogatory epithet depicting himself as some kind of dog-headed baboon! After all the trouble he had endured on behalf of Ish-Bosheth, Abner must have concluded, that he had taken to reestablish Saul's rule over Israel, and the fading fortunes of Ish-Bosheth's rule, why was Ish-Bosheth making this sort of a charge against him? Moreover, Abner claimed he had been loyal not only to Saul's house, but he had shown that same loyalty to Ish-Bosheth's family along with his friends as well (3:8b).

With that, Abner took a strong oath of imprecation, vowing that he, Abner, would become the very instrument under God to make happen what God had promised to David in 1 Samuel 15:28; 16:1. He would help transfer Saul's kingdom to establish no one less than "David's throne," which would stretch over Israel from Dan to Beersheba (3:10). Ish-Bosheth was so weakened by that time that did not add another word to his charge against Abner, for he was terribly afraid of him (3:11).

Abner swung into quick action as he personally joined the forces of David, for he at once sent messengers on his behalf to David with the rhetorical question, "Whose land is it?" (3:12). Was Abner implying, by this question, that the land up north was his [i.e., Abner's] to give? Or did he mean the land was David's, because of God's longstanding promise to him? Abner promised to help David bring all Israel over to David's side in his rule and reign over them, for he was now changing political alliances (3:12). Abner was claiming that he was, in fact, *de facto* ruler of all Israel, but he would now offer that land to David on condition that he be made the commander of David's army!

Abner's motives are a complex blend of ambition and genuine concern for Israel's future. While Abner looked to strengthen his own position within Saul's fragmented house, his decision to defect to David was not merely a power grab. He recognized the divine promise that the kingdom would belong to David and responded accordingly, taking active steps to help the transition. Abner's anger toward Ish-Bosheth and his vow to help fulfill God's plan suggest that he was pragmatic, but also aware of a larger purpose beyond his own advancement. His actions helped to unite the nation, even if they were initially sparked by personal conflict and political calculation. David, alert to the kind of man he was dealing with, said, "Good," but before he would make an agreement with Abner, he had one pre-condition which had to be met, or there was no use in Abner coming to see him again. Saul's daughter Michal, for whom David had paid 200 Philistine foreskins [even though he was charged only with producing 100 foreskins of the enemy] as a bride price, was to be brought to David before any other transactions would be enacted. David then jumped the gun, as it seemed, by sending his own messengers directly to Ish-Bosheth, demanding that he be given back his rightful wife! David aimed to show Saul's throne was tied to his family, undermining Abner's efforts to claim the title for himself. Ish-Bosheth surprisingly gave the order to send to David Michal, and therefore Michal was taken away from her new husband Paltiel to whom Saul had wickedly given her to spite David, and she was sent off to go back to David. Meanwhile, her husband Paltiel trailed behind her for twenty miles weeping all the way up to the town of Bahurim, where Abner told him, "Go back home." So, he finally left following Michal (3:16). This return of Michal, then, strengthened David's claim to the throne that Saul had so recently vacated. David's repossession of Michal (say commentators) did not violate the terms of Deuteronomy 24:1-4,[1] where a man once divorced from his wife could not go back and remarry her again if she had been married to someone else in the meantime. If Mesopotamian law applied in Israel in the same way as it

1. Ronald F. Youngblood, *The Expositor's Bible Commentary*, vo. 3, Grand Rapids, Zondervan, 2009, p. 328.

did in that country, however, then the reunion of the original marriage was possible since the separation from David's wife Michal had been involuntary and not agreed to by David. However, no divine judgment is given on this matter from the Deuteronomy passage.

Abner met with the elders of Israel where he remarked,

> "For some time, you have wanted to make David your king. Now do it! For the LORD promised David [saying], 'By my servant David I will rescue my people Israel from the hand of the Philistines and from the hand of all their enemies.'" 2 Samuel 3:17-18

Abner also went in person to the Benjaminites, the tribe from which Saul came, and he spoke with them about David taking the reins of government. Then Abner and 20 of his men went to David in Hebron, where David prepared a feast for Abner and his 20 men. Abner then asked David if he could go to assemble all Israel for David. In that way the men of Israel could make a "compact" with David and thus he would be able to rule over all that his heart desired. (3:21). With that agreed on, David sent Abner away with his men and Abner left Hebron in peace.

Abner is Murdered by David's Commander, Joab – 3:22-39

Just after Abner had left Hebron in peace, Joab and all his soldiers returned to Hebron from a raid, only to find out that Abner, the commander of Ish-Bosheth's army had just been there and David had let him go on his way in peace; in fact, he had sent him off showing no reprisals to him (3:22). Joab was furious, for he demanded of David,

> "What have you done? Look, Abner came to you. Why did you let him go? Now he is gone! …. [He came to] deceive you and to observe your movements [i.e., of your troops] and find out everything you are doing" (3:24-25).

This Abner was not just anybody with the name of "Abner" in Joab's way of thinking; no, he was the "Abner, the son of Ner," "a cousin of King Saul" (25). David allowed Joab to give him such an excoriating speech that one wonders why David took it from him, for David, as the text will confirm, was not yet strong enough to be able to deal with him. In fact, talk about Abner's "deceiving" David, one must likewise look to what Joab had done by way of deceit. Joab called back to where he had just left, as far as the "Well of Sirah" (a site 2 ½ miles north of Hebron, 27), where he pretended that he wanted to talk to him privately about a secret matter (26-27). Joab then took Abner aside in a gateway, and with that he boldly stabbed him in his stomach, as an act of revenge for what he had done to his brother Ashel (27). The blood feud, then, was on, and tempers were rising at the instigation of these sons of Zeruiah!

At Abner's funeral, David added a brief lament and word of praise for Abner (38) and a note showing his exasperation over his sister's sons, the sons of Zeruiah: Joab and Abishai (39). But it is important to note that "all" Israel "knew" that David was innocent of the death of Abner (37) and that a great man, Abner, had been lost to Israel. David called Abner a "prince and a great man" in Israel.

Ish-Bosheth is Murdered by Two Men Who Were Friends of Saul's Son - 4:1-12

Suddenly, if not finally, David had a clear path to the throne of Israel, since all potential claimants, or would be pretenders, to exercise such rights to the throne were now actually dead – that is except for Saul's son Ish-Bosheth and Jonathan's son Mephibosheth. However, when one of those remaining claimants, Ish-Bosheth, heard that Abner had been killed in Hebron, "he lost courage," which was a graphic idiom for one who was ready to "give up" (4:1). Moreover, "all Israel became alarmed" as well (1b).

Yet, opportunists persist, ready to seize whatever is left as the kingdom collapses. These individuals were two men who were associates of Saul's son Ish-Bosheth and served as leaders of raiding groups from Israel. One was named Baanah and the other Rekhav, and both came from Beeroth in Benjamin, the same town from which Joab's armor-bearer came (23:37; cf. 1 Chron. 11:39). This town of Beeroth was found four and a half miles northwest of Jerusalem (2). These two opportunists, Baanah and Rekhav, sons of Rimmon, might have been seeking a reward from David for their crass deed. Moreover, even though they were members of the tribe of Benjamin, yet the people of Beeroth had fled to Gittaim, where they lived as aliens to that very day (3b).

One reason why these two adventurers were so emboldened to do what they did was this: even though there was only one other person who might have wanted to avenge the wicked deed Baanah and Rekhav had carried out against Ish-Bosheth, that was Jonathan's son named Mephibosheth, who was the only other possible contender for the throne and who was lame in both feet and probably would not have been physically able to recompense these thieves for their deed (4). This son named Mephibosheth was a mere 5 years old when the sad news arrived as to what had happened to Saul and Jonathan in the battle of Mount Gilboa, also called the battle at Jezreel. He had suffered his frailty, which came about when in the haste of escaping, his nurse had picked him up, and in her hurry to leave, she dropped the boy, and he fell and became crippled (4b).

As the narrative unfolded, both Baanah and Rekhav set out for the house in Mahanaim where Ish-Bosheth lived, to which they arrived at about the time of the mid-day siesta, supposing that like most, Ish-Bosheth would be lying down for a nap (5). The two men used a kind of subterfuge to gain access to Ish-Bosheth's private quarters, for the text says it was "as if to get some wheat" (6). Three quick actions are listed in rapid fashion: "they stabbed and killed him, [and] they cut off his head" (7). What a national atrocity!

The murderers then travelled by way of the Arabah through the night to avoid detection and arrived in Hebron to present triumphantly to David the head of Ish-Bosheth (7b). To get on the right side of David, they exclaimed, "Here is the head of Ish-Bosheth son of Saul, your enemy, who tried to take your life" (8). The nefarious deeds of Saul had begun to circulate throughout Israel, so these men gladly used it, they hoped, to their advantage. They boastfully added, "This day, the LORD has avenged my lord the king against Saul and his offspring" (8b).

David was not impressed in the least! His judgment came quickly and severely, for he said,

> "As surely as the LORD lives, who has delivered me out of all [my] trouble, when a man told me, 'Saul is dead,' and thought he was bringing [me] good news, I seized him and put him to death in Ziklag. That was the reward I gave him for his news! How much more—when wicked men have killed an innocent man in his own house and on his own bed – should I not now demand his blood from your hand and rid the earth of you!" (9-11).

Therefore, David gave the order to his men, and the two men were killed immediately. The men cut off the hands and feet of the two murderers and hung their bodies by the pool of Hebron for a public humiliation and so the word would get around in Israel that David was not one who would preempt God's right to bring vengeance to evil doers.

Given the death of Ish-Bosheth, there were no remaining candidates for the name of king left in the land to challenge David. Finally, what Samuel had shown 15 years ago, by anointing David with oil, was now fulfilled in the life of David.

David is Anointed King over All Israel – 5:1-5

It was time for "all the tribes of Israel" (1), along with "all the elders of Israel" (3) for David to reign over "all Israel and Judah" (5). The term "all" has become particularly significant in this context. Abner initially engaged the elders of Israel in this discussion (3:17), but following the unfortunate death of Ish-Bosheth, neither he nor Mephibosheth remained obstacles to the prompt anointing of David.

The elders give three reasons why they should now move to make David their king. First, David is one of their own people with the same Flesh and blood (1). Secondly. David was Israel's best army officer, while Saul was king, which fact was conceded even by the Philistines themselves (2). Thirdly, the LORD himself had called David to this task, for he would not only be Israel's "ruler," but he would be their "shepherd" (3). Commentators point out that this is the very first time a leader in Israel is given the title of "shepherd," except for God himself who was given that title earlier (Gen. 48:15; 49:24). The motif of David as a shepherd brings to all minds the first time David was called out of the fields, where he had been shepherding, to be anointed by the prophet Samuel (1 Sam 16:11). So, just as he led, fed, and protected his father's flock, now he would do the same for the nation of Israel.

Now all of this happened when David was 30 years of age. He reigned altogether, including 7 ½ years in Hebron and then in Jerusalem for 33 years, for a grand total of 40 years (4-5). That figure of course was a round number, so there was no reason to adjust the text as the Lucian text of Samuel did to read in v. 5, "thirty-two years and six months."

David's Campaign for Jerusalem and the Sons Born to Him in Jerusalem – 5:6-16

David must have had his eye on Jerusalem as a site for his capital, for as soon as he was coronated by all Israel as king, he marched his men to Jerusalem to attack the Jebusites (6). Jerusalem will be mentioned more often than any other city in the Bible and was regarded as being "in the center of the nations" (Ezek. 5:5). Whether the Jebusites, who inhabited the city at that time were from an Amorite ethnic group or not, we cannot say for certain, but it appears that they began to inhabit Jerusalem as early as about the time of Joshua's conquest (perhaps with a Hurrian or Hittite origin) and were so firmly entrenched in the city of Jerusalem that they could not be dislodged by the Israelites. But soon after David had been named king, he sent out his men to attack them.

An apparent contradiction seems to appear between Joshua 15:63 and Judges 1:8. But the solution seems to be to note that the Jebusites were settled on two hills in Jerusalem, one which was heavily defended (often referred to as the "fortress of Zion" in the southeastern section of the present city (v. 7) while the other section of the city was located more to the southwest. Thus, the "threshing floor of Araunah the Jebusite," from whom David bought the site for the future Temple (24:16), was in an open field outside of the city.

The Jebusites were mightily assured of their impregnability, for they smugly boasted to David that – "even the blind and the lame" -- would be able to defend Jerusalem and ward off the Israelites (6b). But David promised on that day, "Anyone who conquers the Jebusites will have to use the water shaft (Hebrew, *tsinnor*) to reach those 'lame and blind,' who are David's enemies." (8). The only other time this Hebrew word is used in the Bible is in Psalm 42:7, where it means "pipes" for pouring oil. Others rendered it like a "grappling hook" used in our day to pull bales of hay around on our farms.[2]

Whatever the word means, Joab and his men climbed up something like a tunnel or shaft that led from the water source outside the city to somewhere inside of Jerusalem. Charles Warren suggested this concept in 1867, but the use of "Warren's shaft" for water access is now disputed. Later in the 1990s Ronny Reich and Eli Shikron renewed excavations in this area of Jerusalem where they discovered the ruins of two towers: the Spring Tower and the Pool Tower. Even without definitive agreement on the solution to this matter, there is no doubt that there was the existence of a water system in Jebusite Jerusalem that 2 Samuel 5 was aware of that turned out to be the weak point in her defenses. In fact, as recently as October 2008, archaeologist Eilat Mazar, writing in the *Jerusalem Post,* believed she has discovered the ruins of David's palace, but she also

---

2. There is an Aramaic cognate to the word *tsinnor* that yields the meaning of "scaling hooks."

claimed to have found the water tunnel that gave Joab and his men a way to get inside this Jebusite city! So, the story continues.

As a result of the successful attack on the city. David moved his residence in the city of Jerusalem and renamed it "the city of David" (9). David acted to repair the "supporting terraces," also known as "Millo," which means "fill[ing]." This "stepped-stone structure" served as the foundation of a 2,000 square foot level platform on which, probably "the fortress of Zion" was built.

The king of Tyre, named "Hiram," sent David cedar logs along with carpenters and stonemasons and they built a palace for King David (11). As a result of all of this, David now knew that Yahweh had established him as king only over all Israel and that the LORD himself had exalted his kingdom for the sake of his people Israel (12).

The sad news to this story is that after David had left Hebron, he began to take on more concubines and wives in Jerusalem in contradiction to the word of God (Deut. 17:17), so that a considerable number of sons and daughters were born to him (13-14). This passage listed the names of 11 sons.

Conclusions

1. David is finally installed as king by all 12 tribes of Israel. They expressed both military and theological reasons for doing so.
2. David was called to shepherd his people Israel and to become their ruler after a delay for David of 15 years.
3. Abner left as commander of Ish-Bosheth's army and defected to David's side because of the ancient promises of God that were transferred to David.
4. Joab murdered Abner before he knew all the facts, to which he gave the explanation that it was as an act of revenge for his killing his brother. But this created chaos in the nation of Israel.
5. The murder of Ish-Bosheth while he was sleeping in his own bed in his own home was outrageous. David made clear he had nothing to do with this act of injustice either.
6. Joab found a weak spot in the defense of Jerusalem, so he was able to capitalize on it and win the city for David.

Questions for Thought or Discussion

1. Would Israel's coming together been much easier and longer lasting if Joab had not decided to act on his own without authority from David?
2. Was Joab afraid he might have lost his job as commander of David's troops if things got too cozy between David and Abner?
3. What explains the actions of Rekhav and Baanah in their daring regicide at noon time to a man asleep in his bed and then their fleeing to David in Hebron for recognition?
4. How do you think Joab was able to breach the fortifications of Jerusalem when the enemy was so certain that even blind and lame persons could defend the city?
5. What do you think about the three reasons why all the tribes came together to make David king?
6. Why did God still bless David's reign after he disregarded God's command on multiple marriages?

Lesson 3

David Given Rest from His Enemies, the Ark in Jerusalem and the Grant Type of Covenant

2 Samuel 5:17-25; 6:1-23; 7:1-29

Scholars disagree on whether David took Jerusalem right after becoming king of Israel, or if the conquest occurred between his anointing and his victories over the Philistines. The point is that as soon as the Philistines heard that David had been installed as king of all Israel, they came "in full force" "to search for him" (17). When David learned the fact that these Philistines were spread out in the Valley of Rephaim (a flat piece of fertile land west-southwest of Jerusalem), he went down to his "stronghold," wherever that would be, for we really do not know!

David inquired of the Lord, "Shall I go and attack the Philistines? Will you hand them over to me?" (18). The LORD's answer was, "Go, for I will surely hand the Philistines over to you." (19). Therefore, David went to "Baal Perazim," and there he defeated them saying, "As waters 'break out' (a pun on the name, 'Baal Perazim'), The LORD has 'broken out' against my enemies before me" (20). Israel's victory was so astounding that the Philistines in their hurry to flee from the battler scene had forgotten to take their idols along with them, so David and his men carried them off captive as well, to be burned as the law required (1 Chron. 14:12).

But the Philistines had not learned their lesson yet, so once more they returned to the Valley of Rephaim. Once again, David inquired of the LORD whether he should attack them. The answer was "yes." but David was told not to confront them head on in battle, but they were to "circle around behind them and attack them quickly in front of the balsam trees – [for] as soon as [David] hear[d] the sound of marching in the tops of the balsam trees," he was to attack (23-24). That rumble in the trees would mean that "the LORD has gone in front of you (note the LORD's initiative in battle) to strike the Philistine army" (24b). Once more David obeyed the

LORD and he mowed down the Philistines "all the way from Gibeon to Gezer" (25). Gibeon is 6 miles northwest of Jerusalem and Gezer is a city in the foothills of Ephraim's tribal allotment, just east of the Philistine plain, fifteen miles from Gibeon.

With these victories, God gave to David and Israel a season of rest which now leads up to a climactic moment in the theology of the Bible. There were still other smaller skirmishes, but the major blows had settled the issue.

God Gives Rest from David's Enemies, The Philistines – 5:17-25

This section is paralleled by 1 Chronicles 14:8-16. The material is identical, although there are differences. Both texts agree, however, that the Philistines were the aggressors; that the site of the battle was located on the same site, namely the Valley of Rephaim; and that in both cases David inquired of the LORD as to what he should do before he made a move to attack his enemy. These two battles were certainly important, for they both summarized how effective David was against these people who constantly had opposed him and his government, and they showed how effective David was in battle, particularly because the LORD was with him in each of those battles. These two battles, of course, were not the only ones David fought against this persistently antagonistic hostile people, but the two do serve to mark how episodic they were for setting the pace and peace for the new government.

It is important to note the theological significance of the introductory section of 2 Samuel 7 where it begins by saying, "The king was settled in his palace, and the LORD had given him rest from all his enemies around him" (2 Sam 7:1). That gift of "rest" set the scene for the great accomplishments that God was going to effect during the reign of David and then even more dramatically in his son Solomon's reign.

God Gives the Ark of the Covenant as the Center of Worship 6:1-23.

The ark of the covenant was kept at Kiriath Jearim for 20 years after it vanished from view in 1 Samuel 7:2. But that was not all the years it seems to have been forgotten, for those 20 years were measured for the Ark's return by the Philistines (1 Sam. 6:21-7:1) until the battle reported in 1 Samuel 7:7-13, which would have been sometime around the end of

Samuel's judgeship. In addition, forty years are attributed to Saul's reign, with further years added for David's rule. So that Ark has been absent for at least sixty years or more while it was stationed in "the house of Abinadab," which was on a hill, near Jerusalem.

Cities changed or had dual names, "Kiriath Jearim" ("city of forests") was originally called "Baalah of Judah" (2 Sam. 6:2). It also had an abbreviated name, "Jaar" (Ps. 132:6) along with the names of "Mount Jearim" (Josh. 15:10), "Mount Baalah" (Josh. 15:11) and "fields of Jaar" (Ps. 132:6). All these names for the same place suggest that Kiriath Jearim covered quite an extensive piece of real estate.

The solemnity of bringing this central piece of furniture from the tabernacle into the city of David marks the reason for the inclusion of this chapter in the Bible. This ark is called the "Ark of God" (6:2-4), and the "Ark of the ORD" (6:9-11), in which each of these names occur seven times in this chapter. This ark "is called by the Name, the name of the LORD Almighty who is enthroned between the cherubim that are on the ark" (6:2). This expression denotes ownership; therefore, the ark belongs to the LORD.

David was determined to make the act of bringing the ark of God into the city of Jerusalem an incredibly special event. To do this, David set out with thirty thousand men (6:1) to bring the ark from Kiriath Jearim, also called Baalah of Judah (1). To do this, they went to the house of Abinadab, which was on a hill. The two men chosen to guide the ark, Uzzah and Ahio, were sons of Abinadab. Ahio walked in front of the ark and Uzzah must have walked along the side of it. Meanwhile, David and the whole house of Israel were celebrating as never before, dancing and singing with all their might (5). Songs were being sung, and six instruments were being played in accompaniment: Harps, lyres, tambourines, cymbals, and trumpets (1 Chron. 13:8).

However, as the cart and procession approached "the threshing floor of Nacon," Uzzah reached out his hand, to steady the ark and to prevent it's falling off the cart as the oxen stumbled. That caused the Lord's anger to foment, because this involuntary act of Uzzah's part was considered an irreverent act since God had specified from the beginning that the ark was to be carried on the shoulders of the priests (6:6-12; Exod. 25:12-15; Num. 3:29-31). The LORD struck Uzzah down at once and he died right there at that spot beside the ark of God (7).

David was exceedingly angry because of this evidence of the LORD's wrath which the Lord had cause to "break out" against Uzzah. In fact, that place became known from that day on as "Perez Uzzah," meaning "the outbreak against Uzzah" (8). David was afraid of the LORD as he complained, "How can the ark of the LORD ever come to me? (9). Thus, he became unwilling to take the ark into the city of David, but he left it instead at the house of Obed-Edom the Gittite (10). There the ark remained for three months, but the LORD blessed Obed-Edom.

When David heard how the LORD had blessed Obed-Edom and his household, he decided he would give bringing the ark of God into his city another try (12). David sensed that it was now safe to bring the ark into Jerusalem. David now instructs the Levites to carry the ark as Scripture required. After the procession had gone six steps, David the people of Israel with him, offered a bull and a fatted calf as a sacrifice. David wore a linen ephod and was clothed in a robe of fine linen as he danced before the LORD with all his might (14), and so the ark was brought into the city of David. This use of priestly garments worn be David may have prefigured the future priestly functions of the Davidic line of kings.

Things were going well until we come to v. 16 where Michal the daughter of Saul criticized David for acting in an undistinguished way like a vulgar fellow (20). She may have been smarting from her being separated from her former husband Paltiel (3:13-16), for Michal "despised him in her heart" (16c). It is not possible to say what Micha was objecting to in David's alleged state of undress, but David did take pains to dissociate himself from Saul, Michal's father.

God Gives David a Dynasty, Throne, and Kingdom Forever – 7:1-29

From the standpoint of theology, 2 Samuel 7:1-29 is not only the highlight of the books Samuel, but this chapter stands as one of the four mountain peaks of the entire Old Testament (viz., (1) Gen. 3:15; (2) Gen. 12:2-3 and 15:1-6; (3) 2 Sam. 7:1-29; and (4) Jer. 31:31-34). The Hebrew Bible treats David's grants with equal importance as the Sinaitic Covenant with Moses.

Even though chapter 7 surprisingly nowhere mentions the word "covenant," yet this chapter is universally recognized as the LORD's covenant with David, i.e., "The Davidic Covenant." This text significantly contributed to the messianic hope, influencing more than forty Old Testament passages. Among the Dead Sea Scrolls, a midrash on 2 Samuel 7:10b-14 written by the Qumran sectarians pointed to messianic allusions found in this text. But this trend became even more prominent in the New Testament that exploited to its fullest extend the divine promise-plan of God found in this Davidic Covenant.

Interpreters have argued that the Davidic Covenant was a "conditional" covenant, but most other interpreters note that from the middle of the second millennium onwards, a political treaty known from the Hittite empire as the "royal grant." While the "suzerain treaty" emphasized the obligations of the vassal subject to his master or suzerain, the "royal grant" focused instead on the obligation of the king or master to the vassal. Since Yahweh emphasized the promissory nature of the gifts bestowed on Israel, such as the gift of the land of Canaan, the gift of descendants, and the blessing of God for all who will bless this elected nation, this "royal grant" type of covenant must be understood as "unconditional." No obligations are placed on David for the enactment of the Davidic Covenant.

It was clearly after the LORD had given David rest from all his enemies around him (7:1) that the gift of the "royal grant" was made to him. Thus, David first had to subdue these kingdoms: Philistia, Moab, Tzovah, Damascus, Ammon, Amalek, and Edom. It could also be true that chapter 7 is placed after chapter 6 to stress the fact that the promise of a royal dynasty to David is given to him as a reward for his devotion and worship of the Living God!

The Setting for the Davidic Covenant – 7:1-3

What a story of an unexpected ascendancy of a local shepherd boy from Bethlehem to become king of a people who were called of God to fulfill his purposes! The text can hardly get over the fact that he is "king," for it repeats this term three times is three successive verses. Thus, out of deep gratitude to God, David declares that it was now high time he began to show his gratitude to God by building a Temple of the LORD to dwell in (7:2). Moreover, now that he has built his own palace, the fact that the ark is still in a tent is embarrassing! Add to the fact that God had given him rest from all his enemies, he was long overdue to show his thankfulness to God.

David's prophet Nathan, when he heard of David's building plans, urged him to go do all he had in his mind to do, for the LORD had been with him up to that point on everything else. However, the prophet did not use the prophetic formula, which says, "Thus says the LORD." A major correction was needed in David's plans and Nathan's agreement.

Nathan's Corrected Promise – 7:4-17

The LORD needed to correct Nathan, for in that very night, "the word of the LORD came to Nathan, "Go tell my servant David, 'This is what the LORD says, "Are you the one to build me a house to dwell in?"' (7:5). Therefore, not everything a prophet says is inspired. When it is not introduced as the "word of the LORD," it comes from men and not from God!

The question put to David, the first of two such questions, was given two answers: the first a more practical answer and the second a more theological reason David should not be the one to construct the Temple for the LORD: (1) David was too busy waging war against his enemies (1 Kings 5:3), and (2) there was blood on his hands from his deeds as a warrior (1 Chron. 22:8). In fact, the LORD had never dwelled in such a building, nor had he authorized David to build such a house for him.

What Will be Fulfilled During David's Lifetime – 7:8-11a

The divine grant offered so freely to David can be divided into two parts: (1) those promises that will be realized during David's lifetime (7:8-11a) and (2) those promises that will be fulfilled after his death (7:11b-16). After the LORD has reviewed his earlier blessings to him when he found and taken David "from following the flock" (7:8), the LORD noted that he had in the past been with David as the LORD "mov[ed] from place to place" with his people (7:9).

Then in vv. 9b-11a, the LORD now promises afresh to: (1) make David's name great (9b), (2) provide a "place" for Israel (v. 10), and (3) give David "rest" from all his enemies (11a). But it is also easy to hear in this Davidic Covenant clear echoes of the promise God had also made to Abraham to make his name great (Gen 12:2). Again, the promise made to Abraham was that he would also give them a "place" in a land where he would plant them (Deut. 11:24; Josh. 1:3-4). And when God gave Israel that "place," they would no longer be "disturbed" (v. 10; Deut. 2:25; cf. Gen. 15:13).

What Will be Fulfilled After David's Day – 7:11b- 16

God promises to David's descendants to give them a "house" (= a dynasty), a "throne" and a "kingdom" (11b, 13, 16). Even though David is told that he is not to build a Temple for the LORD, God will "establish/make" a house out of him instead, which in later iterations of this promise, the same point is rendered to "found a dynasty" out of his seed (1 Kings 2:24). Each of the promises mentioned in vv. 11b-16 will happen after David's death, so they point to the future.

In the same way that God so spoke to Abraham about a son and a seed that is yet to be born, so the LORD said the same thing to David. In both cases, this "seed" would come from the bodies of Abraham and David (7:12; Gen 15:4; 17:7-10, 19). In David's case that "seed" would be Solomon, who had not even been born yet; but the "seed" did not mean Absalom or Adonijah, who pretended to be those promised heirs. The word "seed" is a collective noun that can refer to one or many seeds. However, the word "seed" pointed to the "line" in the Davidic family that would end in Yeshua the Messiah being the conclusion of that line. The apostle Paul argued in exactly that same manner when in Galatians 3:16 he stressed that the word "seed" did not say "seeds," but "seed," meaning one person, who was Yeshua the Messiah. It is just as important to note that the Davidic dynasty, throne, and kingdom were meant to endure "forever;" a fact that is repeated seven times in chapter 7 (13b, 16a, 16b, 24, 25, 29a, 29b; not to mention other texts such as 1 Kings 2:23, 45; 1 Chron. 22:10; Ps. 89:4). Add to this discussion the fact that 2 Corinthians 6:18 and Hebrews 1:5 understood the words of 2 Samuel 7:14a ("I [emphatic] will be his father, and he [emphatic] will be my son") as being understood in a Christological and Messianic sense! That is also how the Dead Sea Scrolls in 4Q174 (*Florilegium*) interpreted the words in 2 Samuel 7:10b-14a, likewise, in an eschatological and Messianic sense. "Son" could be understood in a collective sense, thereby making the father-son metaphor another signal that we are dealing with not just familial metaphors, but with covenantal language.

The words found in vv. 14b-15 are correctly understood to mean that the Davidic Covenant is unconditional, for no matter what David's line of sons does, the LORD's love will never be taken away from God's promise made to David.

A further proof of God's love to David can be seen in Yeshua's resurrection from the dead, as mentioned in Isaiah 55:3 and cited in Acts 13:34. God [promised that he would never remove his faithful love and his unfailing kindnesses to David, for they would endure forever (1Kgs 8:26; 1 Chron 17:23; 2 Chron 1:9; Ps 89:37. Therefore, the prophet Nathan reported to David all the words of this divine revelation from God (7:17).

David's Grateful Prayer to the Lord – 7:18-29

David went into the tent he had pitched for the ark of God as one extremely grateful, but humbled man (18). He began with a question of utter humility: "Who am I?" a plea like Moses' question to God in Exodus 3:11. David addressed the LORD as "Adonai Yahweh," a name translated in the NIV as "Sovereign LORD." David used it seven times in his prayer (7:18, 19 [bis], 20, 22, 28, 29). This term occurs in the book of Samuel only here, but it was used no doubt to definitively connect the Davidic Covenant with the Abrahamic Covenant, which older text used it twice (Gen. 15:2, 8). The name for God appeared very rarely in Scripture. For it only appears in five earlier texts: Abraham's prayer (Gen. 15:2, 8); Moses' prayer in Deuteronomy 3:24; 9:26); Joshua's prayer (Josh. 7:7); Gideon's prayer (Judg. 6:22); and Samson's prayer (Judg. 16:28). Therefore, God is recognized as Sovereign and his men are his vassals, a fact that David alludes to ten times (2 Sam. 7:19; 20, 21, 25, 26, 27 [bis], 28, 29 [bis]).

David went on to acknowledge gratefully that God had even better things in store for him, for God had spoken to him about the future of his dynasty and that "this [would be] the charter for all humanity" (7:19b). God had honored his servant beyond all explanations, leaving little more to be said. The NIV rendering of v. 19b as, "Is this your usual way of dealing with man?" is far off the mark for the Hebrew text (*wezo't torat ha'adam*). God had acted for the sake of his word, for his promises, and for David's sake, as he had done "this great thing" (21).

Put in brief terms, God was altogether unique and beyond any comparisons known to mortals (22). This matchless LORD who had no real rivals had done three wonderful things for his people: (1) he had redeemed them, (2) he had made a name for himself, and (3) he had performed great and awesome miracles (23). The LORD had driven out the nations with their gods just as he had delivered his people from mighty

Egypt (23b). Now he had established Israel as his own people and had become their God (24).

Verses 25-29 make up a unit in and of itself, for the LORD highlights his promise repeatedly as he has decided to make the house of David his visible sign of greatness (26), for the word from the LORD's mouth is the truth. David ended his prayer by asking that God would bless the house of his servant and that it would continue forever with God's blessing.

Conclusions

1. David wanted to have the ark of God at the center of Israel's worship, so he made great preparations for its transfer to Jerusalem. However, he forgot to follow God's instructions on how it was to be carried.
2. Saul's daughter Michal lost her love for David and decided instead to despise him as a vulgar fellow, for she did not share in David's joy of seeing the ark of God restored to the city of David.
3. Not everything a prophet says is from God; only what is prefaced with the formula, "Thus says the LORD," can be taken as the absolute truth.
4. God would punish any of David's sons who did wrong and disobeyed his commands, but he would never take away the gift of the dynasty, throne, and kingdom from David as he had taken it away from Saul.
5. At the heart of the promise-plan of God given to David was the gift of the "charter for humanity."

Questions for Thought or Discussion

1. Should Uzzah have been punished for his involuntary attempt to steady the ark of God and keep it from falling off the cart? Were he and his brother members of the Levites? What should they have known about how the ark was to be transported and what did the holiness of God imply?
2. Given the celebration surrounding the bringing of the ark of God to its permanent place, what sort of exuberance in the use of dance, singing, and physical activity best magnifies the holiness and solemnity of God?
3. Was Nathan off base to cheer David to go forward with his plans to build the Temple for the LORD? Should God have rebuked Nathan?
4. What is significant about the collective understanding of the terms for "seed" or "son" in the Davidic Covenant?
5. Why have so many translations of the Bible stumbled over the meaning of "This is the charter/law for mankind?" Were they trying to get rid of the heart of the Gospel in this passage?

Lesson 4

David's Victories Establish His Powerful Reign

2 Samuel 8:1-18; 9:1-13; 10:1-19

There can be little doubt that David's armies were invincible, for no nation could standup against him and his army regardless of their size, power, or reputation. But we must remember that it was not David, his skills, or the men who were in his military employ, but as the text clearly affirmed twice, "The LORD gave David victory wherever he went" (8:6,14).

The Triumph of The Kingdom of God Over Every Challenge-8:1-14

God's kingdom did not and will not come to earth as the result of the work of mortals such as David alone, but such a kingdom will come, as just promised in chapter 7 happens when the Living God is present and when he brings his kingdom in its final form. The key word in this section, therefore, is the Hebrew word *nakah,* "to smite," "to strike down," or "to defeat" an enemy is a verb that occurs five times in this text (8:1, 2, 3, 5, 13).

The Enemy Struck Down in the West – 8:1

God had promised to David that he would "give him rest from all his enemies" (7:11), so it is reasonable to guess that David was preoccupied in his early years with defeating all his enemies before he had time to move the ark of God. The most annoying enemies of all his enemies were the Philistines. David "defeated .... and subdued them" as "he took "Metheg Ammah" from the control of the Philistines" (8:1). We are unsure whether "Metheg Ammah" is a place name or a descriptive phrase, meaning "the bridle of the mother city." However, this total subduing of Philistines took place in 1 Samuel 7:13, where the "Philistines were subdued and did not invade Israelite territory again." Thus, David must have taken control of the chief city or area of the Philistines.

This act by David cannot be underestimated, for up to that point the Philistines thought of themselves as the legitimate heirs and rulers of the land of Canaan, but David's victories soon relieved them of that thought. David no longer had to put up with their constant raids and attacks on Israel! The kingdom belonged to the Lord, and he would both in history and in the final day show who owned the kingdoms and the empires of this world.

The Enemy Struck Down in the East – 8:2

David also struck down the Moabites to the east of Israel, but what offensive act on their part called for this action is unknown. After all, had not Moab been kind to David's parents when David took them there as a place of refuge while Saul was trying to kill David? (1 Sam. 22:3-4). (Ruth 4:10, 13, 16-17). Even the method David used for executing a limited number of his Moabite prisoners is seen only in this passage and is not explained for all its violence. David made his Moabite captives lie of the ground, and he measured them off with a cord so that every two lengths of the cord destined those in that group to be murdered with only the last one third of them escaping to live. As a result of David's victories over the Moabites, they became subject to him and forked over tribute to him as well.

The Enemies Struck Down in the North – 8:3-12

The power and the strength of Aram/Syria during David's reign is not easily available. There is no doubt that the king of Aram, Hadadezer, was rather awesome in its size and power. The Tzovah kingdom should be in the northern part of the Lebanon Valley. Whether the events of 2 Samuel 10:1-11:1 and 12:26-31 describe the identical situation, cannot be determined. It is suggested that the events in 8:3-12 occurred after the battles discussed in chapters 10-12. Hadadezer, whose name means "[The god] Hadad is my help," (which god incidentally was of no "help" to that king whatsoever!) Hadadezer, who was king of Tzovah, believed he had secured control along the Euphrates River; however, he was subsequently defeated by David (8:3). David captured 1,000 chariots and 7,000 charioteers and 20,000 of his foot soldiers (8:4). David "hamstrung all but 100 of his chariot horses" (8:4b). To "hamstring" the horses calls for severing the large tendon above and behind the hocks of the horses to disable them.

The Arameans of Damascus came to help Hadadezer (8:5), but David "struck down 22,000 of them. Moreover, David put "garrisons" in the Aramean kingdom of Damascus, and the Arameans became subject to him and brought tribute" (8:6). David seized the gold shields belonging to Hadadezer's officials and returned them to Jerusalem. The people of Israel used these shields in ceremonies for more than a hundred years, keeping them stored in the Temple.

Three towns that once belonged to Hadadezer (Tebah, Berothai and Cun), were towns that David conquered and took "a great quantity of bronze" from (8:8). There is a modern Bereitan that lies thirty miles north-northwest of Damascus and ancient Cun is perhaps modern Ras Baalbek, thirty miles north-northwest of Berothai, but all three towns can be found in the northern part of the Lebanese Beqa' Valley. (8:9)

When news that David had defeated Hadadezer, Tou, king of Hamath (8:9) (120 miles north of Damascus on the Orontes River), sent his son, named Joram/Hadoram, meaning "The Lord/Hadad is exalted," to congratulate David on his victory over their key nemesis. Joram brought "articles of silver, gold and bronze" to David as a gift (8:10). David dedicated these articles to the LORD as was his custom for all the silver and gold he had taken from all the nations he had conquered (8:11).

The Enemy Struck Down in the South – 8:13-14

This conquest made David famous, especially after he returned from striking down 18,000 Edomites in the Valley of Salt (18:13). There too, David installed "garrisons" throughout Edom, as the Edomites became subject to David (8:14). It would seem, however, that Abishai, son of Zeruiah, was the one who did the actual "striking down" of these hostile forces, but to David goes the credit since he is the supreme commander.

The List of David's Officials – 8:15-18

As would be expected of any strong king in the Ancient World (if not also in the Modern World), the best mark of any rule was that the king acted justly and rightly on behalf of his people and nation. That was the legacy of David as well. Moreover, his government was well established, as might have been learned from the Egyptian rulers.

Joab was his commander of the army, Jehoshaphat was his recorder, Zadok and Ahimelech were his priests, Seriah was his secretary, Benaiah headed up the Kerethites and Pelethites, and David's sons were his advisors (8:16-18).

The Faithful Love in the Covenant Between David and Jonathan – 9:1-13

Scholars love to describe the section that goes from 2 Samuel 9 – 20 and I Kings 1-2 as "earliest and greatest example of Hebrew historiography." This section is labeled "the Succession Narrative," but as others have pointed out, the narrative does not focus on succession.[1] Therefore, it is better to refer to these chapters as "The Court History of David."

This section begins with David asking the question, "Is there anyone left of the house of Saul to whom I can show kindness for Jonathan's sake?" (9:1). The theme of this whole section is the word "kindness," (Hebrew, *hesed*, 9:1, 3, 7). David has had a long-standing covenantal relationship with Saul's son Jonathan, now deceased.

As perhaps forerunners of such an act of graciousness, the Jabeshites of Jabesh-Gilead had shown special kindness to Saul by conducting a nighttime raid on the city where the Philistines had hung Saul and his sons' bodies. These they took down and returned to give them an honorable burial in their city because of his act of kindness as he became king of Israel.

One of the servants in Saul's house, Ziba, was summoned before King David to answer questions about any living relatives in Saul's line. Ziba came to David and asked if there was still a survivor in Saul's house to whom he could show "kindness" from God.

Ziba responded, there was a son of Jonathan, a man who was "crippled in both feet" (9:3). Moreover, Zeba gave David both the specific town and the specific house where this man might be found. This man lived in the town of "Lo Debar," in the house of "Makir son of Ammiel" (9:4). Makir may well have been another name or a synonym for the tribe Manasseh and the town of Lo Debar (9:4-5) was found east of the Jordan River. It

---

1. For example, Robert P. Gordon, *I & II Samuel: A Commentary,* Grand Rapids, Zondervan, 1986, p. 41. Also, James W. Flangan, "Court History or Succession Document? A Study of 2 Samuel 9-20; 1 Kings 1-2," *JBL* 91/2 (1972): 172-81.

was associated with the town, Mahanaim, a former headquarters for Saul's now deceased son Ish-Bosheth. Lo Debar is spelled in different ways, so it is difficult to say whether it really meant "no thing." This town may relate to a modern site of Umm ed-Dabar, found ten miles south-southeast of the Sea of Galilee.

So, a man by the name of Mephibosheth, son Jonathan, son of Saul, was brought to David, where the new arrival respectfully bowed down before David (9:6). Mephibosheth referred to himself as David's "servant" (9:6c). David tried to reassure him by saying he was not to be afraid, for he intended nothing but good for him. Knowing what happened to his uncle Ish-Bosheth, Mephibosheth was understandably uneasy about the meeting.

David's actions in seeking out Jonathan's surviving son, Mephibosheth, reflect not only adherence to an ancient covenant but also highlight the importance of loyalty and remembrance in leadership. Despite the potential political risks associated with showing favor to a member of Saul's family, David's willingness to extend kindness underscores the depth of his commitment to honor past promises and uphold personal integrity. This episode illustrates the complex interplay between political expediency and genuine compassion in the exercise of royal authority. But David had made a strong covenant with Jonathan before God, so he had to be true and faithful to what he had said. There was the character of Jonathan shining through it all.

David's order that Mephibosheth should always "eat at my table" (7,10) is not understood as a gracious and generous offer by all commentators. Scholars interpret David's offer as a way for him to watch the last of Saul's family, given his justified suspicion toward that household. These interpreters credit David with having a genius for doing what is "proper" as well as what is "expedient." Others accuse David of both motives, but it may well be that David did act out of pure and kind motives, for he deeply loved Jonathan and felt he had to honor his word to him.

Mephibosheth, on his part, "bowed down" (6, 8) to the king and referred to himself as "your servant" (6, 8). He seemed grateful that David should even have "noticed" or "paid attention to him" (1 Kings 8:28. In fact, he referred to himself even more humbly as one who was surprised that David would even regard such "a dead dog like me" (8b).

David summoned Ziba, Saul's servant, into his presence to tell him that the king had given to Saul's grandson, the son of Jonathan, "everything that had belonged to Saul and his family" (9). David went on to say that Ziba and his sons, which amounted to the large number of fifteen sons, were to farm the land he had just given to Mephibosheth, and he was to bring the produce of those fields to Mephibosheth so that he could be provided for from their sale (10). Ziba had twenty servants alongside his sons, making him well prepared to fulfil the royal command.

Ziba promised to carryout David's assignment. Meanwhile, Mephibosheth ate at David's table as if he had been one of his sons! (11). So, David really did fulfill the promise of showing "loving kindness" and mercy, which he had pledged to do in the covenant he had made with Jonathan. Mephibosheth always ate at David's table from that time forward (11b, 13). The first time we met Mephibosheth in 2 Samuel 4:4, he was only 12 years of age, but now he was old enough to have a "young son" named Mica(h), whose descendants appear by name in 1 Chronicles 8:35-38; 9:41-44. It might be significant to notice that the name of his son, Mica(h), which means "Who is like (Yahweh)?" is quite a contrast to his father's name of "Mephibosheth," which seems to mean, "One who scatters shame" where the word "shame" is substituted for the name of "Baal" just like "Ish-Bosheth," meaning "man of shame," is a substitute for "man of Baal." The chapter ends with another reminder that he was "crippled in both feet," but he still ate at the king's table (13).

The Loving-Kindness of the Ammonite King Nahash Versus the Humiliating Act and the Subsequent Defeat of His Son Hanun – 10:1-11:1

Both 2 Samuel 10:1 and 13:1 begin with "In the course of time," indicating the beginning of a new section in the book of 2 Samuel. Therefore, the historical notice of the fact that Israel was victorious over the Ammonites and their king (10:1-11:1; and 12:26-31) form a sort of framing device around the central narrative of the David- Bathsheba affair. The name of "Nahash" means something like "snaky" while the name of his son Hanun means "Favored by God," or more appropriately, based on the use of this same noun in Job 19:17, "Loathsome." This Nahash is the same Ammonite king who was defeated by Saul (1 Sam 11:1-11), but the kindness expressed by David toward him may have come for the days when David was a fugitive fleeing from Saul, and Nahash may have shown David help, which is not recorded in Scripture.

When David heard that Nahash had died, he decided to send a delegation to express sympathy to the family of Nahash and the new king Hanun. However, when the delegation arrived in the Ammonite setting, the Ammonite "nobles," who could have been the army commanders, stirred up possible suspicious reasons for David's actions. Their theory was that David's delegation had been sent to "explore" and to "spy out" (3) the region and especially their city of Rabbah, the capital city of the Ammonites known as Amman today (11:1). This city is found about forty miles east-northeast of Jerusalem. They were sure that the men of Israel had come to "overthrow" the Ammonites, so I guess they had decided to pick a fight with Israel. Hanun insulted the Jewish delegation by ordering his men to shave half of each man's beard, signifying contempt and submission.

Hanun then had the garments of each delegate cut vertically up to "the middle of the buttocks" and then they were sent away (4). This may have been good for a real hearty laugh locally, but what did they think might happen because of this internationally? Did they think a warrior like David would just take it and that would be the end of it? Hardly. There were tough times coming, which this new king and his nobles may have finally awakened to, but all too late! Such indignities dished out in such grotesque parody would reap awful consequences, which they did!

When David heard the maltreatment, his men had been given by Hanun (5, 17), he sent messengers to them with instructions that they were to stay in Jericho (some six miles from the Jordan River and a little north of a well-known ancient roadway that led from Rabbah to Jerusalem) until their beards had grown back.

When the Ammonites realized that their actions had made them unfavorable to David (verse 6), they responded by hiring a considerable number of mercenaries to strengthen their forces. Therefore, the Ammonites hired the Arameans from Beth Rehob (8), an Aramean district just north of ancient Laish, more recently called Dan (Judg. 18:28). Also, there were those who came from Tzovah, Maacah and Tob, which added to the troops gathered against Israel.

David sent out his entire army under the direction of Joab to take on this multitude (7). The Ammonite army gathered near their city gate, in Rabbah, while the Aramean troops stayed in the surrounding fields under separate commanders.

Joab sized up the situation as he drew up a strategy (9-10). Joab believed the Arameans were stronger, so he chose top troops to face them and led the contingent himself. The rest of the troops he put under the command of his brother Abishai, who took on the Ammonites. Joab set these terms between himself and his brother: if your enemy is too strong for you, I will come to help you, but if my enemy is too strong for me, then you come help me! His concluding words were words that were often used to encourage the troops just before they went into battle: "Be strong and fight bravely for our people and the cities of our God. The LORD will do what is good in his sight" (12).

As Joab marched into battle against the Arameans, they quickly turned tail and fled (13). And when the Ammonites saw the Arameans fleeing, they instantly decided to flee inside the city and to gain the protection of the city's walls (14). Accordingly, Joab broke off fighting them and returned to Jerusalem for the immediate future. Later he would return and take on the city of Rabbah.

The Arameans must have been embarrassed by their performance on the field, so they regrouped. A leader named Hadadezer got together forces he had contracted to fight with him, and so the ensued on the eastern side of the Euphrates River (15). David learned from his intelligence network that Hadadezer's army was leading a huge Aramean army, so David gathered all Israel, and they crossed the Jordan River and headed east to a place called Helam, about 7 miles north of Tob, to meet a force led by commander Shobach for Hadadezer. Once again, the Arameans formed their battle lines to meet David, but instead they fled before Israel. Israel therefore pressed its advantage as they killed 700 of their charioteers and 40,000 of their foot soldiers. When all the kings who had been vassals to Hadadezer saw that Israel had overwhelmingly defeated them, they sued for peace with Israel and became subject to them. The Arameans had learned a lesson, for from that time forward they were afraid to help the Ammonites anymore!

Kings went out to battle in the Spring of each year, but David had taken the view that it was best if he stayed home while he sent Joab with his army to fight. That is when this army destroyed the Ammonites by besieging Rabbah (11:1).

Conclusions

1. David achieved notable military success and, after overcoming opposing nations, was able to secure peace for himself and his son Solomon.
2. God gave David fame from all his military exploits so that he was genuinely feared by all the surrounding nations. This too added to his "rest."
3. This was also a time in history when there was a power vacuum left by the decline of the great empires of the Hittites, Egyptians, Arameans, and Assyrians. It provided time for the grounding of the kingdom of God!
4. David showed "loving-kindness" to Jonathan's son Mephibosheth as he had covenanted with Jonathan.
5. David showed great "kindness" to Nahash king of the Ammonites when he died. This concept has a wide coverage.

Questions for Thought or Discussion

1. What is encompassed by the concept of Hebrew *herem*? Is it close in meaning or is it quite different from New Testament injunctions for us to be kind, merciful and loving?
2. David showed this kind of kindness to Jonathan's son Mephibosheth and to the leader of the country of the Ammonites. Is the breath of that love and kindness as wide in its extent in the Old Testament as it is in the New Testament?
3. Why would a good man like Jonathan name his son with a name that involved Mephi-"Baal," which had to be changed later to Mephi-"Bosheth?"
4. Could all the military successes have gone to David's head so that he felt he could excuse himself in the affair he had with Bathsheba, which comes in the next chapter of 2 Samuel.
5. If David contributed to the establishment of the kingdom of God, what implications does this have for the nature of that kingdom and its components?

Lesson 5

David's Sin of Adultery with Bathsheba

2 Samuel 11:1-27; 12:1-25

As readers, we are astonished to learn that David, despite all the kind words of Scripture about his piety, and his being "a man after God's own heart," stooped to such acts of temptation as adultery and murder! In this one crime, David violated three of the ten commandments: "You shall not covet your neighbor's wife," you shall not commit adultery" and "you shall not murder" (Exod. 20:17, 14, 13). Here is another case of how plain-spoken and open the Bible is of the faults and sins of its heroes. We could almost wish that it would not be necessary to report such evil, or that these men of God would not need to have such gross sins reported about their lives. But the Bible does not spare the truth where it is needed to be told, so that we too are warned about the conduct of our own lives. Moreover, the scenario of David's sin fits exactly the warning given later in Scripture in James 1:14-15 – "Each one is tempted when, by his own evil desire, he is dragged away and enticed. Then, after desire has conceived, it gives birth to sin, and sin, when it is full-grown, gives birth to death."

David Sins Against Bathsheba – 11:1-5

The narrative begins by telling us that Spring has come to Israel, which is the traditional time when the kings of the ancient Near East go off to war. This is the best time for such activities, since the weather is not too hot yet, the roads are passable by now, and there are crops in the fields that can be raided to supply food for the troops.

But instead of David leading the troops out in conquest, which was his rightful place, we find that David has sent Joab off with the entire Israelite army to crack down on the Ammonites while he stayed at the palace. However, the Ammonites, after being heavily beaten throughout their country, have retreated to their capital city of Rabbah, so Joab has started a siege against that city. Meanwhile David continued to remain in Jerusalem (11:1).

Here is where another story begins, with the Ammonite invasion as the backdrop for this sorry tale of sin, for "David got up from his bed and walked around on the roof of the palace" (v. 2). From his special vantage point, "he saw a woman bathing," and "the woman was very beautiful." (2b -c). Seeing a beautiful naked woman bathing aroused David's sexual and lustful desires. David knew the command of God in the Decalogue as well as we do today, but he decided not to heed the commands of God; instead, he was going to go after the desires of his own heart. David should have resisted both the temptation, and the follow-through act of sinning, but he easily caved in and became a victim of what was too easy a conquest for him as king over the land! Jesus (Yeshua) would later warn, "Anyone who looks at a woman lustfully has already committed adultery with her in his heart" (Matt. 5:28). David did not call out to God for help at that moment but chose to follow his desires instead.

David sent someone to find out what could be learned about this woman (3). Word came back that her name was "Bathsheba" (meaning, "daughter of an oath," or "daughter of seven"), who was the daughter of Eliam, but more importantly, she was the "wife" of one of his soldiers named Uriah the Hittite (3b). The man sent to find out who she was, discovered that she was the daughter of Eliam, also given the variant name in 1 Chronicles 3:5 of "Ammiel." Interestingly, Eliam was the son of David's highly regarded counselor, Ahithophel (23:34), and Eliam himself was one of David's warriors, one who had come from foreign origins. Would that mean then that Bathsheba, mother of Solomon, was also a pagan ancestress of Yeshua (Matt. 1:3-6) just like Ruth? Uriah, whose name means "Yahweh is my light," may indeed have come to help David as a foreign mercenary from a pagan land, but he was certainly a worshipper of the LORD.

David sent messengers "to get her" (4). When she came to him, he slept with her. Previously, when David had seen her bathing, she was purifying herself from her menstrual cycle, which would become an important note later in deciding who the father of the baby was. But a pregnancy did occur; she conceived and so she sent worrisome news later to David saying, "I am pregnant" (5)."

David Sins Against Uriah – 11:6-27

David commanded that Uriah be sent to him, from the battlefront that was fully engaged in attacking the Ammonites (7). David entered a conversation with Uriah that seemed proper and the kind of thing an army man would expect, such as: How is your commander Joab doing? How are the soldiers responding to Joab's leadership? In your view, how is the war going? (7b-c). Soon after this quizzing by the king, Uriah left the king's palace, being urged by the king to "Go down to your house and wash your feet" (8). Uriah may have wondered to himself, "What was that all about? It did not all hang together as it should have! However, Uriah left the palace, but he steadfastly refused to go down to his house (9).

Uriah was both a loyal and a conscientious military man, for while the army was on a military mission, the men "kept themselves from women," as David had noted when he was asking the priest for bread and any weapons he might have had handy (1 Sam. 21:4-5). So, following that ancient military code, Uriah did not feel he was at liberty to violate his military duty. Instead, he stayed in Jerusalem away from the pleasures with his wife until he was given new orders to return to the battle. In addition, if he had taken part in certain aspects of marital life for either of two nights, he would not have been eligible to join the ongoing fight upon his return. Uriah even added, how could be indulge in such martial luxuries when the ark of God and the men of Judah and Israel were camped out in the open fields in tents? (11). It just did not make sense to Uriah. In the meantime, David had sent a "gift" down to Uriah's house expecting he would show up there, but he never did go home as David had encouraged him to do! (8).

David urged Uriah to stay one more day before he would send him back to his post (12), but in the interim, David tried to ply him by eating and drinking with him until Uriah got drunk (13). Still, Uriah refused to go home. Some even think that David's earlier suggestion that he go home and "wash his feet" was intended as a double entendre; a few times in Scripture the word "feet" is used for "genitals" (Exod. 4:25; Deut. 28:57; Isa. 7:20). Poor Uriah! I doubt that he had any idea as to what was going on, but he must by now have felt something strange was happening! But I suppose he was just too loyal to think the worse in this situation, so he guessed the king was hungry for information from the battlefield. If he had had a cell phone, he could at least have called his wife to see how she was doing!

Since David had exhausted all normal avenues to cover up his sin with Bathsheba, on the next morning the king wrote a letter to Joab and sent it by the hand of Uriah. Imagine, carrying your own death-warrant to the battlefield! In this letter, he urged Joab to put Uriah front and center, where the hottest fighting was going on, and then to withdraw from him quickly. This strategy worked the evil plan of the king, for the Ammonites struck Uriah down and he died along with other men of Joab's army (15, 17).

Uriah certainly is the principal character in this chapter, for his name appears seventeen times. But the news was clear, repeated twice: "Your servant Uriah the Hittite is dead (21, 24). The king had murdered him!

Joab therefore sent a full account of what had taken place in the battle. He instructed the messenger quite well, disguising the key point that David wanted to know, i.e. what happened to Uriah? The news was encapsulated in a masterpiece of disguise. Joab told the messenger that David's anger might "flare up" because of the losses in the battle, so be prepared to answer these questions: (1) why did you get so close to the city? (20b). (2) Then, David will ask, didn't the army and Joab know that the Ammonites would shoot from the wall? (20c) (3) Then, the king will no doubt use the illustration of the woman who killed Gideon's son Abimelech when he got too close to the tower (21a; cf. Judg. 9:50-54), (4) Then, David will say, wasn't it a woman who dropped the upper millstone on Abimelech's head when he got too close? (21c). So, if all this comes up, then just say, "Also your servant Uriah the Hittite is dead" (21d).

The messenger went and delivered the news as he had been told, adding details from his own perspective: "The men overpowered us and came out against us in the open, but we drove them back to the entrance to the city gate. Then the archers shot arrows at your servants from the wall, and many of the king's men died. Moreover, your servant Uriah the Hittite is dead." (23-24)

Surprisingly, at least from the perspective of the messenger, David said to the messenger, "Say this to Joab: Do not let this upset you; the sword devours one as well as another. Press the attack on the city and destroy it and say this to encourage Joab." (25).

Bathsheba mourned her husband's death – for more reasons than one. After a period of mourning, David "had her brought" to his palace in Jerusalem (27), but the whole thing "displeased the LORD." Unfortunately, this is the only time the name of Yahweh appears in the whole chapter – which also tells us a lot.

Nathan the Prophet Rebukes David – 12:1-25

This text begins most significantly by saying, "And Yahweh sent Nathan to David" (12:1). Without this intervention by the LORD, this narrative would have been altogether bleak and hopeless. The verb to "send" appears twelve times in this chapter, but the most important person in this action is the LORD himself. It is also a reassuring note that the LORD will not allow his servant David to be satisfied or left alone to wallow in his sin. Instead of abandoning David to his sin, the LORD pursued David with a confrontation of his unfaithfulness and his deliberate disobedience to his law and to his grace.

The LORD sent Nathan to David with a story which becomes the link that joins the man and his sin. Today, interpreters persist in calling Nathan's story a "parable," but apparently as it was being told, David took it as a serious and real case of injustice. After all, it was a story about two men, which as far as David knew at that moment, may have been a situation that had just come to the attention of Nathan. One man, the rich one, can be described in just one line: he "had a very large number of sheep and cattle" (12:2). But the other man, called a "poor man" needed four lines to tell his part in the story (3). However, the rich man, being stingy to the core, could not see himself wasting one of his own animals on such an occasion, so he refrained from preparing and sacrificing one. He decided instead to take the poor man's ewe, perhaps while the poor man and his children were working in his fields. The rich man stole the lamb from his poor servant (just as the king had stolen Bathsheba from David's soldier, Uriah, 4b).

> [Yet the poor man] "had nothing except one little ewe lamb he had bought. He raised it, and it grew up with him and his children. It shared his food, drank from his cup, and even slept in his arms. It was like a daughter to him.

As the story progresses, David still thinks he is going to be asked to function as the judge on a case that is quite simple and self-evident. Suddenly, the story intensifies, for a "traveler" arrives, but Nathan does not use an ordinary word for "traveler; he used the Hebrew word *helek,* meaning a "walker," which was the word that described how David had gotten in trouble by "walking" around on the roof of the palace (11:2).

Was Nathan beginning to load the story a bit to ring certain alarms in the guilty heart of David?

The rich man, being a good practitioner of hospitality such as he was, got ready to prepare a meal for his traveling friend. But as Nathan told the story, he "took" the ewe of the poor man, instead of sacrificing one of his own animals.

David had heard enough, for he suddenly exploded as he burned with anger against this shameful thief. This case involved a huge injustice. He had stolen the poor man's ewe and offered it as if it were one of his own to his guest. At this point, David, with an oath, shouted,

> "As surely as the LORD lives, the man who did this deserved to die! He must pay for the lamb four times over because he did such a thing and had no pity" (6).

It is true, of course, that theft of a lamb did not constitute a capital crime, so David's condemnation of the rich man to death was an exaggeration. But it did show how deeply he was moved by the story. A rich man's stealing of a poor man's lamb, however, did carry a penalty in the law of Moses that required quadruple restitution (Exod. 22:1).

After David had finished giving reacting to this case, Nathan resolutely concluded by saying, "You are the man." (7). Nathan knew better than to try to confront David with a series of charges such as "You are one devious womanizer," or "Don't you have any conscience about murdering one of your key soldiers?" Instead, Nathan carefully coaxed David's ethical instincts until he had judged himself. Then he read the riot act to the rich man for his act. David too, by now, was one of those rich men as well. Nathan was graciously employing, in David's case, the grace our LORD has given to all of us, i.e. those who will pause and repent of sin that is similar. Nathan did not openly accuse or harangue David for his sin; rather, he treated him as a fellow believer who was a child of God who needed to be restored by the same loving God who had saved him.

After Nathan pointed out to David that he was the man he was describing in his story (7), he went on the itemize how grievously David had sinned by listing five specific gifts God had given to him as reasons why he should have been content with what he had:

> I anointed you king over Israel,
> I delivered you from the hand of Saul.
> I gave you your master's house

> and your master's wives into your arms.
> I gave you the house of Israel and Judah.
> I would have given you even more if all this had been too little (8).

Our Lord's question considering all these gifts was this: How could you have despised the word of the Lord by doing all this evil in his eyes? David's sin, like our sin, is so often senseless and without explanation, especially when it is viewed considering what God has done for us already!

Nathan was not finished with David yet, for he went on in v. 9 to speak more particularly of his act of murder. To emphasize how loathsome this was, Nathan used the Hebrew sign for the direct object and placed these first in the sentences with three more charges he was now going to bring against David.

> Uriah the Hittite you struck down with the sword;
> His wife you took as your own [wife];
> Him you killed with the sword of that Ammonites.

Because of these deeds and because David had despised the LORD, and his word, the sword would never depart from David's house! (10). If David could get real worked up over the unfairness and injustice of the rich man in Nathan's story, then he should surely have understood why the Lord God's anger was now so strong against him.

It is true, of course, that the Law of God said that David deserved the penalty of death for what he had done (Lev. 20:10; Deut. 22:22), but instead David received grace. To be sure, Yahweh forgives David of the guilt of his sin, but the Lord inflicted on David the consequences of his sin. The Lord can always cleanse us from the defilement of our sin, but he often continues his discipline because of what we did. Did David then get off too easy for his sin compared to all other murderers? Why did no one die because of his sin? We should not press this issue too hard, but in fact one did die, as it were his substitute – Uriah! Or should we say instead, the son who was conceived in that adulterous affair died because of their joint sin? (14b). The solution to this problem stays in the mystery of the Lord of all, but we can be sure that the Creator of the whole universe did what was right (Gen. 18:26).

The Lord did strike the new-born child born to David and Bathsheba (15b), and so he died. For the seven days that that child lived, David fasted and prayed and spent his nights with his face to the ground (16). When he was urged to eat something, he refused, so his servants became worried about him. However, when he heard his servants whispering, he realized the child had died (19). Upon questioning them if the child had died, they answered directly. Therefore, he picked himself up, showered, splashed on cologne, and changed his clothes. This baffled his servants who wanted to know why this profound change had come over David (23a). He answered:

> "While the child was still alive, I fasted and wept; but when the child died, you arose and ate food" I thought, 'Who knows? The LORD may be gracious to me and let the child live.' But now that he is dead, why should I fast? Can I bring him back again? I will go to him, but he will not return to me.'" (21-23).

David Completes the Siege of Rabbah of the Ammonites – 12:26-31

We may have forgotten Joab by this time because of David's sin, but he was still engaged in fighting the Ammonites. He sent messengers to David urging him to come and finish off the capture of Rabbah and the Ammonites so that the city could be named after him; otherwise, Joab would do the honors and name the city after himself (26-28). Moreover, Joab tells David he has captured Rabbah's water supply, so their days of holding out against Israel were numbered (27).

In 1969 an archaeological excavation of this site uncovered the outline of the city walls of Rabbah. Within that enclosed area, a six-foot tunnel had been cut through the bedrock to a stairway which descended to a deep underground chamber, twenty-five feet wide, fifty-five feet long and twenty-three feet high, like the water chamber cut through the rock in Megiddo.

So, David came with the entire army of Israel and took the city of Rabbah. Also, he took the crown off the head of the Ammonite king, which weighed a talent of gold and was inset with precious stones. They placed it on David's head. David took a large quantity of plunder with him.

David assigned the captives from that city to tasks such as using saws, running iron picks, and making bricks. Then David and the entire army returned home to Jerusalem.

Conclusions

1. One fatal walk on the roof of the palace one warm Spring evening was enough to bring heaps of guilt and discredit to a man who up to that point seemed to have walked beautifully with the LORD.
2. David violated at least three of the ten commandments in one action that began with temptation but went all the way to murder to disguise and cover up his sin.
3. Uriah, David's commanding general, was also lured into sin by acting on David's behalf on the battlefront.
4. Nathan, a prophet, was sent by the LORD to guide David in confronting his wrongdoing and encourage him to seek forgiveness and purification from God.
5. David should have been with the troops in the field, but instead he was left at home bored and unoccupied, all of which provided the occasion for sin.

Questions for Thought or Discussion

1. What do you think about Uriah's refusal to take a moment to go visit his wife when he had an unexpected chance to do so? Might that have saved him from being murdered? Was he at all suspicious that something may have been occurring?
2. What do you imagine went into the grief of Bathsheba when she learned her husband had died in battle? Do you think she ever learned the full story of all that took place? Did the story leak out from those who had access to the story?
3. Did Nathan design the story he told about the two men or did the LORD give him that story as a way of getting beyond the defenses of David?
4. Why did God choose the second son of David and Bathsheba, named Solomon, to be the king who would follow him? After all, David was guilty of polygamy, wife stealing, and murder?
5. How can we describe the enormous extent of the grace of God and yet at the same time protect the holiness of God as he extends such grace to such sinners?

Lesson 6

David's Son Amnon Rapes His Half-Sister Tamar

2 Samuel 13:1-39; 14:1-33

The judgment of God for David's sin with Bathsheba was not long in coming, for David had been told by Nathan the prophet, "Out of your own household I am going to bring calamity upon you" (12:11). Sure enough, the family tragedy that occurred in chapter 13 was in ways a recapitulation of the events of chapter 11. Just as David had seen from the roof top of his palace a beautiful woman and had then lain with her in the palace, only to learn that to keep his paternity of the pregnancy from being discovered he had to arrange for the death of her husband, so David's oldest son Amnon, likewise sees his beautiful half-sister and conspires to trick her into getting close enough for him to grab her, and then lie with her, only to be himself conspired against two years later and also murdered. Sin leaves a terrible tangle in its wake!

This new episode of wickedness, however, involved two brothers of David: Absalom, the third son of David and Amnon David's firstborn son, for Tamar was sister to Absalom, but she was also the object of Amnon's passionate sexual desires as well. Absalom's name appears about 100 times in the Old Testament with over 90 % of them occurring here in chapters 13-20. Commentators see chapters 13-14 as being very closely related to each other. Therefore, we shall combine their presentations into one lesson as part of the study of the life of David.

Amnon Rapes His Half-Sister Tamar – 13:1-22

Three persons of the royal household frame the pericope of 2 Samuel 13:1-22 – viz., Amnon, Tamar, and Absalom in vv.1 and 22b. The introductory, "In the course of time" of 13:1, marks a new beginning, but since it shares so much with the episode that has just been presented in 2 Samuel 11 and 12, it is not particularly new, especially when you get right down to the basics.

Absalom is very much involved with what goes on in this narrative, for Tamar is his sister, the one that his older brother Amnon coaxes into a violent rape scene. Moreover, Absalom, by this time may already be involved in a quest to become the next king and to succeed his father, David. But Tamar, whose name means "Palm tree," we may suppose is so named because of her stature and the clusters of fruit of the Palm that are imitated by Tamar's breast. Tamar is called "beautiful" (13:1), just as her brother Absalom was also declared "handsome" (14:25).

Tamar is furthermore also described as a "virgin" (13:2), but David's third son named Amnon developed such a tremendous sexual longing for his half-sister Tamar, to the point that he was beginning to feel ill over his intense desires (13:2). Tamar was so protected by her family that it did not appear a possibility to do anything such as what Amnon envisaged (2). But Amnon's "frustration" and "distress" over her increased so that he was totally "faint with love" as the expression went in Song of Solomon (SS 2:5; 5:8). Here was one lovesick puppy, who was frustrated and distressed to what he thought were his physical limits.

The story shifts, however, as we are told that Amnon "had a friend named Jonadab, meaning "The LORD is noble" (3). The word "friend" may indicate something like a cabinet post, one who gave counsel and wisdom to those in the royal cabinet (cf. 1 Kings 4:5, "king's friend," = personal adviser to the king). Jonadab visited Amnon in his home, and he began by asking Amnon why he as the king's son looked so "haggard" all the time. Amnon gave him a straightforward answer: "I'm in love with Tamar, my brother Absalom's sister" (4b).

Jonadab's advice to Amnon was one that promoted evil and an inordinate amount of calamity from sin, for he told him "Go to bed!" (5). "Pretend to be sick," Then Jonadab craftily surmised that Amnon's father would come to see him when he heard he was sick. That would be the moment for Amnon to act! Jonadab instructed him, when he could ask his father, here's what you are to do and to say:

> "I would like my sister Tamar to come and give me something to eat. Let her prepare the food in my sight so I may watch her [....do what? for this text has no object!] and then eat it from her hand." (5b-c).

Now what father would fall for that line of distorted therapy, for the whole story smacks of some kind of undisclosed mischief. But Amnon took the counsel of his "friend" Jonadab as he laid down on his bed and pretended to be ill (6).

Tamar, as ordered by the king, arrived at the "sickroom" of Amnon's house and began to prepare the meal as Amnon watched her. She was the object Amnon wanted to watch, not the food she was making, as perhaps David wrongly thought. It could at this point be questioned whether Jonadab was acting alone when he gave this advice to Amnon, for Absalom, the king's third-born, may already have had plans to run for kingship in Israel, and he many have had plans to make sure his brother, David's firstborn, would not be a competitor, but a man with a ruined reputation. We cannot say for sure.

Tamar was hard at work as she took dough and kneaded it into bread in the sight of Amnon, then she put it into a pan to bake it. When it was ready, she went to sick Amnon to feed him, but he refused to eat it (9). Instead, Amnon ordered everyone out of his house except the two of them (9b). The Amnon said "Bring the food here into my bedroom so I may eat it from your hand (10). Tamar followed her sick brother's request, but when she took it to him to eat, "he grabbed her and said, 'Come to bed [lit. "lie down"] with me, my sister'" (11). Did Amnon use the term "sister" as a loving metaphor for a sexual companion as does Song of Solomon 4:9-10, 12; 5:1-2? It is possible.

Tamar's response came frantically and with a strong note of indignity:

> "Don't my brother!" she said to him. "Don't force me. Such a thing should not be done in Israel! Don't do this wicked thing. What about me? Where could I get rid of my disgrace? And what about you? You would be like one of the wicked fools in Israel. Please speak to the king; he will not keep me from being married to you." (12-13).

Tamar begged her brother Amnon to not indulge in sexual relations outside of the marriage bond. However, the Mosaic law also disallowed marriage between a half-brother and a half-sister (Lev. 18:9, 11; 20:17; Deut. 27:22). Therefore, Amnon may have been guilty of incest as well as rape. What, then, was Tamar talking about when she assured Amnon that the king would allow them to get married if the law disallowed it? Was she grasping at straws in her desperation (or just anything to free her) to stop him from finishing the rape. However, Amnon was stronger than she was. He raped her.

Amnon suddenly hated Tamar more intensely than he loved her. That is why he so cold-heartedly ordered her, "Get out; get away!" (15). Did Amnon suddenly realize all too late the "wicked thing" (12) he had done ended in an even more tragedy? But her questions to Amnon are left unanswered: "What about me?" "What about you?"

Tamar pleaded with Amnon not to send her away (16), for this would only add insult to injury, a greater injury than the scandal he had just committed against her. Amnon called his servant to help him clear this woman out of his bedroom (17). So, the servant put Tamar out of the house and bolted the door after she left (18).

Tamar left heart-sick in mind and soul as she put ashes on her head and tore the richly ornamented robe she was wearing as a virgin daughter of the king. She lifted her hand to her head and went home weeping bitterly and sobbing loudly as she went (18-19).

Absalom, Tamar's brother, saw the woman in such deep anguish that he asked, "Has Amnon your brother been with you? Be quiet now, my sister; he is your brother. Don't take this thing to heart" (20). Did Absalom already have an idea of what could have happened to her? Why was he so knowledgeable? Had he been in on the plot to stigmatize Amnon's record so that he would not compete for the kingship? We do not know!

As a result of all of this, Tamar started living in Absalom's house, but she lived as a "desolate woman" (20d). When David heard what had happened, "he was furious," but did he ever raise a word of rebuke against Amnon, or was he silenced by his own fall from grace with Bathsheba? Absalom, however, never said a word to his brother, one way or the other! But clearly, he hated Amnon for the way he had disgraced his sister, Tamar (21).

Absalom Kills His Brother Amnon for Raping His Sister – 13:23-39

Absalom waited patiently for two years before he took revenge on Amnon for what he had done (23). The site for this revenge would be at Baal-hazor, about fifteen miles north-northeast of Jerusalem. This site is the same site as the city named Hazor, a city that dominated the area as the highest peak in the hill country of Ephraim, at 3,333 feet above sea level.

Here Absalom invited the kings with all his sons to join in the festive season of sheepshearing (1 Sam. 25:2). However, the king turned down the invitation to join, protesting that the entire royal retinue that accompanied the king would be too burdensome for Absalom.

Despite the king's turndown to take part in the festival, Absalom still asked that the king allow his brother Amnon to attend. David asked, "Why should he go with you?" (26b). But Absalom persisted it would be an enjoyable time for all, so David yielded to his persistence, thinking, "I suppose the Tamar stuff was two years in the past by now. The king felt that with the rest of Amnon's brothers there, that would be a sufficient cover for any potential uproar! So, all the king's sons attended the festive sheepshearing celebration, but it would turn out to end up on a macabre note!

Absalom certainly must have orchestrated what was to happen down to the minute, for his word to his men was this:

> "Listen! When Amnon is in high spirits from drinking wine and I say to you, 'Strike Amnon down,' then kill him. 'Don't be afraid. Have not I given you this order? Be strong and brave'" (28).

After Absalom gave the order, chaos erupted as David's sons panicked and quickly fled the festival grounds on their royal mules. It is hard to see how this would have helped Absalom's chances to ascend the throne of Israel, for he too now was a murderer, but he was not thinking of that.

Before the princes returned, David heard fake news that Absalom had killed all the king's sons, which was not true. Meanwhile, David's response to the news is better understood when considering his first reluctance to encourage Amnon's attendance at the festival. David stood fully upright, tore his clothes, and lay down on the ground, followed by his servants, who imitated his actions (31).

Once again, the narrative is interrupted by a man who has already had too big a hand in the shaping of these events, Jonadab (32). He is the son of Shimeah, one of David's brothers. His words of comfort were these:

> "My lord should not think they have killed all the princes; only Amnon is dead. This has been Absalom's expressed intention ever since the day Amnon raped his sister Tamar. My lord the king should not be concerned about the report that all the king's sons are dead. Only Amnon is dead" (32-33).

Did this mean that Jonadab was a co-conspirator with Absalom? Jonabad seems to know too much before the princes arrive with all the real news of the day. As Jonadab had assured, not all his sons were killed, but only Amnon (35). A watchman atop Jerusalem's walls reported seeing David's sons on the road toward Horonaim—a ridge road running east-west about 10–12 miles from Jerusalem, connecting Upper and Lower Horon, which the sons may have joined near Gibeon from the north.

In came the king's sons, "wailing loudly," along with the king and all his servants (36). In the meantime, Absalom fled to his mother's father, Talmai, king in the land of Geshur, where he self-quarantined for the next three years.

Joab Employs the Wise Woman of Tekoa – 14:1-20

Joab is the man behind this whole episode, for he knew that King David's heart and mind longed to see Absalom again, for he had been gone now for 3 years. Joab craftily set out to engage the talents of a "wise woman" from the town of Tekoa, a town on the edge of Israel's wild west and desert region, 10 miles south of Jerusalem, also the birthplace of the prophet Amos (Amos 1:1).

Joab directed the woman to present herself as mourning her son by wearing appropriate attire and refraining from using cosmetics for her meeting with the king (14:2). When the woman from Tekoa approached King David, she pleaded, "Help me, O king!"—using the Hebrew term *hoshi`nah*, the same word shouted as "Hosanna" on Palm Sunday (Matt. 21:9). David responded by asking, "What is troubling you?" "What to you?" (Heb. *mah-lak*). The woman began by telling the story that Joab had concocted that her husband was dead (5b). Now, left as a widow, she had only two sons in this world. But they got into a fight with each other out in a field, where there was no one to intervene, or to separate them (6). Thus, it happened, continued the Tekoite, that one struck the other, and killed his brother (6b). Then the whole clan rose up to demand that the murderer, should be handed over and put to death for striking his brother to death (7). If that happened, the Tekoite sobbed in her completely fabricated story, they will get rid of the heir as well, and the whole clan would have been successful in putting out the only burning coal left in her life, with the result that her deceased husband would be left without someone to bear his name in Israel, without a descendant on this earth! (7c-d).

David wanted to conclude this interview quickly, so he told the woman "Go home and I will issue an order on your behalf" (8). But this wise woman was not going to be brushed off so easily. To get the king to act more decisively and quickly, she confessed her own guilt saying, "Let the blame rest on me and on my father's family," but "let the king and his throne be without guilt" (9). The king still did not get the point she was driving at, for he volunteered to deal with anyone if they complained and made things rough for her. They just will not bother you again, once I am through with them, declared the king! (10).

Finally, this Tekoite woman came to the nub of what she was after in v. 11a. If the king is favorably disposed towards me and my case, "then let the king invoke the LORD his God to prevent the avenger of blood from adding to the destruction, so my son will not be destroyed." David simply responded, "not one hair of your son's head will fall to the ground (11b). That certainly should have settled the whole matter, for here was the head of the whole government pledging that every hair on her son's head would be protected.

With that assurance to her first request, the Tekoite woman is ready to make a second, so she asks permission to speak further (12), permission granted by David.

The woman from Tekoa boldly launched into the lines Joab had drafted for her. She addressed David directly, asking,

> "Why then have you devised a thing like this against the people of God? When the king says this, does he not convict himself, for the king has not brought back his banished son? Like water spilled on the ground, which cannot be recovered, so we must die. But God does not take away life; instead, he devises ways so that a banished person may not remain estranged from him (13-14).

Just as the Tekoite woman asked, that the fratricide of her remaining son not be punished, so on behalf of the people of Israel she was asking that the fratricide of Amnon not be punished by putting the punishment on Absalom! (13). She was not asking that in either of the two cases that the murderer be regarded as innocent or even granted a pardon and excused for his sin. But would it not be possible to took at the issue of suffering and hurt raised in their cases? She even implies that God himself will make a way for Absalom to return from Aram to Israel and that the one who had been banished would not remain banished or estranged from the LORD himself.

This wise woman constantly referred to herself as the king's "servant." The king will decide to deliver me, his servant, from the man who is trying to cut me off from my son and from the inheritance God gave to us (16).

By this time, the king is smelling a rat, for he urged the woman not to hide from him the answer to the question he was going to ask her: "Isn't the hand of Joab with you in all of this?" (19). The woman responded. She could not wiggle out of answering the king, for "Yes, it was Joab who instructed me to do this and who put all these words into the mouth of your servant" (19d). But Joab did this to change the situation for Absalom. Your wisdom, O king, is like the wisdom of an angel of God (20).

Joab Engineers Absalom's Return to Jerusalem – 14:21-33

The wise woman from Tekoa had recited quite a story for King David about the alleged circumstances of her two hypothetical sons. Whether Joab listened in from another room as she told the king her story or not cannot, she surely was the woman for the job. But now with Joab's constant pestering of the king to bring Absalom back to Israel from Gesher, David, finally conceded (14:21). Joab was so relieved that he fell on his face to the ground and blessed the king, saying that now he knew on that very day that he had found favor in the eyes of the king because the king had granted his request (22). The 3-year, self-imposed exile of Absalom at Geshur in Aram, had now ended and he was free to return to Jerusalem (23). However, Absalom was not welcome at the king's palace, so Absalom had to return to "his own house," near the palace precincts.

Surprisingly, though, all Israel seemed to rave over the good looks and handsome appearance of Absalom. This is not surprising since David had good looks, and his daughter Tamar was "beautiful." In fact, "From the top of [Absalom's] head to the sole of his foot there was no blemish in him" (25b). This led to his being "highly praised" (25). Whenever Absalom cut his hair, i.e., when it became too heavy for him, he would weigh it (a real sign of his vanity) and its weight would turn out to be "200 shekels by the royal standard" (26). The "royal standard" in Hebrew is literally "the stone of the king" (Hebrew, *'eben Hamelech*). Such stones of assorted sizes appear in archaeological excavations, where they were meticulously polished in antiquity and inscribed with various sets of weights.

Absalom became the father of three sons and a daughter, who he named Tamar after Absalom's sister, whom Amnon raped. But since 18:18 says that Absalom had no sons to continue his name, these three unnamed sons must have died prematurely.

Absalom lived two years in Jerusalem without seeing David's face. Despite Absalom's repeated attempts to get Joab to arrange such a meeting, nothing was happening. So, he decided to get Joab's attention by setting his field of barley on fire, which Absalom's servants did for him (30). Joab did go to Absalom's house, as this mischief-maker had guessed, with this question: "Why have your servants set my field on fire?" (31). Joab had a ready answer for him, for he complained that Joab repeatedly did not come to him when he summoned him to come (32). Absalom then complained, "Why have I come from Geshur? It would have been better for me if I were still there! Now I want to see the king's face, and if I am guilty of anything, let him put me to death" (32). So, Joab granted him his wish and when he saw King David, he bowed down to the ground and the king kissed him, I suppose out of royal protocol more than out of familial love. It was not a happy conclusion to a story filled with tragedy!

Conclusions

1. Amnon's sexual encounter with his sister Tamar illustrates how closely aligned both love and hate are in the same person, for as passionately as he loved her, in a swift moment of time he was just as passionate in his hatred of her. How could this be?
2. Amnon's refusal to heed Tamar's plea against sending her away from his house is even more reprehensible than the former act of rape, for it reveals the whole plot was all about his needs and his refusal to care for any of her concerns.
3. Absalom's slow burn of hatred over three years shows that he had not come to any kind of forgiveness or reconciliation with his brother. No wonder Yeshua taught that anger in the heart was just like murder.
4. Absalom arranged to have all the brothers and sisters present at the time that he would call for his brother's murder. Was he making a statement about his royal aspirations, hoping to get them on board his train?
5. Joab found a way to confront a royal superior with his failures in raising a family by using the wise woman of Tekoa.

Questions for Thought or Discussion

1. What do you think about the role of Amnon's "friend" named Jonadab (the son of David's brother Shimeah, no less) in his advice on the rape of Tamar? What sort of blame does he carry? Why is he still being used to give advice later when David wants to know if all his children have been killed at the festival of sheepshearing?
2. Was David so handicapped because of his own sin with Bathsheba that he did not go the short distance to the King of Geshur to chastise Absalom?
3. What quality attributes, of David, if any fell on the king's sons except his good looks? Why do you think that is so?
4. Was Joab's use of the wise woman of Tekoa a good move on his part to confront the king?
5. Was Absalom justified in burning the barley field of Joab to get his attention? Is any part of the Mosaic law involved here?

Lesson 7

Absalom's Conspiracy Against David's Reign

2 Samuel 15:1-37; Psalm 3:1-8

Our narrative opens with the words: "In the course of time," which phrase is rare in Hebrew. It served, nevertheless, to move the narrative forward (15:1). But that introductory formula is followed right away with the next move in the story: "Absalom provided himself with a chariot and horses and with fifty men to run ahead of him." (1b). Absalom was not only showing off a bit of his style and presumed prestige, but he was also showing flash and was ready to present the world with the gift they had been missing. He would not only show he was more than available to hear the complaints of his fellow countrymen, but he wanted also to ingratiate himself to the people so that in their frustration with King David's government, there was a ready substitute available: it was him! Thus, the fifty men who ran interference for him in front of his chariot paraded forth the trappings of royalty in the making! Absalom presented one huge ego-act of super overconfidence and a readiness to replace the present government.

Absalom's Conspiracy Gets Under Way – 15:1-12

People in David's kingdom were clearly unhappy with his rule over Jerusalem. Absalom had decided that this was the weak point in David's rule he was waiting for, so Absalom would get up early each morning and station himself by the side of the road that led into the gates of the city of Jerusalem. Whenever he saw someone whom he suspected was coming to the capital city to complain to King David, Absalom would call out to this citizen, "What town are you from?" This is the kind of question that one who is superior might ask one he had never met before, to start a conversation.

When the person who had been addressed responded that he was from one of the tribes in Israel (2), Absalom would continue the conversation at once by presuming that he was a plaintiff with a grievance he wished to bring before the king. But instead of encouraging this citizen into seeking relief from the king, Absalom would undermine the king's authority and effectiveness by bemoaning with him that there was no representative of the king to hear his claims, even if they were true and valid (3). Then Absalom would deviously add, "if only I were appointed judge in the land![1] Then everyone who has a complaint, or a case, could come to me and I would see that he got justice" (4). Talk about *chutzpah*! This kid had the nerves of a brass monkey. He was openly fomenting a rebellion against his own father. Didn't David get even a hint that such underhanded activity was going on? What kind of upbringing must Absalom had – or rather, did not have? Shouldn't David have nipped this in the bud? Or was David incapable of doing any correction or offering any rebuking?

But Absalom had some more tricks up his sleeve, for when anyone approached him, he would reach out his hand and take hold of him and kiss him (5). This guy really wanted to be king in a bad way, so he did everything he could to win the approval of the populace. Absalom would intercept anyone on his way to seek justice from the king, and in this way, he stole all the hearts of the men of Israel (6).

Had something gone so wrong with David's government that Absalom's words would carry a ring of authenticity? Psalm 3 can supply us with a little bit of the background. This Psalm is attributed to David during his flight from Absalom. That Psalm begins by saying that David faced a considerable number of insurrectionists:

> "O LORD, how many are my foes!
> How many rise up against me!
> Many are saying of me,
> God will not deliver him. Selah!" (1-2).

People believed that God would not deliver David because he took another man's wife, Bathsheba, and arranged for her husband, Uriah, to be killed—mirroring the poor man's lamb in Nathan's rebuke. That was the reason David's government was slipping from his hands. The rumor must have gotten around so he was no longer seen as "Mr. Clean!"

---

1. Ronald F. Youngblood in his *Expositor's Bible Commentary* on 2 Samuel, *ibid.*, (pp..492-93) pointed to a clear Ugaritic parallel of the tactic of a son usurping power from his father. Here prince Yassib challenges King Kret to "Let me sit on your throne," [since] your illness has made you derelict and unable to hear the case of the widow, the poor, the orphan.... Step down from your kingship, Allow me to reign. Relinquish your power."

However, David knew that the Lord would forgive him of his sin, even though he was leaving Jerusalem not in a kingly style, but rather barefoot, head covered and weeping (2 Sam. 15:30). But the LORD would be a shield around David, and God would answer from his holy hill (Ps. 3:3-4). So, let the ten thousand rebels revolt against David, but the LORD will still sustain him (Ps. 3:5-6). The number of persons revolting against David will be nothing in comparison to the LORD's rising up on his behalf (Ps. 3:7). God will humiliate his enemies by striking them on the jaw and breaking their teeth (Ps. 3:7-8).

Absalom waited for four years before he began to put his plan into action (7). He began by asking his father David for permission to go to Hebron to fulfill a vow he had made to the LORD while he was still in Geshur of Aram. He explained to his father that he had promised to the LORD, that if he ever took him back to Jerusalem, he would worship the LORD in Hebron (8). But the reader can be assured that Absalom knew full-well that Hebron had been the place where David had been anointed as king over Judah. It is possible that Absalom used his three years in Geshu to build substantial support.

The king believed what Absalom had told him, for David seeming once again to be over-indulgent with his children, gave his permission, "Go in peace." So off went Absalom to Hebron, but he went fully bent on introducing mischief to his father and the government of Israel.

Absalom sprang into action at once. He sent "secret Messengers Throughout the tribes of Israel to say, 'As soon as you hear trumpets, then say, "Absalom is king in Hebron."'" Two hundred men, who had been invited as guests of Absalom, all were from Jerusalem, and had gone down to Hebron with Absalom. However, they had no idea what was happening, or why they had been invited. Meanwhile, Absalom was offering sacrifices, and he had also sent for David's counselor named Ahithophel to join him in Hebron. Ahithophel means "my brother is foolish." If it is asked, why was Ahithophel, who was such a valuable part of the Davidic governmental team, should be deserting David to join David's son's rebellion, the answer may lie in the fact that Bathsheba's father was "Eliam," which happens to be the same name as Ahithophel's son. It would make sense, then, if Bathsheba's grandfather was Ahithophel, that he would have been an enemy of David for David's part in arranging for the death of his granddaughter's husband, Uriah!

David is Forced to Flee Jerusalem – 15:13-37

By now it is clear that Absalom has had enormous success in winning over the hearts of the people to his way of thinking (13). Therefore, David sensing the enormity of what was happening, issued the orders to all his officials that they must leave Jerusalem in haste. In fact, if they do not act swiftly, Absalom will overtake them, and ruin will come to all of them, and to the city of Jerusalem (14). King David sees no other choice than to flee the city (14). So, the officials of David's court, who were as loyal to a fault, were ready to act on the plan the king chooses (15).

David's entire household followed his lead and left Jerusalem with him. David, however, appointed ten of his concubines to take care of the palace, so they stayed there (16). David halted the retreat momentarily as all his men marched past him in review, including his special secret police that protected him. They consisted of the Kerethites and Pelethites, and the 600 Gittites who had come to follow David, men and families who were from the Philistine town of Gath (18).

The king told one of his high officials, who led this corps of foreign mercenaries, named "Ittai the Gittite," that he should not bother coming along with David; instead, he should return and go back to stay with Absalom in the capital city of Jerusalem (19). As David argued his case with Ittai, this loyal friend had nothing to gain and everything to lose by staying with David. Ittai, David reasons, is already abroad from his base in the Philistine city of Gath. Moreover, he had just arrived to help David only yesterday, so David is embarrassed to make Ittai wander about in the desert for who knows how long. That was no way to treat a guest (20). David wished him "kindness and faithfulness" as his portion, but he should leave (20c). But Ittai would not be put off so easily, for he replied to David's entreats, "As surely as the LORD lives, and as my lord the king lives, wherever my lord the king may be, whether it means life or death, there will your servant be" (21). Wow! Here was a soldier of the first rank, for he was ready to face unflinchingly anything that was in the future for David. He was determined to stick with David come whatever may. Therefore, David conceded the argument and told Ittai to "Go ahead and march on" (22). And that is exactly what Ittai did with all his men and the families that were with him (22b).

If David had lost popularity with the urban crowd in Israel, he seems to still have kept it with the folks in the countryside, for as he and his retinue passed by in their retreat from Jerusalem, the people wept. At this point, however, David had a change of mind, for Zadok the High Priest and all the Levites who were with him carrying the ark of the covenant of God (which had been set down as Abiathar the priest offered sacrifices until all the people had completed the line of march away from the city), were instructed to take the ark and go back to the city of Jerusalem (25). David urged that if he found favor in God's eyes, he would see the ark and the dwelling place of the LORD again; but if the LORD was not pleased with David, then David was ready for whatever the LORD had (26).

David also reminded Zadok that he as priest was likewise a "seer," meaning a "prophet" (see 1 Sam. 9:9), so if that was so, then Zadok and Abiathar should take their two sons named Ahimaaz and Jonathan, and go back to the city to learn what they could discover, and David would wait at the fords of the River Jordan to bring word of what was going on to David (27-29). Thus, the ark returned to Jerusalem along with Zadok and Abiathar, the priests.

David and those with him continued up the Mount of Olives weeping as they went. David's head was covered, and he walked barefoot over the Mount of Olives (30). Ronald Youngblood [2] recalled the famous line from William Shakespeare (*King Henry* IV, part 2, 3.1.31, "Uneasy lies the head that wears a crown," which clearly fitted David's head at the moment.

At the summit of the Mount of Olives, where people once worshipped, Hushai the Arkite met David as he fled the city, his robe torn and dust on his head (32). Hushai's clan called the Arkites lived near Ataroth, in northeast Ephraim on the border of Manasseh. But as was the case with Zadok and Abiathar, David once again argued the case with Hushai that he would be more valuable to him if he too would return to the city of Jerusalem and promise to Absalom the same kind of service Hushai had given to David as one of his counselors (34). If he could win the confidence of Absalom as part of his inner counsel, then his main objective in being on that counsel would be to frustrate and oppose any advice Ahithophel would give to Absalom, for when that man spoke, so accurate and valuable was his advice that it was like an angel speaking.

Then if Hushai was successful, he was to tell what he had learned to Zadok and Abiathar, whose two sons, Ahimaaz and Jonathan, would then bring to David that word (36). So, Hushai went off to Jerusalem on his new royal assignment!

---

2. Ronald F. Youngblood, The Expositor's Bible Commentary, Ibid, p. 500.

Conclusions

1. David's number three child, Absalom, worked hard to gain the confidence of the people so he could be their king. He pretended that he would listen to their complains and get them better and quicker justice. Something seems to have happened in David's reign!
2. Absalom stole the hearts of the people from his father David. How is that possible with as famous and appreciated a man as David was?
3. Absalom got the ear and confidence of Ahithophel the Gilonite, presumably because Ahithophel was Bathsheba's grandfather.
4. The 600 Gittites were from the Philistine town of Gath. They and their leader Ittai were loyal to David. How did that alliance form?
5. David had the confidence of the countryside while Absalom had the urban city vote for his venture.

Questions for Thought or Discussion

1. Why do you think David did not rebuke or chastise his children? How could a man be so good at leading a country and yet fail with his own family?
2. Why do you think that Absalom thought he might be successful in overthrowing the government of his father? How much did his sin with Bathsheba and Uriah figure into this picture? Why did Absalom think the people would not remember his murder of his brother Amnon if he and his father were both being evaluated by the people for kingship on the scale of righteous living?
3. Which ones of David's official team was Absalom able to draw away to his side and why?
4. How was David able to attract 600 fighting men from the city of Gath along with their leader Ittai? Were these Philistines believers?

Lesson 8

Assessing David's Enemies and Judging Royal Advice

2 Samuel 16:1-25; 17:1-23

2 Samuel 15:13-37 concluded its anticipation of the overthrow of David's government by depicting three of David's friends: Ittai, Zadok and Hushai. Chapter 16, however, focuses on three of David's enemies: Ziba, Shimei, and Ahithophel.

It is important to keep in mind that the man David's enemies are opposing is no one other than the anointed king of Yahweh named David. The LORD chose this man David as king over all Israel, therefore any opposition or rebellion against that anointed man was an open rebellion against Yahweh himself and his kingdom. Absalom was dead wrong in thinking that his coup was the only way he could rally the people in favor of getting needed refinements. True, David was under God's judgment for his sin with Bathsheba, yet he stayed as Yahweh's anointed choice as king until God said otherwise. Consequently, all attempts to oppose him, depose him, or betray him were simultaneously an attempt to oppose, despise and betray the very LORD himself, the One who had placed David where he was as king over Israel. This thinking must be the solid background against which we must now view this attempted coup by David's son.

Zeba the Manipulator – 16:1-4

As David and his followers crested the Mount of Olives, they were met by the steward of Saul's grandson Mephibosheth named Zeba. It may seem strange for us to label this man as one of David's enemies, especially since he arrived with him a string of donkeys, loaded down with 200 loaves of bread, 100 cakes of raisins, 100 cakes of figs, and a skin of wine (16:1). But despite this demonstration of loyalty to David, yet Zeba will lie bold-facedly that the man he servant to, Mephibosheth, was hoping that as part of Absalom's rebellion, the former kingship over Israel of his grandfather Saul would revert to him, i.e. to Absalom (3b).

But Zeba's story does not hold up if one thinks about it carefully. In fact, later, Mephibosheth will give an altogether different story in 2 Samuel 19:24-30 for this same episode. Since Mephibosheth was not present for David to check or verify Zeba's story for authenticity, David accepted it at face value. David did ask, skeptically, however, "where is Mephibosheth?" (3). That is when Zeba gave his cooked-up story about Mephibosheth's desire to stay in Jerusalem on the excuse that the kingdom of Saul might be given to him. But that was all a lie and utterly ridiculous, for why would a son of David want to transfer the kingship back to any in the line of Saul?

But think for a moment: How would the rebellion of David's son Absalom give rise to any descendant of Saul gaining from this overthrow of David? Zeba was boldly working the sympathy angle from David to feather his own nest. He was trying to blacken the reputation of Mephibosheth while he made an impression for himself. What a fake! What a demonstration of Zeba's true colors - that will come out as he and his men did later in a future incident when they stayed behind David and stayed on the farm (19:17-18). He was a real manipulator, one who was trying to get as much as he could for himself.

Shimei the Cursing Rebel – 16:5-14

David and his growing group of followers continued their flight east of Jerusalem, until they came to a place called Bahurim, where they ran into a most violent man named Shimei, son of Gera, one of the descendants of King Saul's family. He proceeded to pelt David and his entourage with abuse, stones, dirt and whatever else he could get his hands on. Shimei must have been walking alongside David's group on a parallel hill, from which he could aim his projectiles at the royal entourage to his advantage and satisfaction (13). However, to protect David, all his troops and his special guard marched along on the right and left sides of David.

Shimei was filled with a ton of rage and hate, for as he went along throwing anything he could at David and his company, he yelled, "Get out, get out you man of blood, you scoundrel" (7). Shimei scoffed,

> "The LORD has repaid you for all the blood you shed in the household of Saul, in whose place you have reigned. The LORD has handed the kingdom over to your son Absalom. You have come to ruin because you are a man of blood" (8).

Didn't Shimei know that to curse a descendant of Abraham was a sure way to invite retribution from God (Gen. 12:3). We know from reading ahead in the story that what Shimei did, in fact, was to get his punishment (1 Kings 2:8-9) even though he repented later of what he had said at this time (19:18-20). The remarkable fact, however, is that David had in an earlier context denied he had anything to do with the blood of Abner (3:28). Moreover, it was Saul's house that had stained its hands with blood and not David's hands as Shimei claimed. It is difficult to rectify a rumor once it has been started, even though the facts may clearly be against the accusations being made! And what about the theology that will be spelled out in Romans 13 that the authorities are all ordained of God, so opposition to those who are already in government is direct opposition to God.

At this point, Abishai, son Zeruiah, wanted to put a quick end to Shimei and make an example of him as someone who was just part of the ordinary, trashy, common, lowlife. He begged David, "Let me go over [to the parallel hill] and cut off his head" (9). Abishai thought David and his company had enough on their mind, so they certainly did not need this guy's cursing to add to it. Abishai also reasoned in part:" People without heads do not curse!" That would end Shimei's trash and filthy talk. But David would have none of such actions (10), for according to his rationale, Shimei was cursing this company because Yahweh had allowed him to curse David, so there was no other basis for asking why he was doing that.

So, Abishai was ordered by David, "Leave him alone, ... For Yahweh has ordered him" (11). Therefore, Abishai had to cool his heels and sword while he let Shimei spit out his venom, for it could also happen that the LORD would look on David's iniquity and one day he would return good to him in place of Shimei's cursing (12).

Dale Ralph Davis comments as follows:

> Here in 16:12 is the secret of David's peace. Not in having Shimei's head on a platter, but in this astounding statement: 'It may be that Yahweh will look upon my iniquity and return good to me.' Let that sink into your gray matter. David had a deep-seated confidence in a God of unguessable grace, who tends to replace cursing with goodness! He assumes that Yahweh has this strangely wonderful way of looking upon guilt and yet returning blessing instead of curse. He senses that though the mouth of God has declared his punishment (12:10-12), the eye of God may long to spare him from it.[1]

---

1. Dale Ralph Davis, *Expositions on the Book of 2 Samuel: Out of Every Adversity,* Believer Focus, Ross-Shire, Scotland, 1999, p. 167,

How does David even think for one moment that such a gift from God is possible considering what he had done to Bathsheba and Uriah? Even though David is not certain this is so, for he says, "It may be," still he could never have come up with this concept unless he had found it in the character of his God! There certainly must have been quite a shared fellowship and real compassion between the LORD and his servant David to have thought this way! David hoped that the LORD might look on his iniquity and return to him his divine goodness instead of his royal curse!

Meanwhile Shimei continues the rage of his anger and hate against David and his government. Eventually, however, the king arrived at his destination, exhausted but still alive. There David refreshed himself (13-14).

Ahithophel the Betrayer – 16:15-22

Ahithophel is one of the turn-coat men in David's cabinet, for on earlier occasions, when he gave David advice, that advice was as if someone had made an inquiry of God, or an angel himself (16:23). But he decided he did not want to work for David any longer. It may be that his granddaughter was Bathsheba, and if that is so, though we are not 100 % sure, then he had a solid reason for wanting to get out of David's advisory council.

In the meantime, Hushai had gone back to Absalom and there he had pledged his loyalty to David's son Absalom instead of to David (16:15). Absalom was completely taken in by Hushai's deceptive loyalty, even after he asked Hushai why he had left his allegiance to his friend David. Hushai gives the response which Absalom thinks applies to him, but it is exactly the reason Hushai is devoted to David: "[The king is] the one chosen by the LORD, by these people and by all the men of Israel" (18). Hushai was ready, at least in this wartime setting of deception from his son, to serve David's son just like he had served David!

Now it was time for learning what advice these two men would give to Absalom (20). Ahithophel was to the first to offer his advice:

> "Lie with your father's concubines whom he left to take care of the place. Then all Israel will hear that you have made yourself a stench in your father's nostrils, and the hands of everyone with you will be strengthened" (21).

That was the advice Ahithophel gave, so faithful to his counsel, they pitched a tent (like a wedding *huppah*?) for Absalom on the roof and then in sight of all Israel, Absalom lay with his father's concubines. There would be no turning back now, for Absalom had cast his lot and what had been done had been done!

The Dual Advice of Two Royal Counselors – 16:23 -17:23

There was little doubt in anyone's mind that the advice of Ahithophel was so good that it was as if someone had asked the LORD himself for advice! (16:23). On this point, both David and Absalom were agreed – Ahithophel was good in giving advice.

But when Ahithophel gave his second piece of advice, he was tactically as good as any general in battle strategy. His advice was this: he told Absalom that he had no time to waste. He should at once choose 12,000 men [did he mean a 1000 from each of the 12 tribes?] and set out to attack David that very night while David was still weary and weak from all he had been through that day (17:1). His plan called for all David's men to leave him and to flee from the king so that the king could be taken by himself alone (2). Once Absalom had the old king out of the picture, then the new king could bring back all the people with the new king leading them! Strike down David alone and all the people, now unharmed, will come over to Absalom's side and way of thinking (3). That plan sounded like the right way to go according to Absalom and the elders of Israel (4).

However, Hushai had just arrived promising loyalty to "the one chosen by the LORD and by all the men of Israel." He carefully avoided attaching any name, such as Absalom's or David's, to his oath of endearment; that way he could double-speak with integrity! When Hushai was told what the advice of Ahithophel was, he had the courage to say, "The advice Ahithophel has given is not good this time" (7). Then Hushai went into a sales-pitch that was full of blustery talk and ego-enhancing exaggerations suited to puff up Absalom's macho-self. Hushai reminded Absalom and his elders that David was a fighting man *par excellence* (8). Moreover, he would not spend the night with his troops, but he will hide in a cave or another place (9). But how could Hushai be sure about that social distancing of Absalom's father from the troops, except that that was the very point which was essential for the success of Ahithophel's plan. Hushai went on with his speech to derail his fellow advisor's wise counsel by depicting a great slaughter among the troops, so that a rumor could get out that Absalom had suffered an enormous slaughter. That would finish any of the rebel's chances for the future, for even the bravest of any of the soldiers would evaporate with fear, for the reputation of David will make everyone assume that he was the one who has triumphed and you, Absalom, will be out of luck (9-10).

To top this whole flamboyant bit of bravado spinning of the future, Hushai ends on a triumphant note. First, let all Israel, from one end of the country to the other, from Dan to Beersheba, be gathered to you and you lead them into battle. Then, go and attack that elderly warrior, wherever he may be found, so that you and your men may fall on him like the dew covers the ground. Should David choose to retreat to a city, then all Israel will bring ropes and together they will pull on those ropes until they all drag that old city right off its foundation and right down in total collapse into the valley, so that not even two scraps of it will ever be found together (12-13).

That kind of talk massaged Absalom's ego just the right way! Absalom and all the men of Israel cheered the good advice of Hushai, but what he had done was this: he had played to the vanity and ineptitude of the rebellious son and his men.

Now the task was to get this word to David without being discovered. Hushai, as previously planned, got the word of these two separate and different pieces of advice to Zadok and Abiathar, the priests, who in turn gave it to a servant girl, who transferred this advice to Jonathan and Ahimaaz, the sons of the two priests, who were staying at En Rogel. The important part of the message was that David and his entourage were not to stay that night at the fords in the desert; instead, they were warned to cross over the river Jordan at once, or the king and his men would surely be swallowed up (16).

However, an unplanned catch in the whole plan threatened to unravel the whole scheme, for a young man loyal to Absalom, happened to see these two young messengers, even though the two men had stayed out of the city of Jerusalem. This young man went and told Absalom what he had seen, but just as quickly the two men rapidly went to the house of a man in Bahurim. But this home in Bahurim also had a well in the courtyard, so the two of them climbed into the well and the man's wife put a covering over the well and scattered seed or grain over the top of the covering (18-19).

When Absalom's men arrived, they asked the woman of the house had she seen these two men and she answered that they had already crossed over the brook. The men did further search, but they found nothing (20). After the men had left, the two men, Jonathan and Ahimaaz, climbed out of the well and were off to tell David these valuable pieces of information (21). They stressed the point that David must cross over the river without delay, which is exactly what David and all his men did (21-22). By daybreak, David and all his people had crossed over the Jordan River. No one was left back at the fords.

When Ahithophel learned that his advice had not been heeded, he saddled up his donkey and set out for his house in his hometown, where he put his house in order and then hanged himself. He died and was buried in his father's tomb (23). He had no need of hanging around (pun intended) to see what was going to happen, for he knew; that is why he advised Absalom the way he did. But from this one piece of information, he could tell: Absalom was a loser and his bid for the kingship would come to naught!

Conclusions

1. Zeba was trying his best to get as much for himself as he could. Therefore, he outrightly lied to David about Mephibosheth.
2. Shimei is a member of Saul's family line who had not gotten his facts straight about the relationship between Saul's government and David, so he repeated the lies he had heard and cursed David freely.
3. Hushai the counselor to the king was careful in his praise of the king to leave off the name of the person he meant to be the object of his praise.
4. Ahithophel gave the best advice to make sure Absalom would become king, but Hushai countered that reasonable plan by stroking Absalom's desire for having his ego massaged and therefore he countered a perfectly good plan to protect David.

Questions for Thought or Discussion

1. What is the danger in a Believer fomenting open rebellion against the government that has been set up in a country legally? Does this take place among Believers today?
2. When Zeba, Shimei, and Ahithophel rebelled against the duly established government, were they also directly opposing God himself (cf. Romans 13:1-4)? How can that be when governments are evil and wicked themselves?
3. Was David correct in quickly assigning everything that had been deeded to Mephibosheth over to Zeba, especially when he lied about what had happened back at the palace? What should David have done in this case?
4. Was Ahithophel acting on good Biblical grounds when he committed suicide when he saw he had backed the wrong man?
5. How can a Believer show obedience to a government while still reserving the right to critique that government on those areas where the government does not act ethically and justly?

Lesson 9

Absalom's Death and David's Mourning for Him

2 Samuel 17:24-29; 18:1-33; 19:1-8a

David and his troops had crossed the Jordan River (17:22), thereby staying just one step ahead of their enemy army, as they came to the site of Mahanaim, which had been the earlier headquarters of David's rival, Ish-Bosheth. Mahanaim was seven miles from the Jordan River. By this time, Absalom had made an appointment to lead his army, a man named Amasa, in place of Joab.

Amasa's father was Jether, the real name for Nabal, and his mother was Abigail, Nahash's daughter. Amasa appears to have been a relative of Joab and of David as well.

When David arrived in Mahanaim, he was befriended by three friends who had come to help him. There was first Shobi, the Ammonite, from Rabbah; then there was Makir, the son of Ammiel from LoDebar (who had provided haven for Mephibosheth); and finally, there was the octogenarian, Barzillai, meaning "iron man." These men arrived with an impressive number of provisions: beds, basins, pottery ware, wheat, barley, flour, parched grain, beans, lentils, honey, curds, sheep, and cheese from cow's milk. They did all of this because they said, "the people are hungry and tired and thirsty in the wilderness" (17:29b).

In the view of these three men, Israel's king was in place as part of God's covenant, hence they were not free to abandon him. As far as they were concerned, God was in heaven, and his kingdom would continue to stand despite the worse of tragedies that could befall them as mortals!

David's Friends and Supporters Show Up – 17:24-29

In 2 Samuel 16:23, David's counselor Ahithopohel had been described in laudatory terms. His term of service was one that was marked by enormous amount of brilliance, and his advice was altogether dependable and on the mark. But when Ahithophel decided to join the coup of Absalom for some unnamed reason, he realized all too quickly that his advice was not being followed and Hushai's advice, which was being adopted, would not result in the death of David, but instead it would mean the man he had backed was doomed. So off he went to his city of Giloh, his hometown, where he hung himself in suicide and was buried in his father's tomb (23).

But as we have already mentioned in the introduction, David was royally aided by three friends who did not assess things as Ahithophel had sized up his world. They were the source of refreshment and encouragement to the man God had chosen to lead them.

David Organizes the Troops with Him – 18:1-5

Now that David had a moment when he could get his thoughts together, he mustered the men who had followed him out of Jerusalem along with those he had picked up along the way. His first task was to appoint commanders over thousands and commanders over hundreds. Therefore, David put a third of the troops under Joab, another third of the troops he put under Joab's brother Abishai, the son of Zeruiah, and the final third of the men he put under Ittai the Gittite (18:2).

When David informed the men that he too would march out with them, they strongly protested and warned him that he must not go into battle with them. No one would care if up to half of their men perished in the battle, but David was easily worth ten thousand of them. No, he had better go back to the city and give them support from that base (3). So, the king yielded to their objections.

Thus, king David stood beside the gate of the city as the men marched out in units of hundreds and thousands (4). David, however, gave a final order to all three of his commanders that they were to be 'gentle" with the boy (5).

The Battle Between David and Absalom's Armies – 18:6-9

But then everything goes wrong in this battle. First, David made a request of his three commanders that was altogether unrealistic (5), for that is why it was so ruthlessly ignored (14-15). Add to that Israel's poster boy, with his good looks and full head of hair gets trapped in a most embarrassing way (9), and then they toss his body into a pit and pile a heap of stones on it to form a most undignified monument ever erected for the son of a king (17). Finally, Joab's intent that the Cushite be the runner who reaches David first with the bad news that his son has died is in this instance eclipsed by Ahimaaz who took the more circuitous route, but one in which he was able to outdistance the Cushite and reach David first (19-32).

We are given extraordinarily little if any description of the battle and the way the fighting went ahead. Verses 6-8 have an extremely brief synopsis of the battle, but it does place most of its focus in ten verses (9-18) on Absalom's inadvertent encounter with David's troops. The writer has no interest in telling us what happened in the battle; no, he wants to tell us what happened to Absalom.

However, we are told that the battle spread out over the whole countryside (8), yet the heart of it must have taken place in the "Forest of Ephraim" (6b). The army of Absalom was defeated by David's troops and there were an enormous number of casualties on that day—20,000 men (7). The forest, however, claimed more lives than the sword! (7b). Normally we would have expected a site named the "Forest of Ephraim" to be on the west side of the Jordan River, but we are also told that there were Ephraimites who settled in Gilead (cf. Judg. 12:4).

The Death of Absalom – 18:9-18

Absalom, now riding through the "Forest of Ephraim" astride his royal mule got his head caught in the tangle of low lying thick branches (9) Perhaps he had been looking back to see if he was being chased by anyone when his celebrated full head of hair was caught by some beautifully spread out branches, only to have his mule moving forward, once he was caught, without Absalom as his rider. Thus, in this way, as Absalom lost not only his mule, but he also lost his planned kingdom. If God is in control, how could the disaster have been unplanned? There Absalom hung in midair, without any support, which would now be true! He had abandoned the man God had appointed as king; now he too would be abandoned without any support hanging between heaven and earth!

One of David's soldiers saw what had happened and told Joab this news: "I just saw Absalom hanging in an oak tree" (10). Joab could not believe his ears. "What!" he cried out, "You saw him [hanging there]? Why didn't you strike him to the ground right there?" Joab went on to say he would have rewarded this man, but the man declared that he would not have done that even for 1000 shekels, for "In our hearing the king ordered you three commanders: you, and Abishai, and Ittai, 'Protect the young man Absalom for my sake.'" (12). The soldier was not going to put his life in jeopardy – anyway, nothing is hidden from the king and you Joab would have kept your distance from me (13).

Joab had had enough of all this talking, for he was eager to get this whole affair over with, so he decided to take things into his own hands and go out after Absalom by himself. He grabbed three javelins and went off to see where Absalom remained swinging in the air – a terrible position for a man about to become a king to find himself in! When Joab got to the site, he plunged the three weapons into Absalom's heart while he was still alive swinging in the oak tree. The ten armor-bearers of Joab surrounded Absalom, struck him down and killed him (14-15).

Joab then sounded the trumpet, and the troops ceased fighting and pursuing Israel, for Joab had stopped all such activities (16). The men took the corpse of Absalom and threw him into a huge pit in the forest and piled up an enormous number of rocks over Absalom and his instant grave and memorial!

During his lifetime, Absalom had taken a pillar and erected it as a monument for himself in the king's valley, which he named after himself. It is called "Absalom's Monument" to this day. There is, however, a 52-foot high, bottle-shaped monument cut out of the cliff in the Kidron Valley east of Jerusalem, but it is incorrectly named "the Pillar of Absalom," and incorrectly named.

David's Mourning for Absalom – 18:19-19:8a

Ahimaaz son of Zadok, who was known for his athletic skills, pleaded with Joab to be allowed to "run and take the news to the king that the LORD has delivered him from the hand of his enemies" (19). Joab, however, refused to allow Ahimaaz to carry the news to David, who had been forced by the troops to remain behind in the city of Mahanaim, where he was now staying. Joab did not feel that Ahimaaz was the right man to deliver the news (20). Ahimaaz could run with the news at another time, but today was not the day, argued Joab (20).

Joab then called a Cushite and instructed him, "Go, tell the king what you have seen" (21). With that the Cushite bowed down before Joab and then off he went. Ahimaaz still was not deterred in his aspirations to run with the news, so he asked if he could run behind the Cushite (22). Joab was not convinced that this was the right job for him, so he asked "My son, why do you want to go? You don't have any news that will bring you a reward" (22b). But Ahimaaz was unassuaged. He still wanted to run! (23). So finally, Joab said, "Run!"

Off ran Ahimaaz, but he took a different route than the Cushite. Even though Ahimaaz's route was less direct than the one chosen by the Cushite, Ahimaaz's route was along level ground, even though it was a mile or two longer. This enabled Ahimaaz to get to Mahanaim first, for he had gone by way of the plain instead of the forest and therefore he was technically able to outrun the Cushite.

Meanwhile David the king was sitting between the inner and outer gates of city of Mahanaim, where a watchman was up on the roof of the gateway calling out to the gate keeper what he saw. When the watchman saw a man running along, he called out to the gate keeper what he had just seen. The king shouted to his watchman that "If he is alone, he must have good news" (25b). His thinking must have been so set on good news that David was willing to psych himself into believing it. But then the watchman reported that he saw another man running, so once again the watchman called down to the gatekeeper, who gave the message to David who was seated nearby with the message: "Look, another man is running alone!" (26).

The watchman recognized the running style of Ahimaaz. King David, however, still filled with optimism, announced for the third time, "He's a good man," which he said once again after he was told that the first man was Ahimaaz son of Zadok (27). When Ahimaaz arrived, he greeted the king with the words, "All is well," as he bowed down before the king (28).

Then he added, "Praise be to the LORD your God! He has delivered up the men who lifted their hands against my lord the king."

But David was so fixed on one question and one only that he asked again: "Is the young man Absalom safe?" Now that was a question Ahimaaz was unable to answer. The only thing he could say was: "I saw great confusion just as Joab was about to send the king's servant and me, your servant, but I don't know what it was" (29). That did not satisfy the king, so he told him to stand down and wait there. For now, it was time for the Cushite to arrive. He began his report this way: "My lord the king, hear the good news! The LORD has delivered you today from all who rose up against you" (31). But it was as if the king were tone-deaf and unable to grasp what was being told him, for he asked the Cushite the same question he had asked Ahimaaz: "Is the young man Absalom safe?" (32).

The Cushite responded again with these words this time: "May the enemies of my lord the king and all who rise up to harm you be like that young man" (32b). That did it; the king finally grasped the message, then he was badly shaken and went up to his room over the gateway and wept. As he ascended the stairs, he cried, "O my son Absalom! My son Absalom! If only I had died instead of you – O Absalom, my son, my son!" (33).

It was time for Joab to swing into action, for if he did not do something soon, Israel was headed for a worse disaster than the one that had just been averted. Joab was told that the king was weeping and mourning for Absalom. This conduct on the part of the king had such a harmful effect the troops that the victory of the army was turned upside down as the men heard that "the king is grieving for his son" (19:2). As a result, the men stole away into the city in the way that men do when they are so ashamed when they flee in the face of battle. The king covered his face and kept crying out and wailing about "O my son Absalom! O Absalom, my son, my son! (19:4).

Joab decided he had to act quickly, so he went into the house where the king was. Joab began by excoriating the king with these words:

> "Today you have humiliated all your men, who have just saved your life and the lives of your sons and daughters and the lives of your wives and concubines. You love those who hate you and hate those who love you. You have made it clear today that the commanders and their men

> mean nothing to you. I see you would be pleased if Absalom were alive today and all of us were dead. Now go out and encourage your men. I swear by the LORD that if you don't go out, not a man will be left with you by nightfall. This will be worse for you than all the calamities that have come upon you from your youth till now" (19:5-7).

So, David decided he had better go down and take his seat in the gateway. When he did so, and the men in his army were told he was now sitting in the gateway, they all came before him (19:8a). The day was saved for David and the army!

Conclusions

1. David had a natural affection for his son Absalom, but there surely was a deeper dimension to his sorrow. The prophet Nathan had told him that "the sword will not depart from your house forever" (12:10), and it had not, for his infant son from his adultery died (12:19), his son Amnon was murdered (13:), and now Absalom was killed. David's sin had let loose the sword on his household. But wasn't he forgiven? Then why this mischief?
2. When David arrived on the east side of the Jordan River at the city of Mahanaim, he was met by three friends, the Ammonite Shobi, Makir from Ammiel, and the octogenarian Barzillai. They brought an enormous amount of provisions to refresh the party after their flight from Jerusalem, which shows the value of friends.
3. David organized those who had fled with him appointing commanders over thousands and others over hundreds.
4. Tears of regret when calamity arrives hardly compensate for years of teaching and raising a family that is not trained in all the ways of the LORD.

Questions for Thought or Discussion

1. What is the difference between shedding tears for suffering unexpected guilt and anguish and shedding tears over missed opportunities to train up children in the way they should go?
2. Would the advice of Ahithophel have worked and Absalom would have been king had it been followed? Why was Hushai's advice heeded and Ahithophel's rejected?
3. Why do you think David's key staff abandoned him? Were they right in the stand they were taking?
4. Why does Scripture spend so much time over whether Ahimaaz or the Cushite should bring the news to David of the outcome of the battle?
5. Had David humiliated the army by his mourning so effusively over his son Absalom? Would he have presented an opportunity for an even greater tragedy had he not snapped out of it?

Lesson 10

Welcoming David Home to Jerusalem Again

2 Samuel 19:8b – 43

The horror of the recent tragedy, in which the number three son of the king had been killed on the battlefield, despite specific instructions that David had given to the troops that they were to handle Absalom "gently," was difficult to deal with. But there were so much commotion and furor over what had happened and how the nation was to go forward, that many Israelites had fled their homes (19:8b). The nation was in turmoil and without a real sense of direction or leadership. In fact, all over Israel, the people of Israel and Judah were arguing with each other about how valuable King David had been in the past and how he was to be evaluated for the present and the future (19:9).

David got wind of this ongoing controversy. People were saying, David delivered us from our enemies, while others were recalling that David had saved them from the hand of Philistines. On the other hand, David had fled the country when just the first pieces of information that his son Absalom was leading a revolt against the nation's government had arrived. Moreover, the people in this controversy admitted that they had been the ones who had anointed Absalom to rule over them. But their appointed and anointed hero had died in battle. So, the question of the day was this: "Why [were all of them] say[ing] nothing about bringing the previous king [David] back?" (19:10b).

King David decided that something had to be done, for all this talk was just so much chatter, which had resulted in nothing happening. David decided to send a message to his two priests, Zadok and Abiathar, saying:

> "Ask the elders of Judah, 'Why should you be last to bring the king back to his palace, since what is being said throughout Israel has reached the king at his quarters? (11).

David tried to appeal to the sense of pride of his two priestly friends and loyal supporters. Moreover, since blood was thicker than water, what about their common blood relationship? Were they not his own "flesh and blood" (lit. "bone and flesh"). These men from David's tribe, the tribe of Judah? (12). There was, to be sure, a special tie between David and the Judahite elders and priests, so why, asked David, should they be last to bring the king home (12b)? The men of northern Israel would not agree that Judah had been the "first" to welcome David back from his quarters in Mahanaim (43), but any such sentiment was not by any means unanimous throughout the tribes of Israel; there were too many conflicting views to claim anything was unanimous in those days!

David added a surprising note to his message which he sent to his two priests. He told them to inform Amasa, who had previously been appointed the commander of Absalom's army of rebels (17:25), "Are you [Amasa] not my own flesh and blood? May God deal with me, be it ever so severely, if from now on you are not commander of my army in place of Joab!" (13). Of course, Amasa was a blood relative of David's, as was Joab. But David was still hurting from the severe rebuke he had received from Joab over his continual mourning over the loss of his son Absalom. Even though, David needed a strong wake-up call, for the good of the nation, he was nevertheless miffed over an underling in the government talking to him in such a manner – whether it was needed or not. Nevertheless, David replaced Joab on the spot with a new commander named Amasa, which must have angered Joab after he had saved the day for David, his men, and his kingdom, and had been his army commander for years.

David replaced Joab with Amasa to appease northern Israelites who had supported Absalom's rebellion. It still might be a valid question whether it was David who won over the hearts of all the men, or was it the work of Amasa, giving the king a result that was favorable to him. Word was sent to David that the hearts of the nation were as one [over his leadership], so he should return home. Therefore, David returned as far as the Jordan River, where he waited for any further guidance and a symbolic acceptance from the leaders of the nation by leading him across the Jordan.

Prior to these events, David met individuals— Ittai, Zadok, Hushai, Ziba, Barzillai, and Shimei—who became either allies or foes. Now, when David was returning, the same cast of characters reappear.

A Divided Nation with a Divided Loyalty – 19:8b -15

We have already seen that things were in a real mess throughout the land of Israel. David had been crowned king long before all this furor had broken out, but then so had Absalom more recently also been anointed as king. But Absalom was now dead; did that mean that everything in the government had reverted to David? What or who would function as the authority? It was clear that something needed to be done quickly, but what were the people of Israel to do and who should take the lead in this matter?

Meanwhile, David continued to hold up in his quarters at the site over in the land of Jordan at the city of Mahanaim. It would seem, however, that one of the things that broke the logjam was David's demotion of Joab as commander of the army and his instantaneous on the spot appointment of Amasa in his place. That must have really offended Joab, but David's choice of Amasa sent a signal that was no doubt greeted with high approval by those in the Absalom party and those who found much to criticize in the Davidic government.

Whether it was Amasa or David who won over the hearts of the men of Judah is difficult to decide, but this decision provided another step for real progress was to be realized.

Shimei, The Stone-Thrower Goes Free – 19:16-23

Shimei was a most deceitful character who could change in a matter to seconds his position on opinions he previously held like a chameleon. In fact, he was more like a snake than anything else, for somehow, he had managed to link up with the men of Judah as he hurried down to go with them from Gilgal to meet King David as he crossed the Jordan River (15-16). This Benjamite, Shimei, son of Gera from the town of Bahurim, joined a 1,000 other Benjaminites along with Ziba, the steward of Saul's household (another liar and snake in the grass) and Ziba's 15 sons and 20 servants – an impressive number to say the least! They all rushed down to the ford at the Jordan River, where King David had been waiting, to take the king's household over the river and to serve him in whatever tasks he needed help with.

After Shimei son of Gera forged the river, he felt prostrate in front of King David and begged for mercy, asking that David "not hold [him] guilty" for his vitriolic temperament and the slew of curses he had heartlessly hurled at David and his company as they fled from Jerusalem (19). He wished the king would put all of that out of his mind, for he knew he had sinned and that he had been in the wrong (20). That is why he wanted to be the first the household of Joseph (Benjamin at the time was part of the northern tribes) to come and greet the king whom he now called his "lord" (20b).

It was at this point that Abishai had had enough of this phony posturing as if Shimei were truly repentant. He was willing to give Shimei his just desert in one fell swoop of his sword (21), but David would not allow it. After all, Abishai had protested, Hadn't Shimei cursed the LORD's anointed? (21b). Was that different from blaspheming the Lord himself? Of course, Abishai was correct in his thinking about Shimei's huge transgression, but leaders have to be careful to keep the larger picture in mind: if David would have allowed Abishai to behead Shimei, the other Benjaminites and northern tribes might sense a possible purge was in the making and that might have started a lot more heads rolling, so David took the route of clemency (23). David rebuked Abishai for his desire to chop off Shimei's head, for Abishai as one of the sons of Zeruiah, had along with his brothers had become David's adversaries – and that of course included Joab too! Moreover, David knew full well that on that day he was once again the real king over Israel, so there would be no more need for any more people to die, including Shimei.

This word from David about Shimei in no way absolved Shimei of his crime and his cursing of David along with his entourage. Shimei had not had a huge change of heart, for he shows no genuine sorrow for the wrong he had done, not only to David, but to the LORD who had anointed him as sovereign over the nation! Shimei functioned as a realist who can detect power and bow to policy when he is forced to do so. So, of course, when someone aligns himself with the authorities, regardless of his present or ultimate ambitions, there is the advantage of gaining notice for who one is, even though it may be no more than a token submission to the winning form of authority.

Mephibosheth, Deceived by the Liar Ziba – 19:24-30

Saul's grandson. Mephibosheth, whom we have not heard from since 16:1-4, was among those who went down to welcome the king back home (24). His servant, Ziba, had outrightly lied about him and his ambitions to become the king, when Ziba reported to David that Mephibosheth had not joined the king's entourage because he was staying in Jerusalem hoping that Absalom's revolt would end up with the kingdom being handed to him as the legitimate heir of Saul's dynasty (16:3). But now, to Ziba's discomfort, Mephibosheth "came down to meet the king" (24a, was this with someone else's help) at the Jordan River and claimed he never said such a thing as Ziba had claimed.

The sudden appearance of this man, however, raised David's hackles and sudden suspicions, so he just asked Mephibosheth straight out: "Why didn't you go with me?" (25b). Mephibosheth response consisted of a sign and a speech. First of all, he pointed out to David as proof of the opposite view that he had not taken care of his feet, or trimmed his mustache, or washed his clothes all the while he was away from the palace, indeed from the day the king had left Jerusalem – which conditions, Mephibosheth asserted would remain until the day David returned safely (24). He also reminded the king that he was lame and that he had to have his donkey saddled so he could ride on it. But his servant Ziba betrayed him, and he had slandered him -- before you O king (26). But then he went on to add that David was his "lord" and that David was as wise as an "angel of God;" therefore this whole episode was in his hands, and he could do with it as he wished (27b). To all this, he further added,

> "All my grandfather's descendants deserved nothing but death from my lord the king, but you gave your servant a place among those who eat at your table. So, what right do I have to make any more appeals to the king? (28).

David had heard enough, for he quickly was sensing what had happened. Ziba had been trying to work his own deal on the king! Even though David had hastily given all the lands over to that liar Ziba, he ordered Mephibosheth and Ziba to divide the fields between them. But Mephibosheth magnanimously said, "Let him take everything now that my lord the king has arrived home safely (30). Rather than being able under the circumstances to see that justice was done, David settled for pragmatism. I wonder if the greedy liar, Ziba, ever made things right with the one he was supposed to have served as his servant?

Barzillai, Decliner of David's Gratitude – 19:31-39

Barzillai (meaning "iron man") was the elderly, but wealthy, Gileadite farmer from Rogelim, who had provisioned David and his entourage during his stay at Mahanaim (32). In a show of gratitude, the king invited him to cross over the Jordan and to go back with him to live in Jerusalem, but Barzillai protested that he was much too advanced in years to consider such a kind offer (34-35a). At 80 years old, he would not be able to appreciate the gourmet tastes of the king's food, nor enjoy flavor of the drinks available there, much less enjoy the entertainment of the male and female singers at the king's residence; he figured he would only be another burden for the king.

However, if the king wished to do him a favor, he would take along Kimham, Barzillai's son, as his substitute and allow Kimham to enjoy what he could not (37b). David was ready to do for Kimham whatever would please Barzillai. So, with the formalities now at a conclusion, the king and his party are ready to cross over the Jordan River. But before David does that, he kisses Barzillai as an act of royal protocol and gives him a blessing as they bid each other farewell.

But during all the negotiations, feelings got hurt. All the men of northern Israel were constantly coming up to David and complaining, "Why did our brothers (at least they were kindly being called "brothers"), the men of Judah, steal the king away and bring him and his household across the Jordan, together with all his men?" (41). This all the men of Judah denied doing deliberately, for they explained that David was more "closely related" to them and their tribe (42). It was for that reason that things turned out the way they did! The men of Judah did not think that the men of Israel should be angry over that gesture of preference. Moreover, they had not eaten any of the king's provisions nor had they taken anything (42d). So why was there all this talk about "kidnapping" the king?

The men of Israel were not satisfied with that explanation, for they answered back that they owned "ten shares" ("ten hands,") in him, meaning Israel was made up of ten tribes, whereas the Judean tribe was only one tribe, so when you do the math, Israel had the greater claim on David. Israel felt they had been treated with contempt. Anyway, had not they been the first to bring up the subject of bringing back the king to Jerusalem with the men of Benjamin? (43c). The men of Judah were not among the peacemakers that day, for they answered even more "harshly" than the men of Israel had spoken to them, which tactic set the stage for the rough treatment Israel was to get later on in the harsh words of King Rehoboam, as he gave his awaited answer to reducing the tax burden of the tribes after they had been abused under King Solomon's heavy load on their lives previously. The die was set for the division of the kingdom even in these earlier stages.

Conclusions

1. The outbreak of the argument after the death of Absalom caused a great disruption in the unity of the nation and their loyalty to David.
2. David had to ask the two priests Zadok and Abiathar to go to the elders of Judah to see if they were ready to bring him back to Jerusalem.
3. David must have been extremely angry with the harsh way Joab talked to him about mourning so long and so ostentatiously over the loss of his son Absalom when the whole nation had just fought to save David's neck and that of his family. So, he appointed Amasa as commander of his troops.
4. Shimei was a real snake in the grass, while Mephibosheth and Barzillai were true loyal friends. Why was David just as gracious to both parties here?
5. The tribes fought over who owned David and who it was who had been first to welcome him home. However, this fuss stood for more the confusion among the tribes to explain what had just happened in their country in a rebellion from the king's own family.

Questions for Thought or Discussion

1. Do you think that the Shimei incident, (who was a Benjaminite), reflects more that the nation was more settled on a king from the tribe of Benjamin than they were happy with one from the tribe of Judah? Was the influence of Saul and his leadership still present?
2. Did David make a good decision appointing Amasa in place of Joab as his commander? What signals did this send to the various parties in Israel?
3. What sort of deal was Ziba trying to pull against his master Mephibosheth? Should Mephibosheth have let Ziba get off so easily?
4. Why is Barzillai made part of the story at this point? What does he represent to David and to the story being told here?
5. Did the elders of Judah steal (or "kidnap") the king away from the other eleven (or ten) tribes? Where did such a partisan view come from in Israel?

Lesson 11

David's Men Quell the Attempted Sheba Rebellion

2 Samuel 20:1 – 22

A new troublemaker named Sheba son of Bicri from the tribe of Benjamin started things rolling by sounding the trumpet and shouting out: "We have no share in David, no part in Jesse's son! Every man to his tent, O Israel!" (20:1). With That rousing rebel outcry, all the men of Israel deserted David there at the Jordan River to follow this new rebel, Sheba, son of Bicri (20:2). Only the men of Judah stayed with their king all the way from the Jordan to Jerusalem (2). Let us examine this event in more detail.

Stop Sheba the Troublemaker and The Ten Concubines -20:1-3

High priority is given to this troublemaker named Sheba, for he is mentioned eight times in this chapter, and it is no wonder either, for he could have split the kingdom without delay! He is always given his full name – "Sheba son of Bicri." Commentators have argued that Sheba is called the "son of Bicri" because he is compared to "a swift she-camel [*bikra*] running here and there" in a rebellious manner (cf. its usage in Jer. 2:23 and Isa. 60:6). The point is that Sheba was well-known for his stubborn, self-willed, and rebellious manner. He is labelled in the NIV as a "troublemaker," a translation of the literal Hebrew: "man of Belial," 20:1. A man who disregarded the rights and properties of everyone else!

Sheba is also called a "Benjamite," so he was marked as being partisan to the Saul's dynasty and the causes of the northern tribes. It is also more than just a coincidence that Sheba was present at the time when the nation had gathered at Gilgal (19:40), which more than likely ties him to Absalom's rebellion. Was Sheba interested in picking up the baton that Absalom had dropped, or was he there if a spoiler was needed to remedy the situation by offering himself as a candidate for being king?

Suddenly Sheba sounded the ram's horn as a herald to all Israel that he was going to make a major pronouncement. The words he will use here are the same that will be used in future acts and words of secessionists (e.g., 1 Kgs 12:16). He boldly announced that he and all he stood for no longer had a "share" in David's realm. What is more, he referred to King David in a belittling and disparaging way, which he did by reducing David's title to "Jesse's son" (20:1b). He, without any authority or right to do so, ordered "every man to his tent." Where did he get this authority? Who died and left him boss over his compatriots? And by commanding each to go to his own "tent," did he mean each to his own "home," in an archaic manner, or was he commanding all to go to their military tents and get ready to challenge David and his rule? No wonder he is considered a "troublemaker," for he surely was an egomaniac, to say the least! It is a relief to the reader to learn that nowhere does the text say Sheba started an armed rebellion, but he was as close to doing so, in fact as close as a rebel can get.

The men from the tribe of Judah "stayed by their king" (2) as they showed the most loyalty and affection for David as they escorted him "all the way from the Jordan to Jerusalem." But there was other business to deal with. David had left ten concubines to care for the palace (3), but for someone who had pretentions of taking over the rule of the land, a former wife, even if she were only a concubine of the previous king, would have helped the case for the pretender to advance his cause of the search from the kingship. But David was wise to this possibility, for as soon as he got back home, he put the ten women under military guard in a "house" (instead of the palace), which would prevent any surreptitious attempts by outsiders to commandeer the situation. Thus, the ten women were virtually incarcerated in what turned out to be a type of "house arrest" or a prison for them. David purposely abstained from having any sexual relations with any of the ten from that time onwards, so there would be no political gains achieved, for no one would be able to get access to one of these women to gain access to the throne. The physical needs of the women were cared for by David, naturally, but they had to be kept in confinement under "house arrest."

Engage Joab in a Pursuit of Sheba – 20:14-22

David gave orders to his newly appointed commander of the army, named Amasa, to "summon the men of Judah to come to me within three days and be here yourself" (4). However, somehow missing the urgency of the situation, Amasa, the former leader of King Saul's army, "took longer than the time the king had set for him" (5). David was not accustomed to having his orders modified, nor was this a time for slackness when rebellion was in the air, so David commanded Abishai to complete the king's order to pursue Sheba before he ensconced himself in a fortified city, Abishai was to take the king's men and cut off Sheba's aspirations to take over the rule of the land (6).

With those orders, Abishai gathered all those in the king's secret service, called the Kerethites and Pelethites, along with Joab's men (for Joab had trained this army for years), along with all the mighty warriors left in Jerusalem (7). His goal was to stop Sheba. Thus, the war was on, but its focus was solidly on Sheba. While the troops were at the great rock of Gibeon, who should come out to meet them but Amasa himself. Where had he been and what had he been doing? But no answer is given to these questions. Amasa gives no reason he was so tardy in showing up. Moreover, who also should be there among the troops -- none other than Joab, who was wearing his military tunic and strapped over it at his waist was a belt with a dagger in its sheath. Joab stepped forward, but as he did so, the dagger dropped out of its sheath (8). Was this a military trick to distort Amasa's concentration or did the dagger drop out of its sheath accidentally?

Joab, with what seemed to be an unsuspecting greeting, inquired of Amasa, "How are you, my brother?" (9). Then Joab grabbed Amasa by his beard in his right hand presumably to kiss him, but Amasa was not on his guard, for in the interim Joab must have stooped to pick up the dagger, which had fallen out of its sheath, only to plunge the dagger into Amasa's belly so that his intestines spilled out on the ground. That was the end of life for Amasa. No record is given of any protest from the men, or even an explanation from Amasa. Poor Amasa lay in the middle of the road wallowing in his own blood. The men were called to attention by one of Joab's men, who stood by the deceased Amasa and announced: "Whoever favors Joab and whoever is for David, let him follow Joab" (11). As the men marched by, they all came to a temporary halt at the spot where Amasa lost his life, so to cure this situation, they dragged Amasa's body off the road into a field and covered it with a garment (12). With Amasa removed, the men went on with Joab to pursue Sheba. How Abishai felt about this or what he said is not told to us in Scripture. Moreover, the man had a long journey ahead of them for altogether they would cover close to 90 miles to the extreme northern boundary of Israel.

Accept the Wise Woman of Abel Beth Maacah's Offer – 20:14-22

The town of Abel Beth Maacah is really in the far north part of Israel, just four miles west of Dan, with the modern name of Abil el-Qahm. Thus, Sheba had travelled as far north in the land as one could go, 90 miles north from where this whole campaign had begun in Gilgal. In Sheba's hasty retreat he had only enlisted the "Berites" (14), whom he had "gathered together" to follow him. Whether these Berites stood for his own clan (in a scribal error called the "Bicrites") is impossible to say. But their number, in comparison to the army that now followed Joab was a pittance in comparison.

Joab lost no time in setting up a siege of the town of Abel Beth Maacah. First, he built a siege ramp up to the city wall and set up battering rams to knock down the wall down. While all of this was going on, an unnamed wise woman called out from inside the city. "Listen! Listen! Tell Joab to come here [at the wall] so can speak with him" (16). Joab stepped forward and the woman checked him out with the further inquiry, "Are you Joab?" (17).

When Joab acknowledged that he was Joab, the wise woman began her plea to him. She began by bringing Joab up to speed on who he was talking with and the reputation of the city he had placed under siege. She continued in this manner: "Long ago they used to say, 'Get your answer at Abel,'" and that settled it" (18). Joab and his army were unaware that his town was among those who were "peaceful and faithful in Israel," so why, asked our wise woman, were they trying to destroy a city that was regarded as a "mother" in Israel? (19). Why was Joab and his men trying to "swallow up the LORD's inheritance?" (19b). This action was ludicrous to the wise woman!

Joab must have been taken back a bit, for he declared that such a charge was the most remote and distant idea of what he was trying to do (20). Now it was time for Joab to bring this wise woman up to date, for Joab explained that a man named Sheba son of Bicri from the hill country of Ephraim had started an insurrection against David the king and had taken refuge in their city.

Joab had a compromising idea: "Hand over this one man, and I'll withdraw from the city!" (21d). The woman, with all her wisdom agreed, and at once without any more coaxing or argumentation she left to talk to her fellow citizens, for she stated what would happen in as concise a manner as wisdom demanded was this: "His head will be thrown to you from the wall." That was playing "heads-up" ball as far as Joab was concerned. If the wise woman from Abel would do so, she would easily win the "toss" for the city, thought Joab.

Now it was the wise woman's turn to produce, so she went to all the people with the typical wise advice she was famous for, and she convinced them it was better for them to "head" Sheba's skull over the wall than it was to lose the whole city to an army (22). Out came the head of Sheba and the rebellion had summarily been "headed off" and stopped. Thus, Joab sounded the trumpet (22), matching Sheba's sounding the trumpet for a different reason in verse 1 as this chapter 20 began, and the army of Joab dispersed from Abel Beth Maacah as each man returned to his home. Meantime, Joab returned to King David in Jerusalem. There was no word on how Abishai felt about this whole deal, for he had enjoyed his rank as commander of the army for a brief time indeed!

A historical footnote closes chapter 20:23-26, just as 2 Samuel 8:15-18 had closed an earlier unit in this narrative. The list of officers in 8:15-18 came from the earlier years of David's reign, while this list in 20:23-26 is a list of the cabinet members of David's government in his later years. This later list has Joab over the whole army, Benaiah the son of Jehoiada as being over David special guard to the king, called the Kerethites and the Pelethites, Adoniram, who was in charge of the forced labor, Jehoshaphat son of Ahilud as recorder, Sheva as his secretary, Zadok and Abiathar as his priests and Ira the Jairite as David's priest.

Conclusions

1. It was providential that this problem with Sheba the son of Bicri as a "troublemaker" was dealt with quickly and summarily.
2. The seeds for a future split of the kingdom, however, were sown at this time with the trumpet sounding and the little aphorism Sheba spelled out.
3. David took measures to ensure that the ten concubines were not abandoned, thereby preventing any potential successor from forming alliances with them to strengthen their claim to the throne.
4. Joab pursued Sheba to northern Israel, set up a siege, and a wise woman saved the city by handing over Sheba's head.
5. The reputation of Abel Beth Maacah was continued and enhanced by the wise advice of this woman who saved the city.

Questions for Thought or Discussion

1. Why do you think there might have been a growing sense of upset with David and his government in Israel that spawned the rebellion of Absalom and now the rebellion of Sheba?
2. Why do you think all the men of the eleven tribes deserted David to follow Sheba except the tribe of Judah?
3. Why is it that David concluded that Sheba son of Bicri would do more harm to him and the nation than Absalom had done?
4. Do you have any ideas or guesses why Amasa was so delayed in meeting David's three-day limit to report back to him with an army?
5. Why do you think Sheba turned into the city of Abel Beth Maacah? Surely, he had passed up a number of cities in Israel in his flight from Joab. He also had a head start over Joab, so why do you think he chose the city the farthest away?

Lesson 12

David's Lament Over Saul and Jonathan's Death

1 Samuel 31:1-13; 2 Samuel 1:1-27

The battle on Mount Gilboa, that David providentially missed by being sent home by the Philistines, went on up north (1 Sam. 29-30), while David was tracking down the raiding Amalekites down south. The verbs in 1 Samuel 31:1-3 carry the sad impact of the story, for the Israelites "fled" rather than face the advance of Philistines (1) as the enemy "killed" Saul and his three sons, Jonathan, Abinadad and Malki-Shua (2). The archers had pressed hard the battle that surrounded Saul in its fiercest form, so that they wounded him most critically and he was at the point of dying (3).

We, the readers, are especially moved in sympathy over the loss of Jonathan, who had played such a major part in David's life up to this point (1 Sam 14, 18-20 and 23). However, long ago Jonathan had acknowledged that the kingship belonging to David in one of their conversations (1 Sam 18:1-4). But Jonathan also remained loyal to his father Saul as well, despite his full knowledge of his father's shortcomings and his mean sins. This chapter 31 can be divided in half, with vv. 1-7 describing the battle on Gilboa and vv. 8-13 picking up what took place after this.

The Divine Prediction of the End to Saul's Life – 31:1-7

The Battle of Mount Gilboa is strikingly different in how the battle progressed from the way David's frequent forays with the Philistines progressed. Instead of the army of Israel going in "hot pursuit" of the Philistines and defeating them (14:22), the tables had been turned against Israel with the Philistines taking the upper hand. Three of Saul's sons had been killed before Saul committed suicide (31:2, 6, 8).

Israel had sustained an awful loss, for three sons had died, his armor-bearer, his bodyguard and Saul himself, including Saul's crack troops, were among the slain. One after another the men of Saul "fell" in death, just as Saul had fallen on his sword; however, there was no falling of the word of God, for it never will fall nor has it ever fallen or failed. Its word always came to pass, and it did not fail to be fulfilled or pass away!

Despite the darkness of the moment, and the apparent failure of the kingdom of God for the moment, even this time of deep sorrow was not an event or an act that was outside of the plan of God. Ronald F. Youngblood [1] has called our attention to three of the stanzas of "Song of Saul before his Last Battle" by George Gordon (Lord Byron) where he imaginatively reconstructed Saul's last words to his men, his armor-bearer, and his son Jonathan.

> Warriors and chiefs! Should the shaft or the sword
> pierce me in leading the host of the Lord,
> Heed not the course, though a kings in your path.
> Bury your steel in the bosoms of Gath!
> Thou who art bearing my buckler and bow,
> Should the soldiers of Saul look away from the foe,
> Stretch me that moment in blood at my feet!
> Mine be the doom which they dared not to meet.
>
> Farewell to others, but never we part,
> Heir to my royalty, son of my heart!
> Bright is the diadem, boundless the sway,
> Or kingly the death, which awaits us to-day!

The Problem of Yahweh's Honor -31:8-13

The next day, the Philistines returned to the battlefield to "strip the dead," but in doing so, they discovered that there was Saul's corpse (which they could identify by his height and his distinctive armor) along with others who had died along with him (31:8). The armor of Saul would soon be put on display in the temple of their goddesses Ashtoreth (Astarte). Obviously, they broadcasted the news of Saul's defeat all over Philistia. The Philistines mangled Saul's body (9a) and chopped off his head, along with stripping his armor.

The Philistines sent back word (9-10) via messengers to proclaim their victory -- no doubt along with Saul's head. Meanwhile, the corpses of Saul and his sons were spiked to the walls of Bethshan (10b).

---

1. Ronald F. Youngblood, *The Expositor's Bible Commentary,* vol 3, Grand Rapids, Zondervan, 2009, p. 290.

Thus, it looked like the gods Dagan and Astarte had won the day; Yahweh for the moment had been defeated. In that day, once the people suffered a major defeat, then so did their god suffer the same defeat. For believers in all generations, the sadness of our hearts is not merely in the fact that Israel had been trounced, but the LORD God of the whole universe had also been simultaneously mocked and defied. There was the real basis of the tragedy.

When those who were living "on the other side of the valley" (7a), i.e., the people north of Mount Gilboa, but who were living on the east side of the Jordan River, saw what was happening, they suddenly abandoned their towns leaving them open to the Philistine incursion, who rapidly occupied the newly provided site.

When the residents of Jabesh-gilead heard how the Philistines had abused Saul's corpse, they had not forgotten how Saul had so dramatically come to their aid at the beginning of his reign (11:2). The people of Jabesh-gilead had faced another mutilator of men captured in battle named King Nahash, the Ammonite (11:6), but Saul had settled that score in favor of the people of Jabesh-gilead. So, their strong men undertook an all-night journey to Beth-shan and removed the desecrated bodies on Saul and his sons from the walls of the city. These men quickly returned to Jabesh-gilead, which was about ten miles southeast of Beth-shan, making a round trip in less than 24 hours of a twenty mile-rescue journey.

Very few things in the Bible look as desperate as the massacre on Mount Gilboa, for it appeared as if both Yahweh and the kingdom of God had been set back in time by years and had suffered unbearable stigma. Yet, all this time God had been preparing a young shepherd boy, who knew how to care for scattered sheep, for our LORD was looking not on the outward appearances of defeat, but on the heart of young David.

An Amalekite Claims to Have Killed Saul -2 Sam 1:1-16

2 Samuel begins exactly where 1 Samuel had concluded by saying: "After the death of Saul" (2 Sam 1:1). That is the identical way that the books of Joshua and Judges began, "After the death of Moses" (Josh 1:1) and "After the death of Joshua" (Judg. 1:1). Moreover, beginning with the lists of the sons born to David in 2 Samuel 3:2-5, a good part of 2 Samuel is replicated in 1 Chronicles as well. In addition to the paralleling of the same information in 2 Samuel, mention should also be made of Psalm 18, which is replicated from 2 Samuel 22.

So, the narrative about David's final arrival and years of experience, first as the king of Judah, then of all Israel, can be found in 2 Samuel. The words of 2 Samuel 1:1 parallel 2 Samuel 1:15-16 that frame this literary unit that had as its subject the "striking down" of the Amalekite(s) by David. Another inclusion can be seen between 2 Samuel 1:1 and 8:13, which section precedes the court history of David in 2 Samuel 9-20, while the section in front of this court history takes us to the time David "returned from striking down" the Edomites (8:13).

2 Samuel began by talking about the Amalekite fugitive, who arrived at David's camp in Ziklag from the terrible battle scene on Mount Gilboa, more than 80 miles, a full three-day trip. This Amalekite fugitive arrived with "his clothes torn and with dust on his head" (1:2). The dust on the "man's" (1:2) head was, of course, a sign of his emotional upset and distress, which could be easily understood for a "lad" (1:5) who had seen such horrible devastation and human carnage. Seeing the man's appearance, naturally David wanted to know where he had come from. His response was that he had just escaped from the Israelite camp on Mount Gilboa where he along with the other Israelites had fled from the battle on Mount Gilboa, led by the victorious Philistines 1:3-4). Then this fugitive blurted out the awful news that King Saul and his sons were dead. This news fell like a ton of bricks even to the battle-weary troops of David.

There is one major problem, however, with the Amalekite's report of what happened at the battle on Mount Gilboa. It did not accord with all the known facts. Some of the more obvious differences would include the following: (1) in 1 Samuel 31, King Saul committed suicide, but in the Amalekite's report, he was the man who actually killed Saul as he was in the throes of dying, (2) in 1 Samuel 31, Saul was wounded by the archers, but in this new account by the Amalekite, his enemies were the charioteers, (3) in 1 Samuel 31, the Philistines took Saul's armor, but here the Amalekite brought Saul's crown and armlet to David.[2] Now, given this disparity, which one was telling the truth? Did the Bible carry two contradictory accounts? But that solution will not fit the evangelical understanding of the bible's claim for inerrancy. Others contend that the Amalekite's story was the correct one, but then that makes the Bible's report in 1 Samuel 31 false. Another view set forth by the ancient historian, Josephus, contends that the armor-bearer refused to finish off Saul, when he requested it, and therefore Saul fell on his own sword;

2. See Bill T. Arnold, "The Amalekite's Report of Saul's Death: Political Intrigue or Incompatible Sources?" *JETS,* 32/3 (1989): p. 290.

however, he was too weak to do so completely, so Saul turned and spied the Amalekite nearby and at the king's request, he killed Saul. After he had killed Saul, he picked up the king's crown and armband and fled.[3]

Josephus has come up with the best conflation of the events that are in tension in this story, however, his basic error is in the assumption that the Amalekite was telling the truth. The way the Amalekite told his story, he "just happened" (Hebrew, infinitive absolute with a finite verb) to be on Mount Gilboa when he met a wounded Saul "leaning on his spear" as the "chariots and riders were almost upon him" (1:6). But what is this Amalekite doing leisurely wondering about a mountain when a battle is going on? (1:7)

Saul is said to have seen this Amalekite and asked him who he was. He answered, "I am an Amalekite" (1:8). That must have brought back to Saul a whole bunch of memories – his failure to obey orders a long time ago! Saul is supposed to have said, "Stand over me and kill me! I am in the throes of death, but I am still alive" (1:9) – like an earlier expression used by Goliath to David, "Stand over me and kill me. (cf. 1 Sam 17:51). The Amalekite was happy to oblige Saul (1:10). That is what happened! Wow!

Neither David nor his men were impressed by this young man's story, for all of them took hold of their clothes and tore them and wept and fasted for the rest of the day until evening came (1:11-12). That evening David recommenced the interrogation of this curious visitor, asking him, "Where are you from?" (1:13). The lad, apparently not up on his current newscasts said, "I am the son of an alien, an Amalekite" (1:13b). Now it was time for David to speak, for he scolded him for not being afraid to destroy the LORD's anointed (1:14). With that, David called for one of his men to "strike him down," and he did so! That ended both the man and the story!

David's Lament for Saul and Jonathan – 1:17-27

David composed a powerfully compassionate poem that depicted his love and deep regard for Saul and especially his son Jonathan. This poem is dated about 1000 B.C.E. and is in the same style as another lament that David composed on the death of Abner (2 Sam. 3:33-34).

The lovely elegy could properly be given the title of "How the Mighty have Fallen" from its lead line at the beginning of the poem (2 Sam 1:19) and in its closing line (2 Sam. 1:27), thus giving symmetry to the poem. The Hebrew word for "mighty" (Hebrew, *gibborim*) is the most distinctive

3. Flavius Josephus, *Antiquities of the Jews, 6.370*-72.

part of this poem, for it appears six times (1:19, 21, 22, 23, 25, 27) in a matter of nine verses).

The first time I ever heard a sermon on this passage was in my young years I heard my father speak at the funeral at the request of his best friend, a past pastor in Philadelphia of a Reformed Church of America, named Rev William Green, but who, more recently, had given up that position to take a key role as a representative of the Pocket Testament League. He and my father had been very close friends, so when the request came for my Dad to give the message at the funeral, he who was only a lay leader in a small suburban Congregation, my father choose this passage for 2 Samuel 1:18-27, as he too, along with the writer of this Scripture, repeatedly asked, "How the Mighty have Fallen!"

Just like Joshua's poetic address to the sun and moon (Josh. 10:12-13), so David's lament was likewise written down in "the book of Jashar" (1:18; cf. 1 Kings 8:13). David Noel Freedman [4] argued that the word translated "glory" (v. 19) should be rendered "the gazelle," a nickname used as a metaphor for Jonathan, who also appears later in v. 25. Thus, the name stood for a "fleet-footed warrior." Later Saul and Jonathan are both compared to "eagles" and "lions" in v. 23, but the image of a deer is used in connection with the "heights" in 22:34. Accordingly, the use of the simile of a gazelle for Jonathan fits here quite well. Thus, the word "mighty" is parallel to the "gazelle" in our revised reading of this text following Freedman's suggestion. Notice that David does not slight King Saul even though Jonathan is given a slight preference.

David warns that Saul and Jonathan's friends are not to "Tell" this news in the Philistine city of Gath, which is a city on the eastern edge of the Philistine territory, nor should they sing it out in a "proclamation" in the streets of Ashkelon, which is by the Mediterranean Sea, and therefore together both represent all of Philistia from east to west. So do not tell and do not proclaim this sad news, lest that pagan country rejoice over Israel's defeat and loss (1:20)!

The third stanza in this lament (vv. 21-22) pronounces a curse on the "mountains of Gilboa," where Israel was defeated. These mountains do not have a solitary peak, but they have a ridge that goes for eight miles in length and three-five-miles wide, forming a watershed between the plain of Esdraelon and the plain of Beth-shan. Because the shield of Saul and

---

4. David Noel Freedman, "The Refrain in David's lament over Saul and Jonathan" in *Ex Orbe Religionum:* Studia Geo. Widengren, Part I, Leiden: Brill, 1972, p. 120.

the bow of Jonathan were defiled on Mount Gilboa, David called for a withdrawal of dew and rain from the fields in the mountain, so that the soil would no longer yield its grain.

In the next stanza, the father and son, Saul and Jonathan, who were both loved and were gracious, yet even in death they were not parted (23). In fact, they were "swifter than eagles" and "stronger than lions" (23d-e).

So, it is right that the "daughters of Israel" should weep for King Saul, for he is the one who clothed them "in scarlet and finery" (24c). Saul also "adorned them in garments with ornaments of gold" (24d). Interpreters call this stanza the central one in David's lament. These daughters who were invited to weep and mourn over the sad happenings of this event may have been professional mourners, who also chanted a lament on behalf of these two dead heroes, as well as on the part of the nation (cf. Jer. 9:17; Ezek. 32:16). It should be noted as well that the words "scarlet" and "clothes" are associated in the acrostic poem on the "Virtuous Woman" in Proverbs 31:21-22.

In the next stanza of vv. 25-26, there is the only stanza where Jonathan appears alone and where David heaps praise on the man he calls "my brother," for he was "very dear to [David]" (26b). Moreover, David went on praising Jonathan by saying, "Your love to me was wonderful, more wonderful than that of a woman." Even though this expression of David's deep "love" for Jonathan has been perversely understood to be homosexual love for each other, this love was instead a "covenantal love" that spoke of a love in which they were bound by a treaty and by a deep appreciation for the devotion each man held for the other man.

The lament closes as it began with the sorrowful words, "How the mighty have fallen," but it adds "the weapons of war have vanished" (27). The expression "weapons of war" seem to hide another metaphor for Saul and Jonathan. Yes, the two of them were used mightily as God's weapons to clear the land and make it habitable for Israel to dwell in the land.

Here then was a most fitting tribute to two of the real heroes in the building of the nation of Israel. It is also significant that nowhere in this lament does David use this as an opportunity to set matters straight and to show the hurt and suffering he had to endure for all that time he was waiting for his inauguration as king under the late prophet Samuel to be realized! Instead, just as God commanded Moses to "teach" his song to Israel (Deut. 32:1-43), so David ordered that this lament be "taught" to Israel as well (2 Sam 1:18). Indeed, "How the mighty have fallen."

Conclusions

1. Saul and Jonathan were both slain in battle on the same day on Mount Gilboa. It was a sad day for all Israel.
2. The Amalekite, who claimed to have given the final fatal blow to Saul, no doubt lied to David, but his story could not to be trusted, so David rebuked him for treating the LORD's anointed in that manner and had him killed.
3. Saul should have obeyed at an early event in his reign by polishing off the Amalekites, so none would have been left for David to fight at Ziklag or for a liar to pretend he had been the last man alive to see Saul still living. These Amalekites will infect the story of Israel all the way up to the life of Esther.
4. David's lament is framed by vv. 19 and 27 with five stanzas in between, viz., vv. 20, 21, 22-23, 24-25, and 26.

Questions for Thought or Discussion

1. Should David have set the record straight in his lament about how Saul and the ten tribes bitterly opposed him when he had been secretly anointed as king already?
2. In what ways was the lament of 2 Samuel 1:18-27 evidence of the character of David as a man after God's own heart?
3. If David had remained with the Philistine King Achish of Gath and fought Israel as one of Achish's servants, being therefore a part of the slaughter of Israel on Mount Gilboa, how would the history of this time have turned out differently?
4. What good characteristics do the men of Jabesh-gilead evidence as they come by night to Beth-shan to steal the bodies of Saul and his sons pined to the walls of that city?
5. Was Saul justified in falling on his own sword and committing suicide since these times were not yet New Testament times?

Lesson 13

The Last Words of David and the Anger of the LORD with Israel

2 Samuel 23:1-39; 24:1-25

David is said to be the author of this section of the text called "The last words of David" (1). It is also interesting to note that in the Dead Sea Scrolls, there is a composition that is not part of the canonical Bible called 11Q Psalms. It has a total of 51 compositions made up of both apocryphal compositions interspersed with pieces from the genuine canonical psalms. In this manner, 2 Samuel 23:7 is placed after the canonical Psalm 150 concludes along with two other compositions known as the "Hymn to the Creator," and "David's Compositions."

The Last Words of David – 23:1-7

David begins his poem by calling it an "oracle" (Hebrew, *ne'um*), a Hebrew term that almost always is associated with what the LORD himself declares. This Hebrew root appears only rarely outside typical contexts, such as with Balaam son of Beor (Num. 24:3a, 15a) and Agur son of Jakeh's wisdom sayings (Prov. 30:1a). But here in our passage it is used in 2 Samuel 23:1b, c; as well as of David in 1 Chronicles 109:14, 1 Chronicles 29:26, and in Psalm 72:20).

David assigns to himself three titles in this section: "The man exalted by the Most High," "The Man anointed by the God of Jacob," and "Israel's singer of songs" (2 Sam. 23:1c, d, e). Of course, at least 73 or 150 Biblical Psalms are attributed to David under various titles as being part of his "Confessions," his "Portrait," or his "Trust" in the LORD.

In verses 2-3 David gives a four-fold explanation of the divine source of his revelations: they came when "the Spirit of the LORD spoke through him," when "the word was on his tongue," when "The God of Israel spoke," and when "the Rock of Israel [talked] to me." Therefore, it was the Holy Spirit of God who came upon David and enabled him to declare the words of God, just as the same Spirit of God enabled Balaam to announce the words of God (Num. 24:2, 4; 1 Chron. 12:18). Moreover,

Yeshua agreed with this assessment of David speaking by the Spirit of the LORD, for he said in Matthew 22:43, "How is it that David speaking by the Spirit, calls him LORD" (Psalm 110:1)? The word of the Lord must have often been on the tongue of David as this text claims!

David followed these assertions with what must have been his list of the qualities of a God-fearing leader:

> One who rules over men in righteousness.
> One who rules in the fear of God.
> One who is like the light of morning at sunrise, on a cloudless morning.
> One who brings the grass from the earth. (3b – 4)

Such a leader who rules in the fear of God and one who is characterized by righteousness. The benefits that come from such a godly rule and reign are like the glories of the morning sunshine. This reign will last as long as the sun shines and the rain renews the earth and promotes growth.

Then David proceeds after this list to ask if it is not true that his house is right with God? (5a). Add to that affirmation this question: "Has not God made with David an everlasting covenant [that is] arranged and secured in every part?" (5b, c). The LORD had used the word "everlasting/eternal" or "forever" repeatedly in 2 Samuel 7:13, 16, 24-26, 29) to describe the Covenant he had with the LORD. Moreover, this Covenant was arranged in every particular and each detail, so secured by God that David knew that this was all part of God's everlasting plan! God would grant David his every desire (5e).

But David also takes time to speak of the wicked and evil men who are just like thorns, whose prickly thorn-filled branches make them downright hard to pick up if one's hands are not protected by gloves for the job (6). It is better to tackle the job of removing such thorny branches with an iron tool rather than with one's hands (7). Of course, one can also burn such branches right on the spot where they lie. The same may be said for one's enemies who are just as prickly at times.

The Mighty Men of David – 23:8-39

These "Mighty men" can be put into two groups. The first group can also be further divided into three equal parts: (1) exploits of the "Three" (23:8-12), (2) the Three that were part of the thirty men (23:13-17), and (3) two especially noteworthy fighters, one of whom was chief of the three and the other who was in charge of David's bodyguard (23:18-23).

The first man to be mentioned was Josheb-Basshebeth, a Tahkemonite, who was "chief of the three" (8). He is also mentioned in 1 Chronicles 11:11 with a variant as the second part of his name (which may be a scribal error). He was noted for lifting up his spear against 800 men, whom he took down in one encounter.

The second man was Eleazar, son of Dodai the Ahohite (9). He was one of the three mighty men who were with David when he met the Philistines at Pas Dammim. However, even when the men of Israel retreated, he stood his ground and struck down the Philistines until his hand froze to his sword. The troops finally returned, but it was only to strip the dead of the loot (10).

The third man was Shammah son of Agee the Hararite (11). He was noted for his stand in the middle of a field of lentils, after Israel's troops had abandoned him. He single-handedly struck down the Philistines, and the LORD gave him a great victory (12).

In another collection of the exploits of David's men, three of his thirty men joined him at the time of the harvest while he was in the cave of Adullam, while the Philistines were encamped in the Valley of Rephaim (13). On one occasion, David wistfully said, "Oh, that someone would get me a drink of water from the well near the gate of Bethlehem" (15). Now at that time there was a Philistine garrison in Bethlehem; nevertheless, three of the mighty men broke through the Philistine lines and drew water from that same well and carried it back to David. David refused to drink the water, pouring it out instead, because he did not want to benefit from the risk these men took to obtain it (17).

In the third subdivision of this first main section, two especially notable fighters came to mind: one, Abishai, the brother of Joab son of Zeriah, was chief of the three (18), and Benaiah son of Jehoiada, from Kabzeel, was in charge of David's bodyguard (20). Abishai lifted his sword against 300 men, so he became famous as chief of the three for killing the 300. In fact, he was held in greater honor and was commander of the Three even though he was not included among them (19).

Benaiah was famous for striking down two of Moab's best men. It was also a snowy day when he went down in a pit and killed a lion (20b). He also struck down a huge Egyptian, who had a spear in his hand, but Benaiah only had a club. Benaiah snatched the spear from the Egyptian's hand and killed him with his own spear. He became as famous as part of the three mighty men and was held in greater honor than any of the Thirty, even though he was not included among the Three (23).

In vv. 24-39 we are provided with a list of David's fighting men, which is paralleled in 1 Chronicles 11:26-41a. This second section of all the mighty men focuses on the Thirty, while the list above in vv. 8-23 concentrated on the Three. The Chronicler did not specify the total number of warriors; however, an added sixteen names are listed beyond those in the Samuel passage. As referenced in 2 Samuel 23:39, the recorded number there is thirty-seven.

The Anger of God Against Israel – 24:1-25

The story of David in the books of Samuel close in 2 Samuel 24 with a plague sent by God because of David's sin in ordering that a census be taken of his troops. Even though David was called a "man after God's own heart," we are given a conclusion to his narrative by letting us see how David's ambition and pride occasionally got in the way of his humility and remorse.

This chapter is often viewed as being set forth in three equal segments: (1) David's sin is described in 24:1-9, (2) David's confession of his sin is viewed in 24:10-17, and (3) David's purchase of the site for the altar to the LORD is recorded in 24:18-25 and identified as the threshing floor of Araunah the Jebusite.

David's Sin – 24:1-9. The LORD was exceedingly angry with Israel, so that it "burned against Israel." He incited David against them by sending him to take a census of Israel's fighting men (1). In the parallel text of 1 Chronicles 21:1 the one who brought the anger against the nation was not the LORD; it was "satan." However, Satan's name does not appear with the article, the, as it does in Job 1-2 and Zechariah 3:1.

Let us first examine why census-taking of the troops was sinful. Some scholars interpret 1 Chronicles 27:23-24 as suggesting that the census described in these verses functioned as a draft notice or a mustering of troops.[1] The basic problem with David, however, was his presumption. God had not authorized David to go into battle. His numbering was seen as a mustering of the troops for a battle that the LORD had not approved. That was what was presumptuous with David's census-taking.

---

1. See my fuller explanation in Walter C. Kaiser, Jr., *Hard Sayings of the Bible,* Downers Grove, IL. Intervarsity Press, 1996, pp. 240-42.

This brings us to the second difficulty in this text: Who tempted David? The LORD or Satan? The concept that God instigated or impelled anyone to do evil is altogether incorrect! In no sense could God authorize what he disapproved of. The LORD may on occasion impel sinners to reveal the wickedness of their hearts in deeds that manifest what they are thinking, for in this manner, sinners may even more quickly see what lies dormant in their hearts and motivates them to act counter to God's will. But God does not sponsor any type of sin.

It is also true in Scripture, that what God permits he is said to commit. Therefore, by allowing this census-taking, the Lord is viewed as having brought about that very act. This is because the Hebrews were not as precise in deciding secondary causes and properly attributing them to their precise cause, since he is Lord over all, in charge of all that happens on earth!

The King ordered Joab and the army leaders to count the fighting men in Israel from Dan to Beersheba (24:2). However, Joab was not so sure this was the right thing to do (3). He could not believe David was going this route, for surely God could multiply the troops a hundred times over if he so wished. Joab must have sensed that David was on a bad and evil track that was not pleasing to God. Did Joab guess that David was preparing for a battle that God had not authorized? In fact, Joab called David's act "repulsive" (1 Chron. 21:6) and "evil in the sight of the LORD" (1 Chron. 21:7).

David, however, overruled Joab and the army officers, so off they went for nine months and twenty days to obtain the number of the fighting men of Israel (4-8). The number they enrolled was 800,000 in Israel and 500,000 in Judah (9).

David's Confession – 24:10-17. As a result of his orders, David was "conscience-stricken" about his numbering the fighting men. "I have sinned in what I have done. Now, O LORD, I beg you, take away the guilt of your servant. I have done a very foolish thing" (10b).

Before David got up the next morning, God sent his word by his prophet Gad, David's "seer," saying: "Go tell David, 'This is what the LORD says: I am giving you three options. Choose one of them for me to conduct against you.'" Naturally, Gad went immediately to David with the three options he was to choose from: (1) three years of famine in your land, (2) three months of fleeing from your enemies while they are pursuing you, or (3) Three days of plague in your land (13).

David opted to take the three-day choice and thus fall into the hands of a more merciful God than go with the other two options. The LORD sent a plague from that morning onwards for three days, so that a total of 70,000 Israelites from Dan to Beersheba died. But when the officiating angel stretched out his hand to destroy Jerusalem, the LORD "was grieved because of the calamity" that had fallen on his people (16a). So, the LORD said, "Enough. Withdraw your hand" (16b). At that point, the angel of the LORD was standing "at the threshing floor of Araunah the Jebusite" (16c).

David was so overcome by seeing 70,000 of his people lying dead, that he again confessed,

> "I am the one who has sinned and done wrong. These are but the sheep. What have they done? Let your hand fall upon me and my family" (17).

Once more, God sent the prophet Gad to David with these instructions:

> "Go up and build an altar to the LORD of the threshing floor of Araunah" (18).

David obeyed the LORD and so he went to Araunah. When Araunah looked up, he saw the king and his men coming toward him. He went out and bowed down to the king with his face to the ground, asking, "Why has my lord the king come to his servant? David's reply was brief and crisp: "So I can build an altar to the LORD, that the plague on the people may be stopped" (21).

Graciously, Araunah offered David whatever pleased him and to offer it up as a sacrifice (22). To this he also added,

> "Here are the oxen for the burnt offering, and here are threshing sledges and ox yokes for the wood. O king, Araunah gives all of this to the king…. May the LORD your God accept you" (22b-23).

But David insisted on the contrary,

> "No, I insist on paying you for it. I will not sacrifice to the LORD my God burnt offerings that cost me nothing" (24).

Things ended up with David buying the threshing floor and the oxen for fifty shekels of silver. The king also built the altar to the LORD and sacrificed burnt offerings and fellowship offerings there. The result was that the LORD answered David's prayer on behalf of the land and the plague on Israel was halted there at the threshing floor.

Conclusions

1. In David's last words, he gives us a most detailed statement of how the Holy Spirit of God spoke the word of God through him.
2. David also gave four excellent descriptions of the qualities of a leader of God's people.
3. David likewise taught that his house was right with God, and the LORD had made an "everlasting covenant" with him; one that was arranged and secured in every part.
4. David gave a list of the most notable among his fighting men including those who were in the highest echelons of his army and those who were among his "thirty.
5. When David ordered that the fighting men of the nation be numbered in a census, he sinned against God and 70,000 Israelites died. He prayed for God's forgiveness and bought the Araunah's Threshing floor in Jerusalem where the angel of death was halted.

Questions for Thought or Discussion

1. Why do you think David wanted to take a census of his fighting men? What was wrong with that from a divine point of view?
2. Who incited David to take this census and why? How do you explain that two different names are given?
3. What was significant about the plague stopping at the threshing floor of a Jebusite? What did this site become important for in the days to come?
4. What do we learn about the work of the Holy Spirit in inspiring David to speak God's word to the people?
5. How could God grant to David his every desire and bring to fruition his salvation?

Epilogue

It was ten years before David was born that Samuel the prophet sadly had to declare to King Saul, the first king of Israel:

> "You have acted foolishly....You have not kept the command the LORD your God gave to you; if you had, he would have established you over Israel for all time. But now your kingdom will not endure; the LORD has sought out a man after his own heart and appointed him leader of his people, because you have not kept the LORD's command" (1 Sam. 13:13-14).

We are not left to guess what the LORD meant by the expression, "a man after his own heart."

> "After removing Saul, he made David their king. He testified concerning him: 'I have found in David, son of Jesse, a man after my own heart; he will do everything I want him to do. From this man's descendants God has brought to Israel the Savior, Jesus, as he promised." (Acts 13:22-23).

What God found pleasing in David was that he had a heart focused on fulfilling God's will. That was the key. That was why God turned down Saul as the one to whom he would give the kingdom and the reason he appointed David instead: David wanted to fulfill the will of the LORD! That was the reason!

But David was accepted as a "man after God's own heart," not because he only outwardly obeyed the word of God; on the contrary, David was a man who was noted for his faith, which preceded his obedience. We are given a beautiful picture of this in the life of Enoch, the "seventh" from Adam. Hebrews 11:5-6 explained:

> "By faith Enoch was taken from this life, so that he did not experience death; he could not be found, because God had taken him away, For before he was taken, he was commended as one who pleased God, because anyone who comes to him must believe that he exists and that he rewards those who earnestly seek him."

But there was another consideration beside his faith in the Lord and his obedience to his word. It centered on the heart attitude of David. This aspect came out clearly when Samuel had been sent to anoint one of Jesse's children. Samuel had quickly assumed that Eliab was that candidate. To his surprise, the LORD carefully corrected the prophet by saying:

> Do not consider his appearance or his height, for I have rejected him. The LORD does not look at the things man looks at, but the LORD looks at the heart" (1 Sam. 16:7).

David's faith was also one that was tied to humility. David showed just such humility, even though he was crowned as king of Israel. One does not find him asserting his rights or demanding that he be honored above others. The Scripture that shows us how David showed the kind of heart God was seeking is found in 2 Chronicles 16:9 –

> For the eyes of the LORD range throughout the earth to strengthen those whose hearts are fully committed to him.

David had learned how to trust and follow the LORD in times of hard trials, such as the time he and the families of his army were living in Ziklag. David had cast his lot with the enemy (the Philistines) instead of placing his case in the hands of the Lord … or the time he sinned with Bathsheba. But David knew the full forgiveness of his LORD as well.

David knew that there would always be someone from his lineage sitting on the throne God had given to him. David rested confidently on God's promise-plan that involved his family and the eternal Kingdom of God. On which he never wavered but remained steadfast!

COMPLETE JEWISH BIBLE
The Lives and Ministries of ELIJAH and ELISHA
Dr. Walter C. Kaiser, Jr.
PRAYING LIKE the JEW JESUS
His Names Are Wonderful
Barbara D. Malda
Come and Worship
Under THE FIG TREE
PATRICK GABRIEL LUMBROSO
Under THE VINE
PATRICK GABRIEL LUMBROSO
Making Eye Contact with God
You Bring the Bagels I'll Bring the Gospel
RUBIN
THE WORLD TO COME
LEMAN
Psalms & Proverbs
David H. Stern
MESSIANIC JUDAISM
STERN
GOD'S APPOINTED CUSTOMS
KASDAN
GOD'S APPOINTED TIMES
KASDAN
GATEWAYS TO TORAH
RABBI RUSSELL RESNIK
CREATION TO COMPLETION
RESNIK
To the Ends of the Earth
On The Way to Emmaus
Dr. Jacques Doukhan
YESHUA
JEWISH NEW TESTAMENT COMMENTARY
MATTHEW PRESENTS YESHUA, KING MESSIAH
KASDAN

Printed in the United States
by Baker & Taylor Publisher Services